A Short Introduction to VEDANTA

other recent books from Cosmo Publications . . .

THE HINDUS. *Bestseller*
Encyclopaedia of Hinduism in 5 Volumes
Edited by Subodh Kapoor

ENCYCLOPAEDIA OF INDIAN HERITAGE. in 90 Volumes
A Descriptive Work of Indological Research in Philosophy, Religion, Sacred Literature, Society, Thought, Traditions, and Ancient Sciences.
Edited by Subodh Kapoor

ANCIENT INDIAN SCIENCES *Bestseller*
in 3 Volumes
Edited by Subodh Kapoor

ENCYCLOPAEDIA OF VEDIC PHILOSOPHY. *Bestseller*
The Age, Literature, Religion, Pantheon, Philosophy, Traditions and Teachers of the Vedas
in 9 Volumes
Edited by Subodh Kapoor

ENCYCLOPAEDIA OF INDIAN PHILOSOPHERS. *Bestseller*
Philosophers, Saints, Sages, Thinkers, Acharyas, Rishis, and great Religious Leaders
in 9 Volumes
Edited by Subodh Kapoor

ENCYCLOPAEDIA OF VEDANTA PHILOSOPHY.
in 5 Volumes
Ed. S. kapoor

Also Available . . .

INDIAN HISTORICAL RESEARCHES *Bestseller*
By Several Authors of International Repute
in 78 Volumes

REDISCOVERING INDIA *Bestseller*
INIDAN PHILOSOPHY LIBRARY
By Several Authors of International Repute
in 71 Volumes

A Short Introduction to VEDANTA

Edited by

Subodh Kapoor

Editor of THE HINDUS. Encyclopaedia of Hinduism, in 5 volumes
THE BUDDHISTS. Encyclopaedia of Buddhism, in 5 volumes
Encyclopaedia of Indian Heritage, in 90 volumes
Encyclopaedia of Vedic Philosophy, in 9 volumes
Encyclopaedia of Indian Philosophers, in 9 volumes
The Indian Encyclopaedia, in 25 volumes

COSMO PUBLICATIONS

2008 New Delhi

SHORT INTRODUCTION TO VEDANTA PHILOSOPHY

First published by COSMO 2008

ISBN 978-81-307-0909-3

Published by
COSMO PUBLICATIONS
for
GENESIS PUBLISHING PVT. LTD.
24-B, Ansari Road, Darya Ganj,
New Delhi-110 002,
INDIA

Printed in India by
Cosmo Publications

Contents

one

VEDĀNTA: AN INTRODUCTION

1. Introductory

ALL schools of Vedānta claim to be based upon the Upaniṣads. Whether this claim can be fully established in every case or not, there is no doubt that they derive a considerable part of their material from that source.[1] In dealing with the Vedānta, we shall accordingly have to refer to the Upaniṣads frequently: but, as we have already given an account of their teaching, it will not be necessary to go into details. It will suffice merely to refer to the relevant points or even to assume the reader's familiarity with what has already been stated. The teaching of the Upaniṣads, we know, is predominantly monistic, though it is not easy to determine what particular form of monism is taught in them. But this did not prevent dualistic interpretations being put on them, and the chief form of dualism that was traced to the Upaniṣads in olden times was the Sāṅkhya. There is a clear indication of this, as already noticed in the *Vedānta-sūtra*, which has for long been the universally recognized manual of Vedānta. One of the chief objects of Bādarāyaṇa in his treatise is to refute this view that the Upaniṣads teach the dualistic Sāṅkhya. There is also another object equally important which he has in view, viz. the refutation of ritualistic Mīmāṁsa, according to which the essential teaching of the Veda is contained in the Brahmanas; and the Upaniṣads, though as a part of revelation are not unauthoritative, are only of secondary significance and should be finally construed with reference to some ceremonial act or other. They may for instance be looked upon as speaking of the self which is the agent in the performance of rites or as glorifying the deities whose propitiation is their aim. In any case it is certain, the Mīmāṁsa contended, that Karma is the sole theme of the Veda and that the Upaniṣads, which form a part of it, cannot be taken to point to Brahman or any other principle as the highest entity whose realization constitutes the end and aim of man.[2] The inherent ambiguity of the Upaniṣads, the glaring contradiction between the purva— and the uttara-kandas of the Veda and, we may add, the growing power of heterodox beliefs, thus account for the attempts made in the Vedānta to systematize the teaching of the Upaniṣads.

There is evidence to show that this systematization was effected in more than one way. In the *Sūtra* of Bādarāyaṇa there is reference to as many as seven Vedantic teachers—whether they were his predecessors or contemporaries is not known; and he alludes to differences of view among them in respect of essential points like the nature of mokṣa[3] and the need of saminyasa[4] for the spiritual aspirant. Even in regard to such an important question as the relation of the jīva to Brahman, Bādarāyaṇa mentions two views other than his own,[5] both implying vital distinctions in general philosophic outlook. Differences like these on fundamental issues show that the teaching of the Upaniṣads was from very early times understood in several ways by Vedantic teachers. Badarayana's exposition is only one; and, in all likelihood, the most influential of them. All current schools of Vedānta, though differing from one another in important matters, alike claim to represent precisely what Bādarāyaṇa himself taught. The extremely laconic form of his sūtras has rendered such variety in interpretation possible. In fact, they are more cryptic than the Upaniṣads, and it is consequently much more difficult to get at their meaning than at that of those old treatises. The result is that even as regards the most essential points there is ambiguity. We do not for instance know for certain there is ambiguity. We do not for instance know for certain whether, according to Bādarāyaṇa, the world actually emerges from Brahman (parinama) or is only a phenomenal appearance of it (vivarta). There seem to have been once commentaries[6] on the *Vedānta-sūtra* upholding both these else views with all their implied differences under theory as well as practical discipline; but they were all superseded by Śaṁkara's great commentary upholding the latter view and are now lost. Attempts were made later to revive some of the superseded views wholly or in part by commentators like Bhaskara and Yadavaprakasa, but without much success. Though these interpretations do not abolish the conception of God, they prefer to look upon Brahman as the Absolute and may therefore be described as predominantly philosophic. There have also been purely theistic interpretations of the *Sūtra*, especially subsequent to Śaṁkara; and among them again we find distinctions due to the identification of the supreme God with Viṣṇ or Śiva. Thus Rāmānuja and Madhva uphold the supremacy of Viṣṇ, while Srīkaṇṭha exalts Śiva above him. Of these various schools of Vedānta, we shall consider here only two—one, that of Śaṁkara to represent the philosophic interpretation and the other, that of Rāmānuja to represent the theistic. Before proceeding to this consideration, we may add a word about the relation between the Mīmāṁsa- and the *Vedānta*-sūtra*s*. The two are regarded by all Vedantins now as complementary to each other and as together exhibiting the totality of Vedic teaching, though they differ in regard to the place that should be assigned in the scheme of Vedantic discipline to karma as taught in the former. Historically the two treatises were probably independent with different authors—Jaimini and Bādarāyaṇa respectively; and they were later put together with suitable emendations by someone who is described as Vyāsa—'the arranger.[7] Upavarsa, the

Vṛttikāra to whom we alluded in the previous chapter, seems to have commented upon them in this combined form. The date of the original work by Bādarāyaṇa is now believed to be about 400 A.D.

2. A. Advaita

The particular type of monism taught by Śaṁkara is very old, though in its final form it owes a great deal to his contribution. Its most distinguishing feature on the theoretical side is its conception of nirguna Brahman as the ultimate reality with the implied belief in the Māyā doctrine, the identity of the Jīva and Brahman and the conception of mokṣa as the merging of the former in the latter; on the practical side, it is the advocacy of Karma-saṁnyāsa or complete renunciation with its implication that jñāna and jñāna alone is the means of release. The earliest extant formulation of this doctrine is found in Gaudapada's *Karika*, which purports to summarize the teaching of the *Māṇḍūkya Upaniṣad*, but really accomplishes much more by giving an admirable summary of advaitic teaching. The main points of Śaṁkara's philosophy—its basic principles such as the inapplicability of the notion of causality to the ultimate reality—are already there. The most important of Śaṁkara's works is the bhāṣya on the *Vedānta-sūtra*, which is as remarkable for the charm of its style as for the logical consistency of its arguments. We have already mentioned that he therein maintains the vivarta-vada or the doctrine that the world is a phenomenal appearance of Brahman. According to him, the belief to be refuted before the Advaita is established is not so much the Sāṅkhya or Prakṛti-pariṇāma-vāda as Brahma-pariṇāma-vāda. On account of the fact that the treatise on which he comments alludes so frequently to the Sāṅkhya, Śaṁkara also considers it at length and shows how far removed it is from the Upaniṣadic doctrine; but his real objective is to establish the vivarta-vada or Māyā-vāda as against the pariṇāma-vāda of certain commentators on the *Vedānta-sūtra*, especially Bhartr-prapañca that preceded him.

Śaṁkara has also another aim in his bhāṣya: Owing to the resemblance, though only seeming, of his doctrine of nirguna Brahman to that of the sunya or 'void' of the Madhyamika form of Buddhistic idealism,[8] one might identify the two and regard the Advaita as alien to the Upaniṣads. So he emphasizes now and again the fact that this teaching is not negative or nihilistic. How far this contention can be maintained, we shall see later. He does not expressly mention this phase of Buddhism except in one place[9] and there he dismisses it summarily; but there is no doubt that he throughout tries to steer clear of these two doctrines opposed to his own, but yet so similar to it, viz. The Brahma-parinama-vada of some Vedāntins and the sūnya-vāda of the Mādhyamikas.

Besides the bhāṣya on the *Vedānta-sūtra*, Śaṁkara wrote commentaries on the principal Upaniṣads and the *Bhagvad-gītā*. Those especially on the *Bṛahadāranyaka* and *Chāndogya Upaniṣads* treat of several points that are not dealt with in comprehension and appreciation of the doctrine of Advaita. In addition to them, we have his *Upadeśa-sāhasrī*, which, though somewhat terse, gives a splendid account of his views. Śaṁkara's doctrine was defended and amplified in matters of detail by various thinkers after him, and this has given rise to some diversity of opinion among his followers. Two of the schools resulting from such divergences of view are in particular well known—the Vivarana school which goes back to the *Pañca-pādikā*, the fragment of a commentary on Śaṁkara's *Sūtra*-bhāṣya by his own pupil Padmapāda, and the slightly later Bhamati school represented by Vacaspati (A.D. 841). The *Pañca-pādikā* was commented upon by Prakāsātman (A.D. 1000) in his *Vivarana,* from which the first school takes its name. The Vivarana has a gloss known as *Tattva-dīpana* by Akhaṇḍānanda, and its teaching has also been most lucidly summarized by Vidyāraṇya (A.D. 1350) in his *Vivarana-prameya*-saṁgraha. The *Bhamati* has been explained by Amalananda (A.D. 1250) in his *Kalpa-taru*, which in its turn has been annotated by Appaya Dīkṣita

(A.D. 1600) in the *Parimala*. There are also various other commentaries of greater or less value on the *Sūtra-bhāṣya,* such as the *Brahma-vidyābharaṇa* of Advaita-nanda (A.D. 1450). Of the numerous hand-books written to explain the Advaita system, we may mention here the *Naiṣkarmya-siddhi* of Suresvara, who was at first probably a Mīmāṁsaka, and the *Saṁkṣepa-śarīraka* by his pupil, Sarvajñātman. Another work of particular value, especially in regard to the Māyā doctrine, is the *Iṣṭa-siddhi* of Vimuk-tatman (A.D. 1050). Later still are the *Nyāya-makaranda* of Anandabodha (A.D. 1050) and the *Panca-dasi* of Vidyāraṇya, a popular treatise. The *Siddhānta-leṣa*-saṁgraha of Appaya Dīkṣita describes the divergences of view, already mentioned, which arose within the doctrine as a result of its wide expansion in the centuries following Śaṁkara. The *Vedānta-paribhasa* of Dharmaraja Adhvarindra gives a technical and systematic exposition of the doctrine, especially on its logical and epistemological side; and the *Vedānta-sara* of Sadananda (A.D. 1550) is an easy introduction to Advaita philosophy. Among the exclusively polemical works written on the system should be mentioned the *Khaṇḍana-khaṇḍa-khādya* of Sriharsa (A.D. 1100), the poet of the *Naiṣadhīya-carita* and the *Advaita-siddhi* of Madhusudana Sarasvati (A.D. 1650) with its commentary, the *Laghu-candrikā* by Brahmananda, whose study is now regarded among the pundits as quite essential to true advaitic scholarship.

I

The Advaita resembles the Sāṅkhya-Yoga in regard to its conception of the psychic apparatus; and it also believes like the other in the theory of representative knowledge. The only difference that may be noticed is that while, according to the Sāṅkhya-Yoga, the ten senses are traced to ahaṁ-kāra, here they are supposed to be derived from elements much as in the Nyāya-Vaiśeṣika.[10] The internal organ (antaḥ-karaṇa) also is here conceived as bhautika and as constituted of all the five elements. Though it consists of all the five elements, tejas predominates, which accounts for its being sometimes described as Taijasa ('made out of tejas'). It accordingly partakes more of the character of that element than of any other and is unstable—always liable to alter its form either where it is or where it is or where it reaches by 'streaming out,' as it is said, through a sense. That is, the antah-karana is always active, except only in states like susupti, where it becomes latent. Each of the forms it assumes by exercising this activity is known as a vṛtti as in the Sāṅkhya-yoga. The explanation that all these organs are bhautika is important on account of the recognition it implies of the indispensableness of physical aids for the manifestation of consciousness. Though indispensable, their distinction from the psychical element is not in the least ignored. It is in fact the constant association of these two incompatibles as implied in common experience that forms, as we shall see, the crux of the philosophic problem according to Śaṁkara.

As regards the nature of the conscious element also, the explanation is almost the same as in the Sāṅkhya-Yoga. It is conceived as extraneous to the apparatus, which yet in ultimately different from the apparatus here as in the other system; for according to the Advaita the apparatus goes back eventually to the same source, viz. Brahman or spirit, the sole reality acknowledged. For this reason, the interaction between the two-the physical apparatus and the psychical principle—is more satisfactorily explained here than in the other doctrine. But, whatever the metaphysical difference, it does not affect the explanation with which we are concerned in this section. Accordingly we may assume for our present purpose that the two are distinct as in the Sāṅkhya-Yoga. The psychical element is viewed as wholly inactive. The activity it manifests only seemingly belongs to it and is in reality to be traced to its physical accompaniment, viz. The internal organ. The element of consciousness is known as the saksin[11] and corresponds to the purusa of the Sāṅkhya-Yoga—the passive observer of the states of the internal organ as they unfold themselves. It appears never by itself, but always in association with the internal organ in its latent or manifest form. The reverse also is true and no internal organ is conceivable without involving a reference to some saksin or other. Thus it is only the unity of the passive saksin and the active antah-karana that is real for all practical purposes. That is what knows, feels and wills. In this complex form it is known as the jīva or the empirical self. Such a conception satisfactorily accounts for what would otherwise be wholly unintelligible, viz. The double character of subject and object which one and the same jīva exhibits in so-called self-consciousness. But for the presence within it of the objective complement of the antah-karana one cold not, it is said, speak of knowing oneself, since what knows can never be the same as what is known—a view which is entirely opposed to that of Kumarila who regards the ego to be simple and yet ascribes this double character to it (p. 305). This complex entity is believed to endure in one form or other till the time of release. When at last it breaks up, the internal organ is absorbed by or loses its identity in its source, Māyā, which for the movement we may take to be the same as the prakṛti of the Sāṅkhya-Yoga, and the saksin losing its saksi-hood, as will become clear later, becomes Brahman indeed. The saksin and the jīva are thus not identical, though at the same time they are not quite different either. While the jīva may become the object of self-consciousness on account of the objective element it includes, it is wrong to speak of the saksin as knowable, for it is the pure element of awareness in all knowing; and to assume that it is knowable would be to imply another knowing element—a process which leads to the fallacy of infinite regress. But the sākṣin does not therefore remain unrealized, for being self-luminous, by its very nature, it does not require to be made known at all. Its presence is necessarily equivalent to its revelation and it is therefore never missed. 'That is self-luminousness,' says the *Pañca-daśī*, 'which is revelation without any aid.'[12] In other words, the jīva is spirit as immanent in the antah-karana, while the saksin is spirit as transcendent.[13]

By jñāna or knowledge in general we must understand in the system neither a vṛtti of the internal organ nor the saksin by itself, but a blend of both-the vṛtti as inspired by the saksin. In jñāna thus understood, the vṛtti element is contingent; the element of consciousness, is eternal, being intrinsically Brahman itself which, owing to its association with the vṛttis that appear and disappear, only seems to be characterized by change, but is really untouched by it. It is sometimes termed sākṣi-jñāna to distinguish it from vṛtti-jñāna to distinguish it from vṛtti-jnana or empirical knowledge which is a result of the interaction of subject and object. It is the light of all our seeing and does not cease to be even in deep sleep. The antah-karana may have modal transformations (parinama) other than vṛtti-jñāna, such as pain and pleasure. In fact, all internal states are viewed as its modes. But the system does not in theory regard those other states as states of consciousness so that they have to be known through a vṛtti-jñāna. This distinction does not mean that pain and pleasure, for instance, may exist and yet be not experienced; for as states or modes of the internal organ they are necessarily illumined by the saksin and are therefore known as they arise just as jñāna itself is.[14] It only shows that the doctrine differentiates the cognitive from the other phases of the mind. If we take this explanation with what we have already stated, viz. That except in states like sleep the internal organ will be ceaselessly operating we see that the jīva is never without some jñāna or other.

Knowledge may be mediate or immediate, the distinction between the two being that while in the former only the 'that' of an object is known, in the latter, the 'what' also is revealed.[15] Both kinds of knowledge are alike vṛttis of the internal organ in which the saksin is immanent. Knowledge which gives the object directly is not here equated with sensory perception, and there may be immediate knowledge not involving sense-perception. The empirical self for instance is immediately known, but it cannot be said to be *presented* to any sense. Hence the word pratyaksa, which literally means 'presented to a sense.' Is here usually replaced by the wider term aparoksa or 'not mediate.' If the following conditions are satisfied, knowledge will be immediate, not matter whether it comes through a sense or not. First, the object must be such as can be directly known (yogya). For example, a table can be so known but not virtue. This is not so much a condition of immediacy as an indication that not all things are perceivable. Secondly, the object must be existent at the time; otherwise even a perceivable object will not be immediately known. Our recollecion of a table that no longer exists cannot for this reason be immediate. Lastly, there should be established a certain intimate relation between the subject and the object in question. The means of such relation is the vṛtti which flows out[16] in the case of external objects, but remains within where it originates in the case of internal ones like pain or pleasure. It will be convenient to take the former variety of immediately knowledge for finding out the meaning of this condition. The subject and object are here by hypothesis removed from each other and occupy different positions in space; and the vṛtti which relates them brings about for the time being what may be described as an identity of ground for the two. The exact manner in which this takes place is stated as follows: When an organ of sense is brought into contact with an object, the antah-karana, like a searchlight as it were, goes out towards it and gets itself determined by it or assumes the 'form' of that object. The existence of the object previous to the appearance of knowledge is thus necessary so that Psychologocally the thoery is realistic. When the vṛtti coincides with the object, perceptual knowledge arises. The coincidence of these two, since the vṛtti is a mode of the internal organ, is really the coincidence of the jīva and the object. They thus come to have the same ground; or the being of the object, as it is stated, ceases then to be different from the being of the subject.[17] It is their identification in this manner that constitutes the third and the last of the conditions for an object being known immediately. Perception as conceived here is accordingly the result of a communion between the knower and the known; and it would therefore be more appropriate to describe the object as 'felt' then rather than known.[18] In the case of internal perception, when the first two conditions are satisfied, i.e. when the object is perceivable and is actually present at the time, the last condition is invariably fulfilled, for internal states like pain or pleasure are not, as already explained, different in fact from the vṛtti through which they are supposed to be experienced. So if those states admit of being directly perceived at all (yogya),[19] they do become immediately known whenever they exist. If knowledge occurs when one or more of these conditions are lacking, it will be mediate. The table beyond the wall can be known only mediately, for the vṛtti cannot flow out to it to bring about the needed relation, contact with one or other sensory organ being a necessary condition for the starting out of the antah-karana towards the object. But even here, we should remember, a vṛtti is recognized, though it remains internal.

The above view of knowledge implies a classification of objects into those that can be directly known and those that cannot be so known. They may belong to the external world or may be states or modes of the internal organ. External objects may be perceivable and may also be present at the time; yet they may or may not be directly known. Internal states, on the other hand, when they satisfy those two conditions are necessarily known immediately. To these two kinds of objects must be added a third which is not only necessarily known immediately but is always so known. That is the empirical ego—the jīva or aham padartha as the same is sometimes designated. It is no doubt that object side that is commonly attended to in knowledge; but it does not mean that the subject remains unrevealed in it, although it may not always show itself quite explicitly. As in the Prabhakara school, all knowledge alike involves a reference to it; and since the jīva, accordingly to the Advaita is never without some jñāna or other, the consciousness of self becomes a constant feature of all experience. It is this sense of self that explains how one person is able to distinguish his experience from that of others. It is absent only in states like susupti or fainting.

So far we have treated of knowledge during the waking state. But there is dream experience as well and even sleep is not quite bereft of experience. We have now to consider these states specifically. As already stated in the chapter on the Upaniṣads, the essential distinction between dreams and waking is that the senses co-operate in the latter, but not in the former. Further, unlike waking, dreaming is not marked by an association with the gross body. Yet there is in it the feeling that the senses are co-operating and that a gross body—not necessarily similar to that of the waking state—is also present. We may dream of an elephant and we may feel that we are riding on it. The consequence is that we experience objects as existent at the time. This peculiarity precludes the explanation of the state as due to a mere revival of past impressions. Dreams are really more than revived impressions; they are new creations. A revival of the impressions left by previous experience is of course necessary for them, but it does not furnish their whole explanation. Dreams, so far as they are direct experience, should be placed on a par with waking; and it is accordingly assumed that objects are present then, apart from their knowledge. In memory on the other hand that is not the case, the reference in it to things as past being quite clear. The character of dream-objects, however, is held to be different from that of the objects of wakeful experience; but the explanation of this point we have to postpone till we reach the next section.

If the internal organ functions by itself in dreams unlaided by the senses, that also becomes latent in sleep. Of the two elements that make up the jīva, one, viz. The antaḥ-karana, is lost in its cause Māyā or, to state it more definitely, in that part or aspect of it called avidyā which constitutes the adjunct of individual jīvas.[20] What endures then is the Sākṣin *plus* avidyā which is known as the kāraṇa-sarira or the 'radical adjunct' of the self as distinguished from its subtle body (limṅga-śarīra).[21] Consequently there is in sleep on subject at all as such and no states of consciousness as in dreams or waking. This makes the 'experience' of dreamless sleep quite unique, though occurring normally and almost universally. What we have in that condition is the sākṣin—not the jīva—associated with its own avidyā, in which the internal organ has provisionally merged. In this state also, we must remember, individuality persists; but the individuality then is due to the union of the saksin with avidyā and not with the internal organ. The avidyā operates in sleep only partially. It obscures the true character of reality, but does not split it up into a variety of 'names' and 'forms' as in dreams or in waking, since the discontinuous and mutually excluding vṛttis of the internal organ are absent there. The experience of sleep involves a reference to both these elements—continuance of personality and absence of all variety—as is shown by the later reminiscence[22] that one was asleep and did not know anything. Over and above these there is felt in sleep bliss which, according to a fundamental postulate of the system, is the very nature of the self and which, owing to the absence of all distractions then, becomes manifest. This unalloyed happiness survives even after waking, as shown by the state of repose that continues for a while; but it disappears as man lapses back into the vortex of common life—a belief which is Wordsworthian in its character.[23] 'All beings visit that Brahma-world day after day, but not one realizes it.'[24] None of these features of sleep, it must be noted, is 'known' at the time, for no knowledge, whether mediate or immediate, is possible in the absence of the internal organ. But they are nevertheless realized then as shown by the fact of their being recalled afterwards.

II

There seem to be strictly but two views in regard to the implication of knowledge—either to deny, like the Yogacara school of Buddhism, that it ever points to an object outside or to admit that it does so always. To postulate the object where knowledge is true while denying it either directly or indirectly where knowledge is erroneous is self-contradictory. To Śaṁkara, all knowledge in the common acceptance of the term points to an object as it does to a subject, and there is no knowledge which does not involve this double implication. Where there is no object, there can be no knowledge.[25] The 'round square' and the 'barren woman's son' are unreal (asat) and there can consequently be no knowledge of them beyond a merely verbal one. But it may be asked how, if all knowledge alike points to an object, illusions occur. In answering the question it will be necessary to refer to the example given in the previous chapter to illustrate the pramana known as arthapatti which the Advaitin also recognizes. If Devadatta continues to be strong and healthy, though not eating by day, we do not at once modify or give up our belief about the need of food for living beings, but try to reconcile the observed fact with it, and in so doing we assume that he must eating by night. That is, when we are face with a fact which contradicts a well-tested view, we do not all at once revise that view, but endeavour to harmonize the new fact with it by means of a suitable hypothesis. In the present case, since it is inconceivable that knowledge should arise without an objective counterpart to it, the Advaitin assumes that there is an object even in the so-called illusion; and, in order to distinguish illustion from non-illusory knowledge, postulates a difference between the *types* of objects cognized in them. The distinction between illusion and ordinary knowledge is not accordingly due to the absence and presence respectively of an object outside corresponding to its content, but to the difference in the character of the object that is pointed to in either. Objects of illusion are not common to several or general, their presence not being vouched for by collective experience. The serpent (say) which a person sees in the dark where there is only a rope is special to him and may not be seen by others. It may therefore be described as 'private' or personal to him, while objects of common knowledge such as a real serpent are public,' for they are cognized by others as well. A second difference between the two types of objects is that while an object of illusion lasts only as long as its knowledge lasts—neither for a longer nor for a shorter period—that of ordinary knowledge is more enduring. The latter is already there before it comes to be apprehended and, generally speaking,[26] continues to be after its apprehension ceases, as is shown for instance by our recognition of it later[27]; the former on the other hand comes to exist as we apprehend it and ceases to be when our apprehension of it ceases. The one is described as vyavaharika or empirical; the other as pratibhasika or apparent. Dream objects, to whole difference from those of the waking state we have already referred, are of the second type.

The objects which we have described as private, it is necessary to remember, are not mere ideas or purely subjective. If they were, the advaitic theory of knowledge would be the same as the yogacara one which Samakara unreservedly criticized,[28] viz. That there is no object apart from its knowledge and that the commonly recognized distinction between them is a fiction. No private object can indeed be conceived except as dependent upon a particular individual; the point to be noted is that it is not mental, but an object of mind. This is brought out clearly in the explanation given of the origin and nature of pratibhasika things to which we shall soon refer. For the present we merely note that the foregoing account shows how mistaken is the common belief that Śaṁkara views the objects of everyday experience to be false or unreal. So far from doing this, he claims some **kind** of reality even for objects of illusion. To be perceived is for him *to be*, and his theory may therefore be described as an inversion of the one associated in western philosophy with the name of Berkeley. This explanation has one great merit. It accounts for illusion as it occurs. What we experience in it is that we *see* the serpent or silver; and this fact of knowing an object as present then and there is not explained, but is rather explained away in other theories of illusion.

In the light of this distinction among the objects of knowledge, we may explain error as arising when different types of things are related in a judgment.[29] In the example 'This is silver,' the 'this' (i.e. shell) is empirically real and 'silver' which is superposed upon it is only apparently so. In other words, error is 'illegitimate transference' or adhyasa as Śaṁkara puts it in his celebrated Introduction to the *Vedānta-sūtra.* Though the empirical and the apparent spheres are both objective, we, for the reasons assigned above, take that which is superposed as less real than that on which it is, That falsity of such knowledge is not realized until we become conscious of the disparity between the objects related in it. When a person is seeing silver where there is only shell, he certainly does not know it to be false. On the other hand, he then feels convinced that it is quite as valid as any other knowledge. But when he approaches the object, picks it up and discovers that it is too light to be silver, he at once realizes that he was in error. What leads to the discovery is therefore this other knowledge[30] whose object, because it is of the emprical kind, is not similarly sublated.[31] Now as regards the relation between the two terms involved in error: It cannot be identity, for things belonging to different levels of being cannot be identified. Nor can it be difference, for then the terms would not appear as subject and predicate in the same judgement as 'This is silver.' We cannot take it as identity-in-difference either, for that conception, as we shall see in the next section, is self-discrepant. The relation is therefore regarded as unique and is called tadatmya.[32] It is not real, because it obtains between terms that belong to two different orders of being. The water that is quaffed in a dream will not quench actual thirst. At the same time the relation is not unreal, for it is experienced. It is therefore like the lower of the two objects it relates, apparent, not empirical. We may further remark that the relation is such that negating the higher of the two relate necessarily negates the lower. But the reverse is not true. If the shell is denied, the silver *is not*; but the negation of the silver is quite conceivable with the affirmation of the shell.[33] This is what constitutes appearance. We accordingly describe the shell as the ground[34] of which the silver is an appearance.

It is necessary to eludicate further the idea of adhyasa. From the fact that wherever there is adhyasa, there is a confusion between two orders of being, we deduce that it presupposes ignorance. It is because we are oblivious of the shell that we see silver in its place. There are other causes also, such as the previous experience of silver, defective eye-sight, etc., to account for the mistake; but it will suffice for our purpose to confine our attention to the most important of them, viz. Ignorance or avidyā. Now avidyā, which is only another word for ajñāna, implies, like jñāna, some person to whom it belongs (āśraya) and some object to which it refers (visaya). The notion of 'knowledge' is not complete until we mention the subject that knows and the object that is known. Similarly, in the case of avidyā, there must be someone whom it characterizes and an object which is misapprehended in it. In the present case, the person that mistakes the shell for silver is its āśraya, and the shell is its visaya. It is avidyā[35] thus determined that is described as the cause of silver[36]; and it operates in a double manner. It conceals the fact of shell and shows up silver in its place. To see silver where there is only shell, necessary condition is the concealment of the shell. Suppression precedes substitution. These two aspects of it are respectively termed avarana or 'veiling' and vikṣepa or 'revealing.' As the avidyā does not put the shell entirely out of sight, it is not lack of apprehension—a mere gap in thought—but misapprehension and is therefore described as positive (bhāva-rūpa). It is the contrary of vidyā, not its conradictory; and the condition for the resulting error to disappear is the removal of avidyā which happen when vidyā arises in the self-same person in regard to the self-same object. It is the reference to a particular individual and to a specific object which this avidyā involves that explains the uniqueness of the silver of which it is described as the source. Because it has a specific external object as its basis, the silver to which it gives rise appears out there—spatially determined—and is not a mere idea; and, because it has a particular person for its āśraya, the illusion which it occasions is special to him. It is this personal character that distinguishes private objects from the empirical ones which, as we shall see later, spring into being directly from Māyā and are 'public' or verifiable by others also. Through the objects we are now considering form an order by themselves, they are not altogether sundered from the other, for avidyā which occasions private objects is dependent upon the same source to which the common order of nature is due, viz. Māyā,[37] and is therefore described sometimes as tūlāvidyā or auxiliary avidya.[38] It is owing to this sameness of the source that when Māyā is overcome in mokṣa both realms of objective being disappear alike. Otherwise though the common order of nature may cease to be then, the other might persist.

There is one important instance of adhyasa which we must specially consider now—the ego or ahaṁ-padārtha. Systems like the Nyāya-Vaiśeṣika and the Mīmāṁsa regard it as a simple and ultimate entity. It is in fact synonymous with the self (ātman) in those doctrines. But the Advaitin denies the integrity of the self in this sense and takes it, we know, to be a complex of the śakṣin and the internal organ. His reasons in favour of this position are chiefly two; One is the fact of self-consciousness which by showing in the same self the contrary features of subject and object indicates its mixed character., The other is the uniqueness of sleep experience. If the ego or jīva were simple and endured throughout, all experience would alike involve a reference to it. But that is not the case, for sleep as interpreted here is without such reference. We are therefore compelled to explain it as consisting of two elements one of which, viz. The internal organ, is common only to waking and dream; and to it accordingly should be ascribed all the specific features of those states. 'Love, desire, pleasure, pain and so forth are experienced when the internal organ functions, but not in sleep; hence they must be of the internal organ.,[39] Now the Nyāya-Vaiśeṣika and the Mīmāmāsa, which hold that the ego is not analysable, maintain that it is distinct from the body, senses, etc. But there is ordinarily an implied identification of these distinct entities, as for instance when one says 'I am stout,' 'I am blind,' where 'stoutness' and 'blindness' which are respectively the characteristics of the body and the sense of sight are predicated of the self. These systems explain the identification as more or less consiciously made, as for example when we describe a man as a 'giant' and as therefore having only a secondary or rhetorical significance (gauṇa)—supporting their position by reference to the equally familiar experience finding expression as 'my body,' etc., where the distinction appears explicitly. The Advaitin does not accept this explanation. He contends that the characteristic of gauna or secondary usage, viz. The consciousness at the time of the distinction between the objects identified, is lacking here fand ascribes the identification to an unconscious confusion between the entities involved, viz. Body, senses, etc., on the one hand, and the śakṣin on the other. It accordingly involves, in his view, ignorance of the true character of those entities and is a case of error or adhvasa. There are indeed occasions, he admits, when we do distinguish between the two, as when we speak of 'our body,' but he explains them as only flashes of the truth which are soon veiled from us. This argument is applicable to the antah—karana also and when a person feels pain, for example, and says 'I am suffering,' he is illegitimately transferring to the true atman what according to the previous reasoning belongs to the antaḥ-karaṇa.[40] If the ego is complex and is an instance of adhyasa, the entities constituting it must belong to different orders of being. We get a hint here of a third kind of reality; for the internal organ, one of the two involved in it, is an empirical reality being an effect of Māyā and as such stands higher than appearances having avidyā for their source. The higher reality is the śakṣin or more strictly[41] saksi-svarūpa which is Brahman itself. It is designated true or pāramarthika reality.[42]

If error signifies that the objects related in it belong to different orders of being, truth by implication should consist in relating objects of the same order; but, for reasons to be explained presently, we shall take this definition as holding good only within the sphere of empirical things and not in the case of appearances which are contradicted when we judge them in relation to that sphere. A dream-judgment like 'This is an elephant' is not true although its two terms alike stand for realities of the pratibhasika type, because both are set aside so soon as one awakes.[43] Pramāṇa we accordingly define as that which leads to knowledge whose content is not sublated (abādhita) as the result of later experience.[44] The silver seen where there is only a shell disappears the moment we scrutinize it, but the shell does not vanish in the same manner. The knowledge of the silver is therefore bhrama and that of the shell, prama. True, even the latter may prove a delusion from a higher standpoint; but such a consideration may be excluded when we are contrasting empirical things with appearances. What is meant when we say that the knowledge of the shell is prama is that, unlike that of the silver, it justifies its claim for truth throughout empirical life[44]—not that it is ultimately real. As regards the question whether novelty (anadhigatatva) should be regarded as a necessary element in truth (p. 313), the Advaitin is indifferent; but with his partiality for the Bhatta view, he would prefer to include it among the conditions of validity. In accordance with the orthodox view of revelation (p. 180), this condition is necessary in the case of śruti.[46]

The Advaita recognizes all the six pramanas mentioned in connection with the Kumārila school of Mīmāṁsa and generally agrees with it in matters of detail also.[47] Of the points of difference between the ftwo, it will suffice to touch upon only the following here, all of them having reference to verbal testimony:—

(i) The Mīmāṁsa rejects the view that the Veda was ever composed by anybody (p. 312), and the Nyāya-Vaiśeṣika ascribes its authorship to Īśvara (p. 258). The position of Śaṁkara in regard to this point, like fthat of the other Vedantins, is midway between the two. Like the Mīmāṁsaka, but unlike the Nyāya-Vaiśeṣika, he admits that the Veda is apauruseya; but he re-defines that word so as to make it signify not that the Veda has no author and is eternal, but that it is produced or, more properly, resuscitated at the beginning of each kalpa by one that cannot interfere either with its content or with the order of its words. In the case of works like the *Raghu-vaṁṣa*, the author composes it just as he likes. Here, on the other hand, the first promulgator of the Veda in every cycle who is God repeats it anew, but precisely as it was in earlier cycles. That is, the Veda is self-existent in this view also; only it is not the self-same Veda that always is, but a series of what may be described as re-issues of an eternal edition which goes back to beginningless time. This, it will be seen, it not in substance different from the Mīmāṁsa view, excepting that it finds a place for God in the doctrine.

(ii) Śaṁkara, following Kumārila, admits śabda to be a pramana outside the Veda also; but he does not restrict its independent logical validity, within the Veda, to injunctive statements (p. 318). Assertive propositions found there may be equally valid, so that there is nothing in the nature of the veda as verbal testimony to preclude it from treating directly of matters of fact (bhuta-vastu) like Brahman or the highest reality. Statements like Tat tvam asi which occur in the Upaniṣads thereby acquire independent logical value here; and there is no need to subordinate them in one way or another to ritualistic commands as in the Mīmāṁsa.

(iii) The truth revealed by the scriptures, contrary to what the Mīmāṁsaka thinks, is here the fundamental unity of Being. We shall see later in what sense this unity is to be understood in the Advaita, and may now consider the place in the scheme of pramanas of perception which seems to vouch for the truth of diversity and thus to come into conflict with the teaching of revelation that all is one. The primary aim of perception, like that of the other pramanas, is, according to Śaṁkara, to serve empirical purposes. It gives no guarantee for metaphysical validity,[48] so that what we commonly hold real may not be truly so. Common knowledge is true,' he says[49] so long only as the identity of oneself with Brahman is not realized, as dreams are until one does not awake.' In other words, the transcendental ideality of the world does not exclude its empirical reality.[50] Such a view considerably modifies the notion of inherent validity (svataḥprāmāṇya) which the Advaitin, like the Mīmāṁsaka, accepts. That knowledge is true requires, according to the Advaita also, no explanation, for by its very nature it is so. This self-validity, however, for the reason just mentioned, is to be understood here as relative and not absolute as in the Mīmāṁsa. Even the validity of the Veda, generally speaking, is only such. When it teaches that svarga can be attained through the performance of a certain sacrifice, it is of course true; but the Veda does not thereby couch for the *ultimate* reality of either the svarga or anything connected with it. The fact is that the Advaita recognizes a higher, viz. The absolute standpoint from which all pramanas alike, inclusive of the Veda, lose their relative validity. An exception is made only in the case of Upaniṣadic statements that teach the unity of all being. These statements are pramana in the absolutesense, for the knowledge which they convey is never shown to be wrong. But it does not secure for the pramana itself ultimate reality, for in mokṣa where nothing but Brahman remains, even that pramana as such must disappear. It signifies that a false means may lead to a true end—a position which may appear untenable; but there are many instancesin life where this happens. The image of a person as reflected in a mirror is not real, but it does not therefore fail to serve as the means or showing to him so many facts about his appearance. The roaring of a lion in a dream is not real, but it may wake the dreamer to actual life. It is necessary, however, to remember in thus admitting the utility of error that nothing here is absolutely unreal so that even a false means is not without a nucleus of truth.[51]

So much about vṛtti-jñāna or knowledge fast fit is commonly known to us. But according to the advaitic analysis of it, empirical knowledge is a complex consisting of a physical factor and a psychical one, neither of which by itself is adequate to explain experience as we are familiar with it. We have now to point out the full implication of this analysis on its psychical side. The śakṣin which is the psychical element is always present like an ever-luminous lamp, the enduring and changeless element in experience which does not cease to be even in deep sleep. It is individual and determinate, being defined by reference to the particular internal organ with which for the time being it seems associated. It is accordingly termed jīva-saksin. What comes within the range of one śakṣin—through the medium of its own antahkarana in the waking and dream states and through avidyā in deep sleep—is not necessarily within the experience of other saksins. But existent objects as a whole can be understood only as presented to some śakṣin, for consistently with the eventually idealistic position of the Advaita there can be no reality outside what either knows or is known. This line of reasoning leads to the postulating of a cosmic śakṣin or absolute consciousness (Īśvara-saksin) which sustains everything that is.[52] It is, in reality, the ground of the whole universe and is, as we shall see more fully in the next section, the Brahman of the Advaita. It is designated svarupa-jñāna or pure consciousness. The vṛtti-jñāna draws its breath and substance from it, and the whole complex of empirical or finite knowledge would be nowhere without the light of this absolute or infinite consciousness.

To sum up: Our analysis of experience has led us, on the one hand, to an infinite consciousness or absolute spirit (anubhuti or caitanya); and, on the other, to two realms of objects which, however, have no being apart from that spirit. We may deduce this principle from the nature of the saksin as we have just done or from the nature of those realms of being. We may argue that just as the pratibhasika reality points to a vyavaharika one, the vyavaharika in its turn does, to a pramarthika reality. If an appearance lasts only as long as its jñāna lasts and the empirical persists ever afterwards, this higher reality is timeless. Thus we have altogether three orders of being of which two alone are related to time. The third, which is the same as the svarupa-jñāna referred to above, is the Brahman of the Vedānta. The recognition of this higher reality reveals a new form of error. The one we have drawn attention to thus far is that in which a pratibhasika object is superposed upon a vyavaharika one. It is error as is familiarly known. But if error is illegitimate transference, the superposition of an empirical 'what' on the highest Being also should be erroneous. This is not, however, error which occurs *within* the world of experience like the other, but lies at the root of it. It is involved in the very notion of the ego or the knowing subject (pramata) because in it two incompatibles are, as we have seen, confounded with each other. It therefore vitiates all our knowledge at its source. The whole of the universe in the form in which it is experienced by us is due to this metaphysical error wherein the empirical is mistaken for the real, and is an abstraction apart from its ground, viz. Brahman.[53] That is, there is a higher standpoint from which even empirical things are only appearances. It is in this sense that the Advaita maintains that the world is not real (mithya) and that Brahman is the sole truth. The conception of truth and error in the system thus becomes relative, and it is essentially wrong to speak of any knowledge as true or false without mentioning at the same time the sphere with reference to which it is adjudged. It was for this reason that we defined truth above relatively to a particular level of being, viz. the empirical. Really, however, even this 'truth' is an error. Only we should not forget that, according to the Advaita, all error is but partially so, for it contains a core of truth—the shell for instance in the case of silver and in the case of the shell itself when we regard it as not real, the higher reality of which it is an appearance.

III

The ontological position of the Advaita has already been indicated generally in dealing with its view of knowledge. We shall now restate the same, adding some details. Of the three types of being mentioned, we need treat only of two here, viz. the empirical and the true or the metaphysical. The former, we have already stated, is common to all and exists independently of individual consciousness. It also, as experienced by different individuals, is no doubt partly divergent, for each cognizes only so much of the world as is within the reach of his limited faculties and is in kinship with his particular temperament. To give the illustration of the *Pancadasi,*[54] a father may think that his son who has gone away from home to a distant place is alive while as a matter of fact he is no more. One and the same object again may occasion different and even opposite feelings in different persons. But these worlds as given in the experience of individuals are not entirely separate. They have, as indeed we ordinarily take for granted, a common basis unlike the dream-worlds, for instance, of two or more persons. That is the world as it is; and it is termed Īśvara-sṛṣṭa ('God-created'), while the same as it exists in the medium of one's individual consciousness is described as jīva-sṛṣṭa[55] ('jīva-created'). Such a view implies that we accept many selves. There is of course nothing preventing us from criticizing this position as a begging of the question, but the only alternative to it is solipsism, which, though as a theory it may be irrefutable, is repugnant to thought and really stultifies all effort at philosophizing. We shall accordingly take for granted the plurality of selves so far as our present discussion goes. These selves or jīvas differ from the common objects of experience in being coeval with time and not in it like them[56]—a belief which the Advaitin shares with the followers of the other orthodox systems. Thus each of the indefinite number of selves we have assumed has been there from the beginning of time or is anadi. The empirical world which is vouched for by collective experience presents both unity and diversity, there being a common and enduring element along with different and changing ones in it. It may be described as a systematic whole, for it exhibits a causal order. It also involves a purpose inasmuch as its creation, as explained in the chapter on the Upaniṣads, rests upon a moral necessity. Such indications of physical and moral order in it, no doubt, are not altogether conclusive; but there is the significant fact that they become more numerous and clearer with the advance of knowledge and the growth of human institutions. When once the cosmic character of the world is admitted, we trace it back to a source which, though simple, accounts for all aspects of it. This source or the first cause is Māyā which symbolizes to us the unitary character of the physical world. Diversity is only implicit in it, while in the objective world that develops from it, it is quite explicit. There is, however, one important difference between Māyā and its products. The latter, as their very description as 'products' testifies, have all a beginning in time; but the former being the first cause can obviously have no such beginning. It also is therefore anadi like the jīvas alluded to above. Jīvas and Māyā thus form a new type of entities and differ from common objects which are all in time; but they are not, it should be added, altogether unrelated to time like Brahman or the ultimate reality.

It has been stated that the sphere of empirical objects is independent of individual consciousness. On the principle, however, to which we have already referred that whatever is, if not itself mind, must be for mind, it should depend upon some consciousness; for otherwise the statement that it *is* would be meaningless. Granting such an all-sustaining consciousness, it is easy to see what conditions it must satisfy. It should last as long as the world in its causal or effect form lasts. That is, it must be anadi. It cannot be any finite consciousness in the sense in which a jīva is, for it must know the contents of the entire universe. Not only this, whatever is known must also be correctly and directly known by it, for error and mediate knowledge which imply limitation of one kind or another are, by our hypothesis, excluded in the case of that consciousness. That is, its experience must be direct, complete and correct. This cosmic subject, as we may term it, to whom the whole of existence is related as an object, is the Īśvara of Advaita and it is the third of the entities coeternal with time along with Māyā and the jīvas. Here we find the triple factor forming the subject-matter of all philosophy and religion. To them we may add a fourth, viz. Time itself to which we have all along been alluding but which cannot be brought under any of the other three heads.

We shall now briefly state the nature of these four entities which, though they are not distinct from the empirical universe, stand on a footing of their own:—

(I) *Jīva.*—This is the empirical self, the true nature of which has already been considered. It is manifold, each jīva having its own peculiar features, although agreeing with the rest of its class in many respects. It represents the spiritual element in the universe; but it is the spiritual element appearing not by itself, but invariably in association with physical adjuncts such as the antah-karana. Its essential associate, however, is avidyā, the individual's share of Māyā which is the adjunct of Īśvara. Just as the whole universe is the effect of Māyā, the portions of the universe which constitute the gross and subtle bodies of an individual self are conceived as the effects of that particular self's avidyā. In fact, the relation of Īśvara to the world is exactly parallel to that of the jīva to its own organism. Considered apart from these individual and cosmic accompaniments, the jīva and Īśvara are one or, more strictly, are not different. That is the significance of Tat tvam asi. The jīvas which we have assumed to be many are in consequence only empirically so; and the individuality characterizing each is due to its adjuncts such as the body and the senses. Intrinsically they are but one, for each is alike the supreme reality.

(2) *Māyā.*—This is the first cause of the physical universe and consequently corresponds to the prakṛti of the Sāṅkhya-Yoga; but there are important differences and metaphysically the two are poles asunder. From it spring into being not only organic bodies that house jīvas but also all inorganic nature. The things arising from Māyā we commonly regard as real; but truly they cannot be described as either sat or asat. They are known (dṛśya) and to that extent at any rate cannot be unreal, for the absolutely unreal, like 'the hare's horn,' is only words. Nor can they be regarded as real in their own right, for they are objective (jaḍa) and hence depend entirely upon spirit for their being. This characteristic of not being finally classifiable as either real or unreal (sadasadvilaksana) constitutes

the uniqueness of the things of experience and should naturally be found also in their cause, Māyā. They are neither something nor nothing, and are therefore termed mithya. They are not unreal as commonly assumed by the critics of the doctrine; only they are not ultimate. Or, in other words, their reality is relative and they may be regarded as appearances when contrasted with the higher reality of Brahman. In giving rise to such things, Māyā resembles avidyā, the source of common illusions, and is therefore described as the principle of cosmic illusion. In this it differs from the prakṛti of the Sāṅkhya-Yoga which is real in the full sense of the term.

(3) *Īśvara.*—We described Māyā as the source of the physical universe. But this source, for reasons already assigned, being altogether dependent upon the cosmic saksin, cannot act by itself. In strictness, therefore, the two elements should together be reckoned as giving rise to the world. Here we find another point of difference from the Sāṅkhya-Yoga where prakṛti is supposed to be endowed with the spontaneity required for manifesting of itself the whole of the physical world. It is the cause of the world in this complex form or spirit together with Māyā that is the Īśvara of Advaita. Or as it is somewhat differently expressed, Māyā is the potency (sakti) inherent in Īśvara through which he manifests the objective world with all its diversity of names and forms.[57] But he at the same time sees through the diversity, so that he never misses its underlying unity as we do. Though the universe as emerging from Īśvara is not around but within him, the exercise of this potency gives rise to a sense of 'the other'; and Māyā may therefore be regarded as the principle of self-consciousness or self-determination. It interpolates a distinction where really there is none. In this sense, Māyā cannot be the source of the universe, but is a mere accessory to

Īśvara in bringing it into existence out of himself. For reasons similar to those adduced in explaining the parallel conception of avidyā—the source of ordinary illusions, Māyā or the principle of cosmic illusion is conceived as more than a negation of jñāna. The very fact that it serves as the cause of the visible universe shows that it should be so far positive. It is again, on the analogy of avidyā, described as having two powers—āvaraṇa and vikṣepa. In its vikṣepa phase it projects the aggregate of names and forms constituting the world. The function of avarana is to obscure the unity of Being; but since that unity is never concealed from Īśvara, Māyā in its avarana aspect is stated to be powerless over him. Nature does not veil spirit from him. This sets a vast gulf between the jīva and Īśvara. It, in fact, accounts for the bondage of the one and the freedom of the other. Owing to the power which the avarana phase of Māyā or avidyā wields over it, the jīva believes in the ultimacy of mere variety, and to this belief, as also to its fragmentary view of the world already mentioned, should be traced all the evil to which it is subject. It ordinarily identifies itself with the organism with which it is bound up and looks upon the rest of reality as wholly external. It develops likes and dislikes for a small part of it, and assumes an attitude of indifference towards the rest. In the case of Īśvara, on the contrary, such preferences and exclusions are impossible according to our hypothesis. He identifies himself with the whole world and the identification is not, as in the case of the jīva and its organism, due to any confusion (adhyāsa) between the self and the not-self, but is the outcome of a continual realization of the true nature of both. The ideal of morality as conceived in the Advaita, we may state in passing, is gradually to replace the narrow view held by the jīva by one like that of the cosmic-self, whose interests coincide with those of the universe.[58] 'Considerations of "mine" and "thine" weigh only with the little-minded; to the large-hearted, on the other hand, the whole world is like a single household.'[59]

Such a conception naturally lends itself to a two-fold presentation, and that is why it is described not only as Īśvara or 'the Lord' but also as the saguna Brahman. The former being personal may be taken as the ideal of advaitic religion—standing for an all-knowing almighty God, the creator, preserver and destroyer of the world; the latter, not being so, as that of advaitic philosophy—standing for the Absolute which explains the world-system as it is. When we consider the universe in reference to this supereme subject, there is only one type of reality in place of the two found in the case of the jīva; and that is of the phenomenal or pratibhasika type. For by hypothesis whatever is, is known to Īśvara and no part of it lasts longer than the time during which it is experienced. In this sense, Īśvara may be described as an eternal dreamer. But we must not think that he is deluded. That would be so if he did not realize the identity of the objective world with himself, or if any aspect of the truth about it remained unrevealed to him. What is meant by describing Īśvara's world as pratibhasika is that its unity with himself being always realized, all variety *as such* is known to him to be mere abstraction. It is just this distinction between the relation of the world to Īśvara on the one hand and to the jīva on the other that critics over-look when they say that according to Śaṁkara the objective world is unreal. It is no doubt an appearance to Īśvara, but not to us who have not realized its unity with ourselves. Till we are able to do so and make our life a mirror of our new convictions, we must view it as real whatever its ultimate nature may be.

(4) *Time*—We have so far assumed an entity like time and taken it as lying outside the remaining three. It really represents the relation between spirit and Māyā.[60] Of these, the former alone is completely real and not Māyā also. Hence the relation between them, like that

between the shell and silver, cannot be fully real. That is, time is phenomenal. In this connection it is necessary to point out the advaitic view of space. It is regarded as an offshoot of Māyā and the first object to be created,[61] so that the Advaitin does not place time and space on the same footing. Its conception presupposes the principle of causation already at work but not so the conception of time. While all things born, excepting space, are in time and space, space is in time only. Jīva, Īśvara and Māyā are neither in time nor in space.

These are the fundamental entities of the Advaita considered from the empirical standpoint. It is not necessary to enter here into cosmological details, for they are practically the same as those mentioned in the chapter on the Upaniṣads. These entities, it should be clear from their description given above, are not disparate. They are interrelated and together constitute a system which, as time is included in it, may be taken to be dynamic in its character. The question now to consider is whether such a conception is satisfactory enough to remain final. The conclusion of the Advaita is that it is not, whether we judge it from the standpoint of practical religion or from that of speculative philosophy:—

(1) Thus to view it as representing a theistic ideal: There is the well-known difficulty—to mention only one—of reconciling God's assumed goodness and power with the presence of physical and moral evil in the world.[62] Even supposing that evil exists only from our standpoint and not from that of God or Īśvara as defined above, the theistic position does not become fully comprehensible. We cannot, for instance, understand why god should have created the world. To ascribe a motive to him would be to admit that he world. To ascribe a motive to him would be to admit that he has ends to attain; and that would be to question his perfection or all-sufficiency (paritrptatvam). To deny a motive and ascribe the work of creation to his intrinsic nature or to some

sudden impulse in him would be to reduce God to an automation or attribute caprice to him; and either way his supposed omniscience is compromised.[63] There are solutions of such difficulties suggested in the Advaita as in theistic doctrines generally; and these attempts at justifying the ways of God to man are not without their appeal to the religious mind. But, as Śaṁkara observes, they are not final because they 'have reference to the world of names and forms founded upon avidyā.'[64] In other words, such solutions, like the problems they solve, keep us tied to the realm of relativity and, as the essence of the relative is to point beyond itself for its complete explanation, the theistic conception cannot be regarded as ultimate.

(2) The same conclusion is reached when we regard it as the philosophic Absolute. The relation for instance which appears to constitute its several elements into a system will on examination be seen to be not really intelligible. Let us consider first the place of the jīvas in it: Since, according to the doctrine, the jīvas do not originate and are anadi like the saguna Brahman itself, the relation between the two should be anadi. So much is certain. But what is the nature of this relation? It is not identity, for the saguna Brahman cannot be the same as any of the jīvas with its fragmentary experience. Nor can it be regarded as a collection of all of them, for that would give us only a collection of individual experiences and not, as required, an integral one which alone can serve as the ground and explanation of the whole universe. That is, we cannot identify the saguna Brahman with either any of the jīvas or with the totality of them. Equally impossible is it to think of it as altogether different from or outside them, for in that case there would not be that intimate connection between the two which is implied in the description of the whose as a system. A similar reasoning applies to the relation between the

saguna Brahman and the physical universe emerging from it; only as the latter unlike the jīvas has a beginning, being produced, the relation is not anadi.[65] It cannot be identity, for an effect as such is not the same as its cause; nor is it difference, for then the two cannot be represented as cause and effect.

But it may appear to us that the relation in question is one of identity-in-difference. Such a conception itself, according to the Advaitin, is self-discrepant. This is a point which is discussed at great length in advaitic works.[66] It is not possible to enter here into all the details of the discussion; so we shall content ourselves with drawing attention to its main features.[67] Let M and N be two entities between which the relation in question is supposed to exist. Now neither of them can *as such* be both identical with and different from the other. It would mean that M is both N and not-N and that N similarly is both M and not-M, which is a violation of the law of contradiction. When two things are distinct in fact, they cannot be the same. We cannot accept both sides of a contradiction to be true. But it may be said that this deficiency if it be one is vouched for by experience and that, since experience is our only guide, we must acquiesce in it. Such an argument seems to the Advaitin like a refusal to think. He admits that we finally depend upon experience for determining the truth about things, but he does not therefore relinquish the right to re-examine the meaning of experience when it results in a palpable self-contradiction and seek for a new explanation of it, if possible. The data of experience, merely because they are such, put us under no constraint to accept them under all circumstances as logical verities. Further, it may be granted for the sake of argument that there is no valid ground for doubting the reality of the content of experience as it ordinarily occurs, when there is agreement among thinkers about it. But the point in question is not one about which we find any such agreement. Even the realist Naiyayika, we know, postulates the new-fangled relation of samavaya in such cases with a view to avoid the necessity for admitting the real to be self-contradictory. Whatever view, therefore, we may hold about the verdict of experience in general, the present case at any rate is not one where it can be accepted without scrutiny. If M and N do not constitute an identity in difference directly, it may be though that they do so mediately through features or elements in them—some of which are identical and others different. Thus we may say that M and N possess one or more common features which may be represented by *a* and, at the same time, exhibit differences represented by x and y respectively. Accordingly to this explanation, what is identical is quite distinct from what is different; yet the entities, viz. M and N, by virtue of such features, it may be said, are identical with and, at the same time, different from each other. Such an explanation may seem to solve the difficulty, but the solution is only apparent of it merely shifts the difficulty to another set of things. It assumes that M and N are characterized by *a x* and *a y* respectively, and the assumption leaves us where we were, for we cannot satisfactorily explain the relation between a thing and its so-called charactgeristics. Now the relation between M and *a x,* to take only one of the entities, cannot be identity, for then the distinction between *a* amd *x* would vanish, both being identical with the same M; and with it also the relation of identity-in-difference between M and N. Nor can *a* and *x* be different from M, for then their character, whatever it may be, will cease to affect m and therefore also its relation to N. So we are driven to think of identity-in-difference as the only possible relation between these. That is, in explaining the relation in question between M and N, we presuppose the same relation within each of them; and pursuing the inquiry further will only lead to an infinite process.[68]

For such reasons the Advaitin views the relation between the saguna Brahman and its constitutive elements as unique or as tadatmya in the sense explained in the previous section—not to be characterized as identity or difference or identity-in-difference. Hence the conception of saguna Brahman involves adhyasa, and like that of Īśvara cannot be regarded as ultimate. Or to state it differently, the saguna Brahman includes not merely reality but also appearance, which is something less than the real. The element of reality in it is the ultimate of Advaita. It should be carefully noted that this reality is not the mere unity underlying the diversity of the universe, for unity and diversity are relative to each other, and it is impossible to retain the one as real while rejecting the other as an appearance. Both of them are alike appearances and the advaitic ultimate is what is beyond them—their non-phenomenal ground (nirviśesa-vastu). It is for this reason that Śaṁkara describes his doctrine as advaita or 'non-duality,' and not as aikya or 'unity.' By discarding the notion of bhedabheda or, more specifically by refusing to accept a chaning Brahman as ultimate, Śaṁkara differentiates his doctrine from brahma-parinama-vada advocated by other Vedantins according to whom both the physical universe and the jīvas actually emerge from Brahman.[69] Brahman according to him does not evolve in this sense, but only gives rise to appearances which, though entirely depending upon it, affect it no more than the silver does the shell in which it appears. He thus enunciates a new view of causation which is different from both the parinama-vada and the arambha-vada with which we are familiar. According to it, the cause produces the effect without itself undergoing any change whatsoever. It is vivarta-vada or the doctrine of *phenomenal* development. Viewed in the light of this theory, Brahman only appears as the world. It is the original of which the world, as it has been said,[70] may be regarded as 'a translation at the plane of space-time'; and Brahman depends as little for its being on the world as an original work does on its translation. This is what is otherwise known as the Māyā doctrine.[71] Though the doctrine as it appears here naturally shows considerable development in matters of detail, it has, as we have pointed out, a definite basis in the Upaniṣads. The charge that it is alien to the Vedānta is therefore really without foundation. Again, by postulating a Reality behind the self-discrepant world of experience, Śaṁkara differentiates his doctrine from the sunyavada of the Madhyamika. The discrepancy characterizing the saguna Brahman or its relativity only degrades it to the level of appearance; it does not dismiss it altogether. If accordingly to the Madhyamika it is impossible for though to rest in the relative, it is equally impossible for it, according to Śaṁkara, to rest in absolute nothing. To use the terminology of the Upaniṣads, the Advaita denies only 'names' and 'forms' but not that which appears under their guise. Or, as an old writer has observed, while the Advaitin negates only distinction (bheda), the Madhyamika negates it as well as the distincts (bhidyamāna).[72] That there is a Reality at the back of all empirical things again is not a mere assertion, for it is maintained here, as we know, that the thinking subject in us is not different from it so that its being becomes an immediate certainty. If we denied it, the very fact of denial would affirm it.[73] We may not know what it exactly is; but its presence itself, owing to the basic identity of ourselves with it, can never be doubted.

What is the nature of this Reality? As indicated in an earlier section, it may be represented on the one hand as the infinite Consciousness implied by empirical knowledge or as the infinite Being presupposed in all finite existence. But it is neither empirical knowledge nor phenomenal being, for each of them has appearance superadded to the real and so far fails to represent the latter in its purity. Such knowledge and being, though revealing the ultimate, do not represent it truly and the same is the case with all empirical things. While they are not apart from it, they cannot either singly or in combination stand for it. That is why Brahman as the ultimate is termed nirguna or 'indeterminat,' which does not amount to saying, as it is ordinarily assumed, that it is nothing, but only means that nothing which the mind can think of can actually belong to it. Whatever we think of is for that very reason objective (drsya) and it cannot therefore be an element in that which is never presented as an object (dṛ). The familiar categories of thought therefore are all inapplicable to it. Hence no direct description of it is possible. But we can indirectly point to it utilizing the appearances as aids; for an appearance, which can never be independent, necessarily signifies a reality beyond itself. In this sense every precept and every concept can be made to indicate the Absolute. The Upaniṣads prefer to direct our attention to it through terms like tvam they, besides dispelling all doubt about its being, afford a better clue to its nature.[74] When such terms are combined with another like tat or Brahman in an assertive proposition like Tat Tvam asi or Aham Brahma asmi, the reference to Reality becomes ensured. For the attributes which they respectively connote of the individual and of the cosmic subject—such as the bondage of the one and the freedom of the other—being mutually incompatibel,[75] our mind abandons the explicit sense of the terms, and travels beyond those attributes to that in which they are grounded (nirvisesa-vastu) as constituting the true import of the proposition. The dropping of these attributes, we should add, signifies little because they are but illusive barriers erected by Māyā between the jīva and Īśvara. It should also be pointed out that we do not here identify the ground of one set attributes with that of the other, for such identification would be meaningless without some difference equally real between them. To avoid this implication we merely deny the distinction between the two, so that what the proposition in strictness means is that the jīva is *not other* than Brahman.

The advaitic Absolute is not merely indefinable; we cannot know it either, for the moment it is made the object of thought it becomes related to a subject and therefore determinate. That is another important reason why the idea of Īśvara or saguna Brahman is rejected as inadequate to be the true goal of philosophy which the Advaita, like the other Indian doctrines, views as not merely arriving at a speculative notion or a conceptual formula of the ultimate reality, but to realize what it is in itself. The ideal of the determinate Brahman has been elaborated in thought and it therefore remains a reality for thought. It is Brahman in 'an empiric dress'—the Absolute as it appears to us, and not as it is in itself. Its internal self-discrepancy to which we have drawn attention is in fact the result of its relation to thought. It is, it is expressed, jñeya Brahman or Brahman that can be known. In itself, it excludes all relations (asaṁsṛṣṭa), including that between subject and objection, and is therefore unknowable. But though it cannot be known it can, as we shall point out presently, be realized.

One should therefore be careful in understanding what exactly is meant when the Upaniṣads describe Brahman as nirguna and therefore as indefinable and unknowable. It is not in every sense beyond the reach of words. To suppose that it is so would be to deprive the Upaniṣads of the whole of their purpose. Even granting that the negative definition is the only possible one, it does not follow that the nirguna Brahman is a blank.[76] For all propositions directly or indirectly refer to reality and negation necessarily has its own positive implication. As matter of fact, however, the Advaitins assign Upaniṣadic statements like neti —'Not this, nor that'—a secondary place while the primary place is given to those like Tat Tvam asi, which point to the reality in us as the ultimate. That is, the negative statement is not to be understood in isolation but along with positive ones like Tat tvam asi. Negation is only a preliminary to affirmation. [77] It means that the Absolute is not conceived here objectively—as merely inferred from outer phenomena; but as revealing itself within us.[78] This alters totally the significance of the negative description, for we are thereby constrained to admit not its positive character but also its spiritual Nature. It is not thus a bare or contentless being for which the Absolute stands here. Nor should the statement that Brahman is unknowable lead us to regard the doctrine as agnostic. It, no doubt, rules out all discursive though as inapplicable to Reality; but it does not represent it as extra-empirical—as something wholly outside the world of experience. The nirguna Brahman is not the negation or the antithesis of the saguna, but is its very truth and is immanent in everything that goes to constitute it. Hence every aspect of experience, whether on the subject or object side, reveals it. Indeed irrepressibility (svayam-prakasatva) is its very essence and, like the sun behind a cloud, it shows itself in a sense even in being hidden. We seem to miss it ordinarily on account of the bewildering mass of appearances. But that is like not seeing the ocean for the waves. It is true that it cannot be grasped as an object of knowledge. But there may be other ways of 'experiencing' it; and the whole tenor of the advaitic theory of perception as well as its scheme of practical discipline, to which we shall refer in the next section, shows that there is such a form of experience and that we can 'know' Brahman by being it. This higher type of experience is not altogether unfamiliar to us. There are moments, though all too rare, when we transcend ourselves and when even the experience that is being lives through is not cognized. We pass in it not only beyond common consciousness in which the though of self is implicit, but also beyond explicit self-consciousness to where thought merges in experience. It may be taken as a distant analogue of the attitude of the sage who, having through long discipline learnt to feel his identity with all that exists, at last succeds in passing beyond even that state, and losing sight of the objective world and of himself as such, is straight away installed within Reality. That constitutes the consummation of Advaitic teaching.

Though the ideal of the saguna Brahman is thus inadequate to be the ultimate of philosophy, it must not be regarded as useless. We have already seen how it furnishes an ethical ideal by following which the disciple can rise above his congenital limitations and acquire that moral fitness which is indispensable for success in achieving the advaitic goal. Even from the purely theoretic standpoint, it is not without its own value, as is shown for instance by the method followed in the Advaita. This method, we know, starts with the more or less diverse worlds as given in individual experience and discovers as their basis a common one. Systematizing the variety that is manifest in it, it then arrives at unity. And it is only afterwards, since this world of unity in diversity is itself an appearance on the reasoning adopted above, that the doctrine concludes to the spirit which lies beyond it as the sole reality. The contradictions and anomalies of ordinary experience have at first to be resolved at least in the seeming orderliness signified by the ideal of the saguna Brahman, if we are to reach the advaitic ultimate unerringly. Without the sythesis effected in it or, to express the same thing differently, without the jiva's avidyā being universalized as Māyā, we would land ourselves in subjectivism reducing the world to a mere private show, for there would then be no reason for postulating anything beyond what is present to individual consciousness. The Advaitin's criticism of the saguna Brahman should accordingly be understood as showing only the inadequacy of that conception to serve as the goal of philosophy and not as signifying that it is valueless.[79] But its value is restricted to the empirical sphere—a view which is entirely in consonance with the general advaitic position that practical utility need not rest on metaphysical validity. It is this distinction that has given rise to what are familiarly known as the 'two grades' of teaching in the Advaita—the higher one of the nirguna Brahman (para-vidya) and the lower one of the saguna (apara-vidya).

IV

Since mokṣa, according to Śaṁkara, is not a state to be newly attained, but is the very nature of the self, we can hardly speak of a means in its ordinary sense for achieving it. It is realizing what has always been one's own innate character but happens for the time being to be forgotten. The Upaniṣadic statement is 'That thou becomest.' The common illustration given here is that of a prince, brought up as a hunter from infancy, discovering afterwards the is of royal blood.[80] It involves no becoming, for he has always been a prince and all that he has to do is to feel or realize that he is one. We might illustrate the point equally well by referring to the distinction between a solar and a lunar eclipse. In the latter, the light of the sun is actually cut off from the moon by the earth coming between it and the sun, so that the passing off of the eclipse signifies a real change in the condition of the moon, viz. the part that was enveloped in darkness becoming lit. In a solar eclipse, on the other hand, the luminary continues to be during the eclipse exactly as it was before or will be afterwards. It only appears to be eclipsed because the intervening moon prevents it from being seen as it really is. The re-emergence of the bright sun accordingly means no change whatsoever in it, but only a moving farther away of the moon or the removal of the obstacle preventing the sun from showing itself as it is. Similarly in the case of advaitic mokṣa, all that is needed is a removal of the obstacle that keeps the truth concealed from us and the discipline that is prescribed is solely with a view to bring about this result. It is therefore only in a negative or indirect sense that we can talk of attaining mokṣa here. Empirical life being entirely the consequence of an adhyasa, the obstacle is ajñāna and it is removed through its contrary jñāna. The jñāna that is capable of effecting it should be, for the reasons mentioned more than once before, direct or intuitive (saksat-kara); and it should refer to one's own identity with Brahman, for it is the forgetting of this identity that constitutes samsara. Such knowledge is the sole means of liberation. Neither moral perfection nor religious acts are required as direct aids to it. The cultivation of the will and the purification of the affections are of course necessary, but they are only aids to jñāna,[81] not to mokṣa. It means that the morally impure will not seriously set about acquiring the saving knowledge. When once jñāna arises, it does of itself dispel ajñāna and the simultaneous revelation of spirit in all its innate splendour is mokṣa. To state the same in another way, ethical improvement and religious discipline are necessary for mokṣa but not enough. That is what is meant by karma- saṁnyāsa as advocated by Śaṁkara. The conception of jīvan-mukti is the logical result of such a view of the world and of escape from it. If knowledge is the sole means of release from bondage, freedom should result the moment it is gained; and there is nothing in the psychical or other equipment of the human being which renders its acquisition impossible here and now.[82]

The discipline is to be undergone in two stages–one, preliminary which qualifies for entering upon the serious study of the Advaita; and the other, Vedāntic training proper which directly aims at self- realization. Of these, the former is identical with karma-yoga as explained in the chapter on the Gītā and its aim is the cultivation of detachment. The latter consists of sravana, manana and nididhyasana. These have been already explained in the chapter on the Upaniṣads, but it is necessary to restate the position calling attention to what is peculiar to the Advaita, (1) *Śravaṇa*. This is study and discussion of the Upaniṣads with the assistance of a *guru*. That has realized the truth they teach. The implication of this requirement is two-fold: First, it signifies that the ultimate philosophic truth is to be learnt through a study of the revealed texts. Secondly, it emphasizes the need for personal intercourse with a competent teacher, if the study is to be fruiful and shows that mere book-learning is not of much avil. (2) *Manana*. This is arguing within oneself, after knowing definitely what the Upaniṣads teach, how and why that teaching alone is true. The main object of this process in not to discover the final truth, for that has been learnt already through sravana, but to remove the doubt (asambhavana) that it may not after all be right. It is intended to transform what has been received on trust into one's own true conviction and brings out well the place assigned to reason in the Advaita. The recognition of the value of analytical reflection, we may note by the way, is rather a unique feature in a doctrine which finally aims at mystic experience. (3) *Nididhyasana.*Manana secures intellectual conviction. But there may still be obstacles in the way of self- realization. For despite such conviction, there may be now and again an unconscious reassertion of old habits of thought (viparītabhāvanā) incompatible with what has since been learnt. Nididhyāsana is meant to overcome this kind of obstacle. It is meditation upon the identity between the individual self and Brahman–the central point of Vedantic teaching. It should be continued till the desired intuitive knowledge arises and that identity becomes immediate (aparoksa).[83] When it does, one becomes a jīvan-mukta. The ultimate philosophic fact is no doubt to be known through the testimony of the Upaniṣads; but if the knowledge conveyed by it is to bring real freedom, one should verify it by one's own living experience in the form 'I am Brahman' or Aham Brahma asmi.[84] It is this immediate experience or direct intuition of the Absolute, which is described as vidvadanubhava to distinguish it from lay experience, that accordingly becomes the final criterion of Truth here.[85]

The jīvan-mukta's life has two phases: It is either samādhi or mystic trance when he turns inwards and loses himself in Brahman: or the condition knows an Vyutthāna or reversion to common life when the spectacle of the world returns but does not delude him since he has once for all realized its metaphysical falsity. Diversity continues to appear then as the sun, we may say, continues to appear as moving even after we are convinced that it is stationary. A jīvan-mukta experiences pain and pleasure, but neither really matters to him. He does not necessarily give up all activity as is abundantly illustrated by the strenuous life which Śaṁkara himself led,[86] but it does not proceed from any selfish impulse or even from a sense of obligation to others. Blind love for the narrow self which ordinarily characterizes man and the consequent clinging to the mere particular are in his case replaced by enlightened and therefore equal love for all. The basis for this universal love is furnished by the Upaniṣadic teaching "That thou art.' We should do unto others as we do to ourselves, because they are ourselves-a view which places the golden rule of moralityon the surest of foundations, 'Who sees all beings in himself and himself in all beings–he will dislike none,' as the Upaniṣad[87] says; or as the Gītā puts it, 'He harms not self by self.'[88] The common laws of social morality and ritual which are significant only in reference to one that is striving for perfection are meaningless for him.[89] The jīvan-mukta, having transcended the stage of strife, is spontaneously virtuous. Impulse and desire become one in him.[90] He is not then realizing virtue but is revealing it. 'In one that has awakened to a knowledge of the self, virtues like kindness imply no conscious effort whatsoever. They are second nature with him.' When at last he is dessociated from the physical accompaniments, he is not reborn, but remains as Brahman. That is videha-mukti.

B. Viśiṣṭadvaita

THIS is the system which is associated with the name of Rāmānuja. Its most striking feature is the attempt which it makes to unite personal theism with the philosophy of the Absolute. Two lines of thought, both of which can be traced far back into antiquity, meet here and in this lies the explanation of a great part of its appeal to the cultured as well as the common people. It resembles in this respect the teaching of the Gītā, though it naturally shows greater systematization both on the religious and on the philosophical side. Historically speaking, the elements of thought combined here are distinct. The first of them, viz. Theism, is of the Bhāgavata type, inculcating belief in a personal and transcedent God who saves, out of mercy, such as are whole heartedly devoted to him and are for that reason described as ekantins ('single-minded'). The second element in the teaching is still elder, being based upon the Upaniṣads. Of the two Upaniṣadic views to which we have alluded (p. 62), neither in its entirety proved acceptable to Rāmānuja, but his teaching is more like what is described as Brahma-pariṇama-vāda[91] than Brahma-vivarta-vāda. The ideas of the unity of ultimate reality and of its immanence in the universe, as also the doctrine that jñāna[92] is the means of salvation, are derived from this source. As to the success with which the two teachings are synthesized here, we shall say a few words later; for the present, it will suffice to mention that the synthesis was not initiated by Rāmānuja, though that should not be understood as minimizing the value of his contribution to the final shaping of the doctrine. The attempt to bring together theism and the philosophy of the Absolute is very old and may be traced even in parts of Vedic literature itself. We know that a similar synthesis is found in the Gītā where, as in the Viśiṣṭādvaita, it appears with the added feature that the theism is of the Bhāgavata type, not directly traceable to the Veda. The same also is found in one or other of its various phases of growth in the Mahābhārata, especially in the section known as the *Narayaniya* and in the Purāṇas such as the *Viṣṇu-purāṇa*. Only, in the time of Rāmānuja there was a fresh circumstance, viz. The reaction against the purely absolutist philosophy of Śaṁkara and its seeming negations calling for a new formulation of this old synthesis. There was, for instance, the advaitic identification of the jīva and Brahman which explains the Viśiṣṭādvaita assertion of the reality of the individual or its attempt to give the Hindus their souls back,[93] as Max Muller has put it. It was as a protest against views like these that the doctrine was given out in the South about 1000 A.D., and systematized somewhat later by Rāmānuja.

The sources of authority for the doctrine are two-fold, for which reason it is described as Ubhaya-vedānta; one, the Veda including the Upaniṣads and works like the Purāṇas which are for the most part based upon it; the other, the literature of the South found in Tamil which, though largely indebted to Vedic teaching, undoubtedly contains elements of non-Vedic thought. Of the immediate predecessors of Rāmānuja in this work of synthesis we may mention Nāthamuni (A.D. 1000), none of whose writings, however, has yet been discovered, and his grandson Ālavandār or Yāmunācārya (A.D.1050), whose several works form splendid manuals of the essentials of the Viśiṣṭādvaita as they were understood before Rāmānuja took up the work of systematization. They are *Agama-pramanya*, *Mahapurusa-nirnaya* which is designed to show the supremacy of Viṣṇu as against Śiva, *Gītārtha-samgraha, Siddhi-traya* and two hymns—*Śrī-stuti* and *Viṣṇu-stuti*. Rāmānuja or the 'prince of ascetics' (yati-rāja), as he is described, is reputed to have been his pupil's pupil and his commentary on the *Vedānta-sūtra,* known as the *Śrī-bhāṣya*, that on the *Bhagavadgitā*[94] and his *Vedārtha-saṁgraha* which gives an independent exposition of the creed, form the chief scriptures of the system. His other works are *Vedānta-sāra, Vedānta-dīpa, Nitya-grantha*, dealing with forms of worship, and *Gadya-traya*. Of those who came after him, we may note Sudarśana Śuri (A.D.1300), the author of commentaries on the *Śrī-bhāsya* and on the *Vedartha-samgraha*. Then came Veñkatanātha, better known as Vedānta Deśika (A.D. 1350), whose many-sided scholarship and long labours contributed much to establish the doctrine of Rāmānuja on a firm basis. First, he formulated even better than his predecessors had done the objections to the Advaita, taking into consideration the defence put up by its exponents since Rāmānuja's time. Not only did he thus render the doctrine stronger on its critical side; he also undertook the task of internal systematization and set aside once for all whatever departures from strict tradition had taken place by his time.[95] His is the second great figure in the history of Viśiṣṭādvaita and the early promise he gave of his future eminence is well indicated by the following blessing which Varadaguru, a famous teacher of the time, is said to have bestowed upon the boy when five years old: 'May you establish the Vedānta on a firm basis, vanquishing heterodox views; may you become the respected of the orthodox and the abode of abundant auspiciousness.'[96] His works are too numerous to mention here. Some of the chief among them are his *Tattva-tīkā*, an incomplete commentary on the *Śrī-bhāsya, Tātparya-candrikā*, gloss on Rāmānuja's *Gītā-bhāsya, Nyāya-siddhanjana, Tattva-muktā-kalāpa* with his own commentary upon it called the *Sarvārtha-siddhi* and the *Sata-dusani* which is a vigorous attack on the Advaita. The *Yatīndra-mata-dīpikā* of Śrīnivāsācārya (A.D. 1700) is a short manual useful for beginners.

I

While Rāmānuja holds in common with many others that knowledge implies both a subject and an object, he differs essentially from them in certain other respects. The most important of these is that discrimination is essential to all knowledge and that it is impossible for the mind to apprehend an undifferentiated object. What is known is necessarily known as characterized in some way, its generic feature being in any case apprehended along with it. The importance of this view we shall appreciate by comparing it for instance with the Nyāya-Vaiśeṣika one of nirvikalpaka according to which isolated reals are all that are apprehended at first. According to Rāmānuja, such a stage in perception is a psychological myth and the savikalpaka of the Nyāya-Vaiśesika is itself primal. Any analysis of it into simpler elements is the result only of reflection and has nothing corresponding to it in the mental process as it actually takes place. This should not be taken to mean that Rāmānuja does not admit the distinction of savikalpaka and nirvikalpaka; only to him, the two alike involve a complex content. Perceptual experience is termed nirvikalpaka when the object is cognized for the first time. It is primary presentation that does not call up any previous impression of the same. A child see a cow, let us say, for the first time; even then it sees the object as qualified in some way. When it sees a cow again, the sight of it is accompanied by a revival of the former impression and it is this second or subsequent apprehension[97]—the cognizing of the new in the light of the old—that is described as savikalpaka by Rāmānuja. While 'This is a cow' represents the form of perceptual experience at the nirvikalpaka level, 'This *also* is a cow' does the same at the savikalpaka. Accordingly the psychological development implied by 'determinate' perception is not from the simple to the complex as in the Nyāya-Vaiśeṣika; rather the complex itself, hitherto new, ceases to be so and becomes familiar through it. To put the same in another way, while according to the Nyāya-Vaiśesika only the savikalpaka involves judgment, the nirvikalpaka merely furnishing the material for it, according to the Viśiṣṭādvaita all perceptual experience alike involves it. The savikalpaka does not thereby become the same as recognition (pratyabhijñā): 'This is that Devadatta,' for the latter refers to one and the same object as perceived twice whereas the former arises when different objects of the same type are cognized. In both alike, no doubt, a present object is associated with the revival of a past impression: but while in the savikalpaka it is only the impression of the attributive element that revives, in recognition that of the particular individual (vyakti) also does. Further, though all perception equally entails judgment, recognition includes a specific reference to the distinctions of time and place in which the object is cognized on the two occasions. It is not only at the primal stage of perception that the unqualified object (nirvisesa-vastu) is not known; all jñāna, including that of the ultimate reality, is necessarily of an object as complex (saguna).[98] This constitutes a radical difference from śaṃkara, who represents the Upaniṣadic ultimate as nirguna. 'If the Upaniṣads describe Brahman as without qualities,' Rāmānuja says, 'all that the description can mean is that *some* qualities are denied while there are still others characterizing it.'[99]

To know the nature of jñāna, according to Rāmānuja, it is necessary to understand the classification of ultimate objects which is peculiar to his doctrine. To the well-known distinction between spirit and matter which are respectively termed cetana and jada in Sanskrit, he adds another which is neither. Jñāna is of this intermediate type. It is unlike material entities in that it can unaided manifest itself and other objects neither of which is possible for them. But what it thus manifests is never *for itself* but always for another. That is, it can only show but cannot know. In this latter respect it is unlike spirit, which knows though it is unable, according to the doctrine, to show anything but itself. To take an example from the physical sphere, jñāna is like light, which can reveal the presence of a jar (say) as well as of its own, but cannot itself know either, its revelation of things being always for another. It exists not for itself but for someone else. Its teleology takes us beyond it. The classification of things here is accordingly not into jada and cetana, but jada ('matter') and ajada[100] ('the immaterial'), where the second term stands for cetana and what is unlike it but is yet distinct from jada. Jñāna pertains to one or other of the two kinds of spiritual entities recognized in the system, viz. Jīvas and Īśvara. It is consequently described as dharma-bhūta-jñāna—literally 'subsidiary or attributive jñāna'[101]—which implies that there is substantive jñāna also. The various jīvas and Īśvara are jñāna in this higher sense. They are compared to the flame of a lamp to which belongs and from which proceeds their dharma-bhūta-jñāna like rays. This jñāna is supposed to be eternally associated with a subject—whether jīva or Īśvara—and constitutes its unique adjunct. When it 'flows out,' as it is expressed, from the subject to which it belongs and comes into contact with an object, it is able to manifest that object to it. Throughout mundane existence, it functions in a more or less restricted manner but it ever endures. Even in deep sleep it it; but it does not function then and does not therefore show itself, the theory being that jñāna is known only along with some object or not at all.[102] Then the jīva remains self-conscious along with the unrevealed presence of its dharam-bhūta-jñāna. In dreams, as will be seen in the next section, the actual presence is postulated of the objects dreamt of. Hence jñāna also it then known; but its action being much more impeded than during waking, the knowledge of dream-objects is dim and hazy. In mokṣa, on the other hand, entirely free action is restored to it. It becomes all-pervasive, with the result that there is nothing then which falls outside its range. The liberated sould consequently knows everything. The analogy of the lamp and the rays may suggest that the dharma-bhūta-jñāna is of the same stuff as the jīva or Īśvara, but only appearing in an attenuated form. That, however, is not the view of Rāmānuja, who takes it as a distinct entity,[103] though always associated with the dependent upon another. It is, however, difficult to see the reason for postulating two kinds of jñāna, except it be the desire to make spirit in itself changeless and thus harmonize the doctrine with the teaching of the Upaniṣads whose whole weight, as Śaṁkara is never tired of insisting, is in favour of its contancy (avikriyatva).[104]

Jñāna operates through the manas alone or the menas as assisted by some organ of sense through which it streams out towards its objects which are supposed to be already there. Rāmānuja describes the process of knowing as starting from the soul, then reaching the manas and then, emerging through the sense, meeting the outside objects. When thus it comes into contact with an object, it is stated to assume the 'form' (akara) of that object and somehow reveal it to the subject in question. It is clear that the conception of dharma-bhūta-jñāna corresponds to that of the antaḥ-karaṇa in the Advaita, which also is supposed to go out similarly towards objects and assume their form before giving rise to knowledge. But while the antah-karana in that doctrine is physical (jada) and requires an extraneous aid, viz. The aids it requires, like the manas and the indriyas, are only for determining its appearance in particular ways—as knowledge of colour, of sound, etc. It is not only knowledge that is regarded as a modification of dharma-bhūta-jñāna; internal states like desire and anger are also its transformations, so that they are forms of knowing at the same time.

II

To turn now to the logical implication of knowledge.[105] We have just drawn attention in noticing Rāmānuja's description of the process of knowing to the fact that objects are viewed as existing before they are known. They are therefore to be reckoned as real; and, since they depend in no way upon the self or the knowledge which brings them into relation with it, their reality is not merely relative but absolute. Rāmānuja traces this realistic view to the old teaching of the Veda, using terms in doing so which are reminiscent of the description of knowledge given in the Prābhākara school.[106] In particular, his view is described as sat-khyāti which means that what exists (sat) is alone congnized and that knowledge in the absense of a real object corresponding to its content (yathārtha) is inconceivable. It is not enough for securing the correspondence here meant, if something or other exists outside to serve as a presentative basis. Consistently with Rāmānuja's view that a bare identity is a metaphysical fiction and cannot be know, the character of the object also should be as it is given in knowledge. In other words, the agreement implied in knolwedge extends from the *that* (prakārin)to the *what* (prakāra) also of the object presented. While it is easy to understand this position so far as normal perception is concerned, the question will arise as to how it cab be maintained in the case of illusions where we seem to have knoweldge without corresponding things. Rāmānuja's explanation of them is two-fold:—

(1) In some cases the realistic position is maintained by him on the basis of the Vedantic doctrine of quintuplication (panci-karana) according to which objects of the visible

world, which are all compounds, contain all the five bhutas or elements though in varying proportions (p. 65). Thus in the case of the mirage, what is being looked at is a heated sandy waste which contains not only prthivi, the preponderating part of it, but also ap and the other elements however slight; and the apprehension of water there, we have to understand, is therefore only of what is actually presented to the eye. But such an explanation may do only in cases where the object of illusion, as in the example given, is one or other of the five bhutas. Illusions, however, are by no means confined to such rare cases. We may mistake shell for silver where neither is itself a bhuta. To explain such cases, Rāmānuja resorts to an extension of the principle underlying panci-karana. The illusion of shell-silver is due, among other causes, to the similarity between the two things, viz. their peculiar lustre. This similarity means to Rāmānuja the presence in shell, though only to an extremely limited extent, of the very substance which constitutes silver. Likeness is to him another term for partial identity of material,[107] and so what is perceived even here is what is actually presented. That is, Rāmānuja justifies his view of sat-khyāti in such cases by pointing to what is a fundamental tenet of his system, viz. the unity of the physical world and the structural affinity that is discoverable among the things that belong so it.

(2) In other cases like the white conch seen yellow by a person with a jaundiced eye a different explanation becomes necessary, for as the yellowness is admitted by all to be there outside the knowing self, viz. in the eye-ball, the point requiring elucidation is not whether it is real but how it comes to be seen as characterizing the conch. The explanation of Rāmānuja, which is based upon the theory of vision current at the time, assumes that the yellowness found in the diseased eye-ball is actually transmitted from there to the conch along with the 'rays'

of the organ of sight (nayana-rasmi) as they travel to it in the process of seeing and that the new colour thus imposed upon the conch obscures the whiteness natural to it. The conch is accordingly supposed to become actually yellow, though only for the time being. Here also then knowledge is of what is given in repect not only of the relata but also of the relation between them. To the objection that if the conch becomes actually yellow others also should find it so, the answer is given that the yellowness here is of too subtle a kind to be perceived by anyone who, unlike the person in question has not followed it throughout its course of transmission.[108] The explanation is no doubt arbitrary and unconvincing; but what our present purpose requires us to note is the spirit of persistent realism that underlies it, not its scientific correctness. The question will readily occur as to how dreams are to be accounted for. There at least we seem to have experience without corresponding objects existing at the time. The explanation once again is arbitrary and it is stated, now on the authority of the Upaniṣads,[109] that objects like the elephant seen in a dream are not subjective but are present there at the time. 'They are created by the supreme Person (parama-purusa),' says Rāmānuja,[110] and adds that the reason for creating such unique things is the same as in the case of objects of the waking state, viz. the providing of *suitable* means for the individual to experience pain or pleasure according to his past karma. 'He creates these objects, which are special to each jīva and last only as long as they are experienced, in order that it may reap the fruits appropriate to the extremely minor deeds of virtue and vice it has done.'[111]

It is instructive to find out the significance of this two-fold explanation. The yellow-conch and the dream-elephant are objects solely of individual experience; and though not unreal they last only as long as the illusion lasts and can, in the nature of the case, be testified to only by the person that sees them. The illusion of the mirage or the shell-silver also in a sense has reference to particular individuals; but the water and the silver perceived there by one because they by hypothesis persist even after the illusion is over as actual parts of what is presented, are verifiable by all. This shows that Rāmānuja distinguishes two classes of objects – one which is cognized by all or many and may therefore be called 'public,' and the other, special to single persons and may therefore be termed 'private.' But it must be distinctly understood that such a classification does not mean that he admits different types of reality—an admission which would place his doctrine epistemologically on the same footing as Śaṁkara's Aḍvaita. In fact, it is in denying that there is such a distinction that he formulates the doctrine of sat-khyāti. In point of reality, private and public objects differ in no way. Both alike are outside and independent of knowledge, and both are absolutely real. a thing's being private does not take away from its reality. Our pains and pleasures are personal to each one of us, but they are not the less real on that account.

However diverse the explanation in the two cases and whatever we may think of its scientific value, it is clear that the aim of sat-khyāti is to show that jñāna, including the so-called illusions, never deviates from reality and that even in the case of objects whose existence can be vouched for only by individuals, there is no ideal or purely subjective element. If all knowledge be equally valid, it may be asked how the distinction between truth (pramā) and error (bhrama), which is universally recognized, is to be explained. It may appear to us from the examples cited above that error here is incomplete knowing. Thus in the case of the yellow conch, it is caused by our failure to comprehend its whiteness or, more strictly by our overlooking the fact that it is obscured. The omission and the consequent error are clearer still in the case of another example given[112]—the 'firebrand-circle' (alāta-cakra) where a point of light, owing to its rapid movement, is mistaken for its locus, because while the fact that is occupies every point on the circumference is apprehended, the other fact that the occupation takes place successively and not simultaneously is altogether lost sight of. But we must remember that there may be elements of omission, according to the doctrine, even in truth. When for instance we perceive shell as shell, there is by hypothesis present in it silver, but it is ignored quite as much as the shell aspect is when the same object is mistaken for silver.

Similarly in the case of the desert when we cognize it as such, our mind lets slip the element of ap supposed to be contained in it. The fact is that while sat-khyāti postulates that only what is given in known, it does not admit that all that is given is known. Knowledge, no doubt, is always of the given and of nothing but the given; but is need not be of the *whole* of what is given.[113] It would not, therefore, be right to conclude that error in general is incomplete knowing. Since complete-ness like validity fails to differentiate truth from error, Rāmānuja enunciates a new principle, viz. that for knowledge to be true in its commonly accepted sense it should, in addition to agreeing with outside reality, be serviceable in life. When the mirage and the shell-silver are described as false what we have to understand is not that water and silver are not present there, for in that case we could not have become conscious of them at all, but that they are not such as can be put to practical use. The distinction between truth and error comes thus to be significant only from the practical standpoint; from the theoretical one, it does not exist. All knowledge without exception is valid and necessarily so, but such validity need not guarantee that what is known is adequate to satisfy a practical need. A geologist may correctly adjudge a piece of ore as golden; but it does not mean that a bracelet (say) can be made out of the metal in it. This is the significance of including in the definition of truth not only yathārtha or 'agreeing with outside reality,' but also vyavaharanuguna or 'adapted to the practical interests of life.'[114] If knowledge should conform to vyavahara, it should satisfy two conditions. It must, in the first place, refer to objects of common or collective experience. It is deficiency in this respect that makes the yellow-conch and the dream-elephant false. Because their being private to a particular individual is overlooked at the time, they are confounded with the corresponding objects of the waking state; and this deficiency when discovered exposes their falsity. In the second place, it should comprehend the pre-ponderating element in the object presented. The object we call shell may contain silver, but the shell part predominates in it; and it is this predominance that exmpains its being put to use as the one and not as the other. The silver, though certainly present, does not count practically on account of its slightness (alpatva); and this feature when discovered reveals the erroneous character of the knowledge in question. Prama not only apprehends rightly so far as it goes, but also goes far enough to be of service in life. Bhrama also is right so far as it goes; but it does not go far enough and therefore fails to help us in the manner in which we expect it to do. So when erroneous knowledge disappears and truth comes to be known, as Rāmānuja's commentator says, the object (artha) is not negated but only activity (pravṛtti) is arrested.[115] The discovery of error, as we said in connection with Prābhākara's view affects the reactive side of consciousness, not its receptive side.

Two important corollaries follow from such a view. The practical activities of life do not require a complete knowledge of our surroundings. It is enough if we know them approximately fully. In other words, purposive thought is selective, not exhaustive; and partial or imperfect knowledge is not necessarily a hindrance to the attainment of the common ends of life. The doctrine also recognizes a social or inter-subjective side to knowledge. so far as theoretic certainty is concerned, there is no need to appeal from the individual to common consciousness; for, as we have more than once remarked, it is in the very nature of knowledge without reference to its being peculiar to one or common to many to point to reality; but its serviceability depends upon the general though tacit testimony of society—upon the 'common' sense of mankind. These observations are sure to suggest a likeness between the doctrine of sat-khyāti and what is now known as Pragmatism. Both recognize the instrumental character of knowledge and adopt practical utility as the criterion of truth. But there is one important difference. Rāmānuja admits the cognitive value of knowledge apart from the practical, whereas Pragmatism in its familiar form makes no such distinction. Even in error, there is some revelation of reality so that in adopting the pragmatic attitude he does not relinquish the logical. In fact, knowledge according to him has not one but two functions to perform—to reveal reality and to serve the purposes of practical life. Both are equally important; and if either is to be emphasized more than the other, it would undoubtedly be the former. In other words, Rāmānuja, unlike the pragmatist, is interested in truth for its own sake and values knowledge 'more for the light it brings than for the fruits it bears.'

The theory which we have so far sketched very much alters the nature of the epistemological problem. The question to be decided about knowledge is not whether it is logically valid or not—for by deficiency in this respect knowledge would lose its very title to that name—but whether it has or has not a bearing upon practical life. In other words, it is not quality that varies in knowledge but relevancy. If we take this along with what was stated above, viz. that even truth commonly reveals reality only incompletely, we see that the sat-khyāti doctrine contains the suggestion of an ideal form of knowledge which is not only valid and has practical value but is also complete or all-comprehensive. This ideal of perfect knowledge, which we may deduce from the premises of sat-khyāti, is actually recognized by

Rāmānuja as characterizing the jīva in mokṣa. Throughout saṁsāra, jñāna operates under limitations for defects of one kind or another interfere with its free activity. Consequently common knowledge, including prama or truth, only half reveals reality. Its full revelation is possible only in mokṣa when all deficiencies are overcome and all possibility of 'error' is removed. Man's vision then becomes extended to the maximum. 'It blossoms to the full,' enabling the liberated to know everything fully and as it is.[116]

As regards pramāṇas, Rāmānuja recognizes only three: perception, inference and verbal testimony. His conception of the first from the psychological as well as the logical standpoint has already been explained, and there is nothing of importance to be noted about the second. In regard to verbal testimony, Rāmānuja follows the Mīmāmsākas in general and holds that its subject-matter is special to it—what never falls within the range of the other two pramāṇas. In agreement with the other Vedantins he also maintains logical validity for assertive equally with injunctive propositions. Though resembling Śaṁkara in his views so far, he differs from him in other respects. It will suffice to refer to two of them here. The Veda, we know, is in two sections, which seem to contradict each other in what they teach: and, since both alike are looked upon as revealed, it becomes necessary for every school of Vedānta to explain their mutual relation in some manner. According to Śaṁkara, the two are really antithetical, and he gets over the antithesis between them by assuming that they are addressed to different classes of persons (adhikarin). The karma-kāṇḍa is intended for one who is still under the spell of avidyā and the jñāna-kāṇḍa, for one that has seen the hollowness of the activities it commends and is striving to transcend them. What is desirable and true from a lower standpoint is thus undesirable and not altogether true from the higher. Such a gradation of the teaching is permissible according to the Advaita with its belief in the relativity of pramanya. Rāmānuja does not admit any such antithesis, and maintains that the two portions of the Veda together form but a single teaching intended for the same class of persons. They are complementary to each other in the sense that the uttara-kāṇḍa dwells upon the nature of God and the purva-kāṇḍa upon the modes of worshipping him.[117] But such a co-ordination of the two sections, it must be added, presupposes that the purva-kāṇḍa is to be understood in the spirit of the Gītā teaching and that the various karmas taught in it are to be performed not for obtaining their respective fruits but for securing God's grace.[118] In thus attaching equal logical value to the two sections of the Veda, he differs not only from Śaṁkara but also from the Mīmāmsāka who subordinates the Upaniṣads to the Brahmana portions (karma-kāṇḍa) of the Veda. The exact bearing of this view on the practical discipline prescribed in the Viśiṣṭādvaita for the attainment of mokṣa, we shall consider later. The second point of difference is that Rāmānuja reckons not only the Veda as revealed but also the Pancaratragama[119] regarding the whole of it, unlike Śaṁkara, as eventually going back to a Vedic or some equally untainted[120] source. The agamas deal, generally speaking, with the worship of idols, particularly in temples; and the Pancaratragama, as distinguished from the Saivagama, is devoted to establishing the supremacy of Viṣṇu.[121]

III

Rāmānuja recognizes as ultimate and real the three factors (tattva-traya) of matter (acit), soul (cit) and God (Īśvara). Though equally ultimate, the first two are absolutely dependent upon the last, the dependence being conceived as that of the body upon the soul. Whatever is, is thus the body of God and he is the soul not only of inorganic nature but also of souls or jīvas.[122] It is in this connection that Rāmānuja formulates the relation,[123] so important in his system, of aprthak-siddhi or 'inseparability' which obtain between substance and attribute and may be found between one substance and another. It may be described as the pivot on which his whole philosophy turns. It is parallel to, but not identical with, the Nyāya-Vaiśeṣika samavaya. The two agree in so far as the relata which they bring together are regarded as quite distinct and real; but while samavaya is an external relation, the conception of aprthak-siddhi is that of an internal one. The example given in illustration of it, viz. the relation between body and souls, brings out clearly its intimate character. The body is defined by Rāmānuja as that which a souls controls, supports and utilizes for its own ends.[124] Matter and souls, being the body of God, are to be regarded as directed and sustained by him and as existing entirely for him. The inseparable unity of matter, souls and God—the first two being entirely subject to the restraint of the third in all their forms—is the Brahman or Absolute of Rāmānuja. Since Rāmānuja identifies the relation here involved with that between the body and the souls, his conception of the Absolute may be described as that of an organic unity in which, as in a living organism, one element predominates over and controls the first. The subordinate elements are termed viśeṣaṇas and the predominant one, viśeṣya. Because the viśeṣaṇas cannot by hypothesis exist by themselves or separately, the complex whole (visista)[125] in which they are included is described as a unity. Hence the name 'Viśiṣṭādvaita.'

This conception of unity may be illustrated by taking a common example like a 'blue lotus.' Here the blueness is quite distinct from the lotus, for a quality cannot be the same as a substance. But at the same time the blueness as a quality depends for its very being upon a substance—the lotus here, and cannot therefore be regarded ad external to it. The complex whole of the flower in question is, in this sense of *necessarily* including within itself the quality of blueness, spoken of as a unity. It will help us to understand this view well if we contrast it with those of some other schools. Ramajuja recognizes a real distinction between the quality of blueness and the substance of lotus. Hence his view differs from the Advaita for which all distinctions are alike only apparent. It differs likewise from the Nyāya-Vaiśeṣika though maintaining a real distinction between the two entities, because it regards that they are not external to each other. but this should not lead us to think that Ramajuja, like Kumārila, advocates the bhedabheda view for he does not admit identity of any kind whatsoever between the entities supposed to be distinct, the unity affirmed being only of the complex whole.[126]The term 'Viśiṣṭādvaita' is more usually explained in a somewhat different manner—especially in interpreting verbal statements affirming unity like Tat tvam asi. But the idea underlying it is the same. If we take the proposition 'The lotus is blue,' the quality of 'blueness' according to this explanation, because of its attributive character, points necessarily to some substance to which it belongs. This blue substance is a complex whole. The lotus also may similarly be looked upon as complex whole, comprising the attributive element of 'lotus-ness' and a substance which it characterizes. The identity that is expressed by the proposition is of these two complexes.[127]Or, in other words, the two terms—'blue' and 'lotus'—have distinct meanings but refer to the same substance (prakāryadvaita). What is signified is not therefore a bare identity which excludes the viśeṣaṇas. It includes them and it is their difference that calls for an affirmation of identity in the above sense. Otherwise we may be misled into thinking that the two complexes are distinct. In the example that we have taken, there is only one visesana. There may be several, which again may be co-existent or may appear in the viśeṣya successively. When for instance we think of a youth whom we knew as a child, the two viśeṣaṇas due to distinction of age appear one after the other; but they do not lie outside the unity of the individual in question. Such identity is found not only in the case of substance and its attributes as the above examples may suggest but also in that of substance and its modes, e.g. clay and jar. In fact, it obtains wherever we have inseparable correlative. Of two such entities, the major member is designated prakarin; and the minor, prakāra.

The central point of the teaching of the Upaniṣads, according to Rāmānuja, is the unity of Brahman in this sense; and he, like Śaṁkara, cites in support of his view the two kinds of co-ordinate propositions that occur in them—one, affirming the identity of the soul and Brahman, and the other, that of Brahman and the material world. But he differs totally from him in their interpretation. Before stating his explanation of them, we must briefly refer to another aspect of the doctrine. According to Rāmānuja all things that are, are eventually forms or modes (prakāra) of God. Similarly all names are his names,[128] so that every word becomes a symbol of God and finally points to him. This deeper significance of words, described as Vedānta-vyutpatti, is what only the enlightened comprehend. According to it no word ceases to signify after denoting its usual meaning, but extends its function till it reaches the Supreme.[129] In fact, it is only the latter that is conceived as the essential significance of a word. Now let us select for illustrating Rāmānuja's interpretation the well-known Upaniṣadic maxim—Tat tvam asi. The term tvam in it which commonly stands for the jīva really points to God who is the jīva's inner self (antaryamin) and of whom the jīva and, through it, its physical body are alike modes. What the term tat means in it is also the same, but viewed in a different aspect, viz. God as the cause of the universe, as shown by the context in which it occurs in the *Chāndogya Upaniṣad.* The identity meant by Tat tvam asi, according to the explanation of the term Viśiṣṭādvaita given above, is of these two complexes—God as the indweller of the jīva and God as the source of the world. The final import of the statement is that though the world and the individual souls are real and distinct, the Absolute in which they are included is one.[130] 'They are eternal with God but are not external to him.' In the advaitic interpretation of the same, the distinction due to the vise sana elements is rejected as but an appearance though, as we have tried to show, no identity as such is taken to be implied by it. Here the distinction is not denied; and, at the same time, the organic unity of the whole is affirmed.

This is only a general account of the Viśiṣṭādvaita view of Reality. To state the same now more in detail: Rāmānuja recognizes, as it is clear by now, the distinction between substance and attribute; but the attributes are not further distinguished, as in the Nyāya-vaiśeṣika, into guna, karma, jati, etc.[131] and are comprehensively termed adravya or 'what is other than substance.' There are thus only two main categories of which the second, adravya, is always and necessarily dependent upon the first, dravya, although neither, in consequence of the unique relation that obtains between them, can be or be thought of apart from the other.[132] The adravyas are reckoned as ten. Five of them are the qualities of the five bhutas—sound, etc.—and the next three are the gunas in the special sense of sattva, rajas and tamas, which are the characteristics of matter (acit) or prakṛti. Three of the adravyas are thus general; and five, specific. Of the remaining two, sakti or 'potency' is that property of a causal substance by virtue of which it produces the effect, e.g. plasticity in clay, attractive power in a magnet, burning capacity in fire. The tenth adravya is samyoga, by which is meant as in the Nyāya-Vaiśesika an external relation like that between the floor and a jar.

Not only is adravya distinct from dravya in this system; the dravyas themselves are to be distinguished from one another. But what is a dravya?[133] According to the Viśiṣṭādvaita conception, whatever serves as the substratum of change is a dravya. It means that Rāmānuja accepts the pariṇāma-vāda or sat-kārya-vāda. But it is the attributive elements (viśeṣaṇa) alone that change, for which reason the complex whole (viśiṭa) is also spoken of as undergoing modifications. The substantive element (viśeṣya) in itself is changeless. God viewed as the viśeṣya is changeless and the soul also is so,[134] but the dharma-bhūta-jñāna which belongs to them changes. Matter, which is entirely a visesana, itself changes.[135] The relation between it and its transformations, say, clay and jar is, as already pointed out, aprthak-siddhi. But if we consider a lump of clay (piṇḍa) which, and not mere clay (mṛt), is regarded here as the material cause of the jar, the relation between them is stated to be identity (ananyatva, literally, 'non-difference'). Whatever difference there is between the two is explained away as the material is the very same, though the disposition of its constituent parts in them may differ.[136] There are six dravyas answering to this description; and they are divided into two classes—jaḍa and ajaḍa, as already explained. The jaḍa includes prakṛti and time (kāla); and the ajaḍa—dharma-bhūta-jñāna, nitya-vibhūti or suddha-sattva, jīva and Īsvara. We shall now add a few words of explanation regarding each of these:—

(1) *Prakṛti*—This is the dwelling-place of the soul and, through it, of God himself. Nature is thus alive with God. 'Eearth's crammed with heaven, and every common bush afire with God.' We shall best understand its character as conceived in this system by contrasting it with the Sāṅkhya view of it with which it has much in common. The chief differences are : (i) The three guṇas-sattva, rajas and tamas—are supposed in the Sāṅkhya to be its constituent factors, and prakṛti is merely the complex of them all. Here, on the other hand, the gunas are conceived as characterizing it so that they are distinct although inseparable from it. (ii) The prakṛti of the Sāṅkhya is infinite, but here it is taken to be limited in one direction, viz. Above, by the nitya-vibhuti of which we shall speak presently. (iii) in the Sāṅkhya, prakṛti is theoretically independent of the purusa, but here it is entirely under the control of spirit, i.e. jīva or Īśvara. The relation between them is aprthak-siddhi so that neither admits of separation from the other. Owing to this difference, Rāmānuja's conception of prakṛti is much superior to the Sāṅkhya one. The entities evolved out of prakṛti andthe order of their evolution are exactly as stated under the Sāṅkhya.

(2) *Kāla*—Time is viewed here as real; but it is not outside the sole reality recognized, viz. Brahman or the Absolute, though it does not merge in it. So it does not subsist by itself, as it does according to thc Nyāya-Vaiśeṣika. Nor is it but a phase of prakṛti as in the Sānkhya-Yoga. Time also, like prakṛti of which it is the companion, so to speak, admits of change or undergoes parinama; and moments, days, etc., are represented as its evolutes. Unlike time, space is derived from prakṛti and is included only through it in the highest reality. Of prakṛti and time, neither can be said to be prior to the other; but the same cannot be said of space, for prakṛti is prior to it.

(3) *Dharma-bhūta-jñàna.*—As we have already dealt with this, only a few words need be added now. It characterizes jìvas or Ìšvara and is always, as its name indicates, secondary to them, the relation between them being inseparable. It is conceived as both a dravya and a guṇa[137]—a dravya inasmuch as it, through contraction and expansion,[138] is the substrate of change; a guna inasmuch as it is necessarily dependent upon a dravya, viz. Jīva or Īsvara and cannot be by itself. It is knowable as in the Nyāya-Vaiśeṣika, but by itself and not through another jñāna, for it is self-luminous and shows itself though it cannot self-conscious.

(4) *Nitya-vibhūti.*—We have seen that prakṛti is characterized by the three guṇas. If of these we leave out rajas and tamas and conceive of it as characterized only by sattva, we get an idea of nitya-vibhūti and see why it is called śuddha or unalloyed sattva. On account of this peculiar character, it ceases to be material (jaḍa) and becomes 'immaterial' (ajaḍa) in the sense already explained. It is sublimated prakṛti, a sort of super-nature. Since, however, the three guṇas are represented here as constant attributes or qualities of prakṛti and not as its constituent factors as in the Sāṇkhya, it becomes hard to imagine how any

one of them can alone be conceived of as a characteristic when the contrast of the other two is removed. Further, according to the explanation given, prakṛti and nitya-vibhuti possess a common feature, viz. Sattva, and therefore prakṛti also to that extent should be non-material. In that case its entire separation from the ajada category would not be quite accurate. These discrepanicies are in all probability to be explained as due to the system being eclectic in its details, and have led the later Viśiṣṭādvaitin to differentiate between the two sattvas and declare that they are altogether distinct (vilakṣaṇa).[139] Except in this important respect, nitya-vibhūti is similar to prakṛti. Briefly it is the material out of which the things of the ideal world, and the bodies of God and of the liberated souls are made. It is 'matter without its mutability' and has been described as a fit means to the fulfilment of divine experience.[140] The domain of nitya-vibhuti is limited below by prakṛti but is infinite above. Vaikuṇṭha, the city of God, is supposed to occupy a part of it. Though a sharp demarcation is made between prakṛti and nitya-vibhuti, the latter, it is stated, is found within the region of the former as for instance in the holy idols worshipped in sacred places like Śrīraṇgam, those idols being viewed as permeated through and through by this material. The reverse cannot happen and prakṛti does not encroach upon the region of nitya-vibhuti.

(5) *Jīva.*—In dealing with dharma-bhūta-jñàna, we have already referred to the nature of the jīva. It is of the essence of spirit and has dharma-bhūta-jñàna always associated with it. In these respect consists its essential affinity with God. The jīva is not here, as in the Advaita, merely the assumed unity of individual experience, but an eternal reality. In its natural condition of mokṣa, its jñàna expands to the maximum, reaching the ends of space, and there is nothing then which it fails to comprehend. In saṁsāra as a whole the jñàna is more or less contracted,

but never absent, not even in deep sleep where it only ceases to function and does not therefore reveal objects. The jīva itself, apart from its jñàna, is viewed as of atomic size—a mere point of spiritual light, and its functioning in places where it is not, as for example in seeing distant things, is rendered possible by the expansion and contraction of its dharma-bhūta-jñàna. 'Though monadic in substance it is infinite in intelligence.'[141] The jīva is not merely sentience; it is also of the essence of bliss. This aspect of the jīva's nature again will remain more or less obscured in saṁsāra, becoming fully manifest only when liberation is achieved. The diminution in its capacity to know or to enjoy is temporary; when released, it is restored to its omniscience and eternal happiness. The jīva with its physical body derived from prakṛti and with God for its indweller is the meeting-point, so to speak of the material and the divine which explains the gulf which often separates man's ideal aspirations from his actual life. The jīvas are infinite in number and in addition to those that are on their trial here (baddha) or have already achived their salvation (mukta), the doctrine recognizes what are described as nitya which have never been in bondage. They are beings like Visvaksena who have from all time. been attending upon God. Each jīva is in reality both a karta and a bhokta, i.e. an active and purposeful being. It is also free and God, who is its 'inner ruler immortal,' must be supposed to control it without interfering with the freedom that belongs to it.[142]

(6) *Ìšvara.*—The conception of God also in the system has by this time become clear, rendering it unnecessary to say much about it now, Ìšvara too is of the nature of spirit of intelligence and is of the essence of unsurpassed bliss.[143] Like the jīva, he also possesses dharma-bhūta-jñàna whose transformations constitute his several psychical states. Owing however, to his omnipresence, there is

really no need for such an aid in his case; and its postulation is intended solely to secure constancy to spirit in itself. The term Ìśvara is used in a double sense. First, it stands for the entire universe with all its spiritual and material elements included in it. In this sense, Ìśvara may be thought of in two stages-as cause and as effect. In dissolution (pralaya) he subsists as the cause with the whole of the universe latent in him; in creation (srsti), what is latent becomes manifest. Subtle matter becomes gross; and souls, expanding their dharma-bhūta-jñàna, enter into relation with physical bodies appropriate to their past karma. The causal form includes within itself everything that is required for the development signified by creation, so that Ìśvara is the whole and sole cause of it. In other words, God is self-determining and the universe develops from within unassisted by any external agency (p.82). It is because he *grows* into this cosmic variety that he is called 'Brahman' (p. 54). That would ascribe change to God which is against the prevalent teaching of the Upaniṣads; but Rāmānuja tries to explain the difficulty away by holding that the change is only to be secondarily understood—as sa-dvaraka. God does not suffer change in himself, but only through the entities comprehended in the whole of which he is the inspiring principle. But it is not easy to see how he can be said to remain changeless when his inseparable attributes are changing. This Ìśvara in himself, regarded as the unchanging centre of the changing universe, is the other meaning of the term. Such an Ìśvara of course does not exist isolated by himself, but it is still legitimate to make the distinction because the viśeṣya element in the Absolute, like the viśeṣaṇas, is real and ultimate. In the former sense, Ìśvara is the Absolute of Rāmānuja; in the latter, he is the antar-yamin and dwells within whatever is—whether soul or matter.

This absolutist view which is chiefly based upon the

Upaniṣads is intertwined in the system with the details of a creed which, historically speaking goes back to a different source. In that phase, God is conceived as completely personal. He is looked upon as having pity for erring man and as actuated by a desire to show mercy to him. Benevolence, indeed, is one of his essential features. He is known as Nārāyana or Vāsudeva, and the latter designation is a sign of the presence in the doctrine of elements drawn from the Bhāgavata religion. He is also known as Para or the Supreme. In this form he dwells in his own citadel Vaikuṇṭha which, as we said, occupies a corner in the domain of nitya-vibhuti. He manifests himself in various ways to help his devotees: One of the most important is known as vyuha. It is four-fold: Vāsudeva—a differentiation within Para Vāsudeva and therefore to be distinguished from him—Samkarsana, Pradyumna and Aniruddha. They are all incomplete manifestations, and God appears in them in different garbs. Another way in which the Supreme manifests himself is as avatars (p. 98) which are well known. They are classed together as vibhava. Still another manifestation is known as the antaryamin whose presence within is common to all the jīvas and who guides them like a friend.[144] It is God incorporate—possessing a rūpa—and should be distinguished from the one referred to above which bears the same name and which, as taught in the *Bṛhadāranyaka Upaniṣad*,[145] is the essence (svarupa) of God.[146] The last of the manifestations, called arcavatara, is as holy idols worshipped in sacred places like Śrīraṇgam.

Now as regards the success with which the two teaching have been assimilated here: The attempt, so far as it aims at identifying the ultimate of philosophy with the ultimate of religion, has its undoubted excellences. But it is one thing to think of the two as the same and quite another to try combining a particular philosophic doctrine with a particular religious creed. The theistic creed that finds place in the present synthesis had, as the result of its long history, developed a host of concrete details, not all of which for lack of adequate rational support could fuse with philosophy. The philosophic doctrine included in it was, on the other hand, the result of one of the most daring speculations in the whole field of thought; and its conception of Reality was the least personal. Hence there are some discrepancies in the doctrine resulting from the synthesis, such as those we had occasion to mention in speaking of the notions of antaryamin and nitya-vibhuti. Another instance of the same disaccord is found in what we shall point out in the next section, viz. The retention in the doctrine of the 'esoteric restriction' of the saving knowledge of bhakti by the side of the popular pathway to release of prapatti. The fact is that the Vaisnava religion was there in all its completeness in the time of Ràmànuja. As a practical creed, it had indeed served human needs in an excellent manner and given rise within its fold to more than one saint of pre-eminent mystical power. But it lacked support from the Upaniṣads and this lack of support should have become the more conspicuous after Śaṁkara had expounded them in a specific manner. The attempt made in the Visistavaita was to secure for Vaiṣṇavism the needed support. It was thus practical exigency rather than any organic connection between the two teachings that led to their synthesis. We may illustrate best the resulting discrepancy by reference to the conception of the Absolute in the system. Rāmānuja admits several ultimate entities, but holds at the same time that there is only one Being—that of the viśeṣya, all the attributive elements deriving their being from it.[147] If all these entities are existentially one, it is difficult to see how the distinction between them can be ultimate. It is just this lack of independent being that the Advaitin means when he denies reality to elements of diversity in the Absolute.[148] If to avoid the above difficulty we assume that each visesana has its own *separate* being, the absoluteness of the Absolute vanishes and it will be hard to think of it as a unity except in a secondary or figurative sense. The only other alternative is to define the relation between the several entities constituting the Absolute as bhedābheda, thus predicating both identity and difference of them. But such an explanation, even supposing it is logically sound, is, as already pointed out, totally unacceptable to Rāmānuja. The notion of apṛthaksiddhi on which the conception is based is as imperfect as that of the Nyāya-Vaiśeṣika samavāya which it is intended to replace. The only difference is that while samavāya tries to unite what are supposed to be distinct, apṛthak-siddhi tries to separate what is supposed to be one. Both alike represent efforts to seek what it is not possible to have, viz. A half-way house between inclusion and exclusion. The system, so far as it is based on Vaiṣṇavism, endeavours to secure ultimate reality for the souls as well as matter; but loyalty to the Upaniṣads drives it to modify it, thus rendering the result logically unsatisfactory.

IV

As in the Advaita, the practical discipline here also begins with karma-yoga in the Gītā sense, which purifies the heart and fits a person for knowing the truth; but it is quite different in what follows. The training that is distinctive of the Viśiṣṭādvaita is two-fold:—

(1) *jñàna-yoga.*—This means meditation upon the jīva after knowing its true character through sravana or study of the scriptures under a proper *guru.* Those only that have achieved success in karma-yoga can enter upon it. Its object is to realize how the self is different from its several accom-paniments like the body, senses and so forth with which man usually identifies it and how attachment to them impedes spiritual progress. When this yoga is carried to fruition, the discipline does not terminate, for according to Rāmānuja, the jīva though an ultimate fact is not the Ultimate. The disciple may have succeeded in realizing his nature in relation to the physical environment; but there yet remains the task of discovering the same in relation to God, the highest fact of the universe. Man cannot, according to Rāmānuja, know himself truly until he knows God. The means prescribed for

such knowledge is termed bhakti-yoga.

(2) *Bhakti-yoga.*—This marks the culminating stage of the discipline. It presupposes a reasoned conviction regarding the nature of God as taught in the Viśiṣṭādvaita, and those alone that have successfully pursued jñàna-yoga in the sense just explained can begin it. Bhakti here is equated with dhyana and may therefore be taken as upasana or meditation taught in the Upaniṣads, provided we remember that it implies also love. It is not a mere austere concentration of the mind on Reality, but a loving contemplation of a personal God.[149] There is also another implication in it which is equally the result of the conception of the jīva characteristic of the doctrine, viz. The feeling of one's absolute dependence (sesatva) upon God as the sole power in the universe. Bhakti-yoga also thus consists in meditation like jñàna-yoga; but it is meditation that is suffused with feelings of love and dependence. Success in this part of the discipline results in the attainment of what may be described as divince vision, actual mokṣa resulting when the soul is severed from the probation of flesh. This is in accordance with the ancient ideal of finding release in a life hereafter, and no jīvan-mukti as such (p. 19) is recognized here as in Śaṁkara's Advaita.

Another important difference from the Advaita is that the obligation to perform karma is not a feature of the preparatory stage only. It continues even when one enters upon bhakti-yoga, so that the ideal of karma-saṁnyāsa as known to the Advaita (p. 339) is rejected here. Man should never abandon karma of the nitya variety or unconditional duties, for he will then become sinful and miss salvation on account of neglecting what is enjoined in the Veda. So far Rāmānuja agrees with Kumārila. But there is here the positive purpose that bhakti, which has been described as 'salvation in becoming,'[150] might grow through karma and ripen into intuition. Adherence to karma in this stage is not therefore for subjective purification as in the earlier one, but for advancing further and further in the life of the spirit. And karma, with its purpose thus transformed, will continue till the very end, for the immediate experience of God is not believed to arise until the moment before departing this life. The discipline for mokṣa thus consists of both jñàna and karma; yet it is the former alone that is regarded as the *direct* cause of release, the latter being taken to be only an accessory and not a co-ordinate aid. Hence, though insisting upon the performance of karma throughout life, the Viśiṣṭādvaita like the Advaita does not advocate what is known as samuccaya-vāda.[151] Before we close this topic we must draw attention to the widening in its scope which karma undergoes in the system. It includes not only whatever is prescribed in the Veda but also prayer and devotional worship as understood in Vaiṣṇavism (kriyā-yoga).[152]

As in the other Indian systems, mokṣa is conveived here also as freedom from mundane existence. But over and above this is the idea here of reaching a supra-mundane sphere and there enjoying in the presence of God the highest bliss. The imperfect prākṛtic body of the jīva is then replaced by a perfect one, so that release does not mean here a disembodied state as it does in many another doctrine. It is this ideal world—'the Highlands of the blest'—that is constituted out of suddha-sattva. Picturesque descriptions are given of the place. There God is seated on his white throne and is served by his consort Laksmi—interceding on behalf of man—and by all the souls of the nitya and mukta variety. It is a place of absolute peace and perfection, and the joy of all there lies in following the will of the supreme. When a bound soul is liberated, it is led to this region and, welcomed by all there, it is at last received by God as his very own. An account of the triumphal progress of the spiritual pilgrim till he arrives at the throne of the Lord is given in the first chapter of the *Kauṣītakī Upaniṣad.*

This is the normal or regular means to release. But a

person, to follow it, must belong to one or another of the three higher castes of Hindu society; for it is only such that are qualified to receive instruction in the Veda and the Upaniṣads. So the course described heretofore becomes considerably narrowed in its usefulness. The Viśiṣṭadvaita therefore recognizes along with it another pathway to God which any one, irrespective of caste or rank, may follow. That is known as prapatti.[153] The word is derived from *pra-pad,* meaning 'to take refuge with' or 'to piously resign,' and points to a belief that salvation is obtained through free grace. It is described as saranagati or flinging oneself on God's compassion. It consists in absolute self-surrender, and signifies a resolve 'to follow the will of God, not to cross his purposes, to believe that he will save, to seek help from him and him alone and to yield up one's spirit to him in all meekness.'[154] In one of its forms described as 'resignation in extreme distress' (arta-prapatti), it is believed to bring deliverance immediately. A single moment of seriousness and sincerity is considered enough; and this also testifies, in the eyes of the Visistadvaitin, to its superiority over bhakti which means a long and laborious process of training. The inclusion by Rāmānuja in his doctrine of a means to salvation which is accessible to all, explains the wide popularity it has always commanded; and the social uplift of the lower classes to which it has led is of great value in the history of India. But it is ouside our purpose to dwell upon that aspect of the Viśiṣṭādvaita at any length. Rāmānuja attaches so much importance to prapatti that he makes it essential to bhakti also in its final stages.[155] He maintains that it represents a form of knowledge and is not therefore in conflict with the Upaniṣadic view that jñàna alone is the means of release—an explanation rendered necessary by prapatti being the distinctive characteristic of Vaiṣṇavism rather than of the Vedānta. The prominent place given to it in the teaching shows the need for absolute self-suppression whatever course of discipline a person may follow. Though zealously upholding the persistence of personality, Rāmānuja commends the cultivation of an attitude which makes one feel and act *as if* that personality did not exist. He means thereby that it is not belief in a permanent self but selfishness which is the enemy of true life.

Foot Notes:

1. The *Upaniṣhads*, the *Bhagavadgītā* and the *Vedānta-sūtra* are known as the prasthāna-traya or, as we might say, the triple foundation of the Vedānta.
2. Cf. I. i. 4 and Śaṁkara's com. On it, The Mīmāṁsakas are styled 'deniers of Brahman' (Brahma-nastika) in Ramananda's gloss on the later.
3. VS. IV. Iv. 5-7.
4. VS. III. Iv. 18-20.
5. VS. I. iv. 19-21.
6. See Dr. S.K. Belvalkar: *Vedānta Philosophy* (Poona) Lectrure v.
7. See Deussen: *System of the vedānta*, pp. 24-5 and 28.
8. Cf. Yatśūnya-vādhinḥ śūnyam tadeva Brahma māyinaḥ. Madhva% *Aṇubhāṣya* on VS. II.ii. 29.
9. VS. II. Ii. 31.
10. It may be noted that the Nyāya-Vaiśeṣika does not recognize karmendriyas, and explains their functions as those of prāṇa or vital air.
11. The word means 'witness' or a disinterested looker-on. The conception is thus relative; and the saksin *as such* is not therefore Brahman.
12. xi. 32.
13. This is expressed as follows in Sanskrit:—Antah-karana-viśiṣṭo jīvah; antaḥ-karṇopahitaḥ sāksī: VP. P. 102.
14. VP. Pp. 79-82.
15. Mediate knowledge removes only the ignorance concerning the existence of an object (asattvapadakajñāna); immeidate knowledge, that regarding its exact nature also (abhānāpādakājñāna).
16. The metaphor is drawn from water in a tank flowing through the sluice to a field to be irrigated and assuming its shape. VP. P. 57.
17. VP. P. 77.
18. 'The theory of perception adopted by the Advaitya Vedānta is rather crude on the scientific side, though its metaphysical insight is valuable.' IP. Vol. ii. Pp. 492-3.
19. For example, religious merit (punya) and demerit (papa), which also are regarded as modes of the antah-karana, are not perceivable because they lack this condition of

yogyatva or fitness. They are only inferable or knowable through verbal testimony.

20. There is some divergence in the use of these terms—Māyā and avidyā. We confine them here respectively to Māyā in its cosmic character and in its 'incidence,' so to speak, on the individual.

21. In place of the two adjuncts of the self as conceived in the Sāṅkhya-Yoga, we thus have three here: (1) karana-sarira, (2) linga-śarīra and (3) sthūla-śarīra.

22. The recollection by the jīva of what was experienced by the śakṣin is possible as the two are not really different. See SLS. Pp. 155-6.

23. *Pañca-daśi*, xi. 74-5.

24. *Ch. Up.* VIII. iii. 2.

25. See e.g. com. On VS. II. ii. 28.

26. See *Gaudapāda-kārika,* ii. 14. An object may of course disappear and cease to be as we are apprehending it.

27. It is possible to say that this feature characterizes illusion also, and that so far the distinction of the objects of ordinary knowledge from those of illusion vanishes. For example, the 'rope-serpent,' once seen may be recognized after some time, if in the meanwhile the mistake has not been rectified. Such a position cannot be proved to be false; and there have been Advaitins who maintained it (Cf. SLS. Pp. 105-6). But it lands us eventually in solipsism and is not the commonly accepted advaitic view.

28 VS. II. ii. 28-32.

29. Cf. VP. P. 153. Satya-mithya-vastu-tadatmyavagahitvena bhrama-tva-svīkārāt.

30. Paratah eva aprāmanyam: VP. P. 338.

31. It should be noted in this connection that pain, pleasure and other modes of the antah-karana, though 'private,' are not thus sublated and are therefore not pratibhasika. The same remark applies to the antah-karana also.

32. Literally the word means 'identity' and is used in the Nyāya-Vaiśeṣika in the sense of the abstract identity of a term with itself. It is also used in the sense of 'identity-in-difference' by some like Kumarila. Here it has neither of these senses.

33. For this reason the silver is described as ananya with reference to the shell which Śaṁkara explains as 'not

existing apart from.' Ananyatvam vyatirekena abhavah. See com. On VS. II. I. 14.

34. That is, the proximate ground. The ultimate ground is always spirit or caitanya.

35. This avidyā should not be confounded with the one described above as the radical adjunct of the jīva. That is constitutive of the jīva; this is only a passing characteristic of it. The one continues till mokṣa is attained; the other disappears with the error it has occasioned.

36. Avidyā is directly the cause of the illusion, but all knowledge has by hypothesis an object and that object, viz. 'silver,' here is ascribed to the same avidyā, not being traceable to any other source. See VP. P. 137.

37. SLS. P. 140.

38. VP. P. 168. Māyā is then termed mūlāvidyā.

39. Rāgecchā-sukha-duḥkhādi buddhau satyām pravartate4:
Susuptau nāsti tannāśāt tasmāt buddhẹstu natmanah.
These are all vṛttis as inspired by the śakṣin and it is their vṛtti aspect alone that belongs to the antah-karana. The resemblance to the Sāṅkhya-Yoga here is clear.

40. The Nyāya-Vaiśeṣika and the Mīmāṁsa also admit that the manas which corresponds to the Advaidin's antah-karana is different from the self; but they view pain, etc., as features directly characterizing the atman. There is therefore nothing, according to those doctrines, that is out of the normal in the experience 'I am suffering' to need an explanation.

41. The notion of the śakṣin, as already pointed out, is relative to an antah-karana and cannot therefore be regarded as ultimate. Saksi-svarupa means the essence of the śakṣin.

42. Some recognize only one kind of being. See VP. Pp. 221-3. Some again do not make any distinction between vyavaharika and prāti-bhāsika being. According to the latter, the reality of the waking state does not stand higher than that of the dream state—what is true according to either being sublated in the other. See Note 2 on p. 350.

43. The ground of the adhyasa here is taken to be spirit or caitanya, as indeed it is in the case of 'shell-silver' also eventually (VP. Pp. 162-3). The only difference is that in the latter the illusion is mediated by an empirical object, viz, the shell, while in the former it is direct.

44. VP. Pp. 19 ff.
45. VP. Pp. 36-8.
46. VP. P. 298.
47. Compare the saying: Vyavahare Bhatta-nayah.
48. Cf. *Naiskarmya-siddhi,* ii. 5; iii. 44 and 83-6.
49. VS. ii. i. 14.
50. See Deussen: *System of the Vedānta,* p. 55. Cf. stanzas cited by Śaṁkara at the end of his com. On VS. I. i. 4.
51. See Śaṁkara on VS. II. I 14; *Naiskarmya-siddhi,* iii. 108-9.
52. VP. pp. 102 ff.
53. Contrast the sāṅkhya-Yoga view where the elements constituting the empiricanego are independently real.
54. iv. 20-35,
55. It is the world as it exists for an individual that is the source of bondage to him, not the world as it is. See *Panca-dasi,* iv. 32.
56. Cf. Śaṁkara on VS. II. iii. 16 and 17.
57. See Śaṁkara on VS. I. iv. 3.
58. See Śaṁkara on *Ch. Up.* III. Xiv. 1 and on VS. I. ii. 1-8.
59. Ayam nijaḥ paro veti gaṇanā laghu-cetasām: Udāra-caritānām tu vasudhaiva kuṭumbakaṃ.
60. See *Vana mālā* on Śaṁkara's com. On *Tait.Up.,* p. 131 (Śrīrangam Edn.).
61. *Tait. Up.*ii. 1.
62. VS. II. I. 34-6.
63. Ibid., 32-3.
64. See com. On sūtra 33 *ad finem.* Cf. *Bhamati* on sūtra 34.
65. If we take, instead of the visible universe, its source Māyā, the relation is anadi.
66. See e.g. BUV. IV. iii. St. 1637-1787; *Bhāmatī,* I. i. 4.
67. Cf. *Iṣṭa-siddhi* (Gaekwad's Oriental Series), pp. 18-22.
68. It does not alter the matter if M and N, instead of being two objects, are two moments in the history of one and the same object, say P. The argument would still be applicable to them, the only difference being that what are described as identical features are truly so in the latter, but are only similar and remain separate in the former.
69. Some like Bhāskara take the universe alone as the parinama

of Brahman and not the jīvas also.
70. IP. vol. ii. 570.
71. If the Advaitin sometimes uses terms implying belief in parinama, he should be understood as speaking from the empirical standpoint See Śaṁkara of VS. II. I in the Brahman in I iv 20.
72. See SAS. Iv. 20.
73. Ya eva hi nirākartā tadeva tasya svarūpam: Śaṁkara on VS. II. Iii. 7.
74. Cf. *Naiskarmya-siddhi,* iii. 100-3. All objects alike reveal being (sat) of some type or other. The subject which cognizes them reveals not only being but also thought (cit). Thus we may say that the Advaita recognizes kinds as well as degrees of reality.
75. As other examples of distinction between the two, we may mention the following: The jīva's knowledge has many limitations, while God is all-knowing; God is mediately know, while the jīva is immediately realized.
76. Being the Absolute in the true sense of the term, it may appear as 'nothing' to the dull-witted (manda-buddhi) as Śaṁkara says (see com. On *Ch. Up.* Viii. I. 1). Compare: 'I still insist that for thought what is not relative is nothing'—Bradley: *Appearance and Reality,* p. 30.
77. See *Samksepa-sariraka,* i. 250-6.
78. If an objective reality be negatively described and all knowable features are abstracted from it, we may conclude that there is nothing of it left behind. The observation that 'pure being is pure nothing' may accordingly apply to another form of Advaita which is named sattadvaita, in contradistinction to the Ātmādvaita of Śaṁkara, and takes mere Being (sattā-sāmānya) to be the Absolute. See *Naiṣkarmya-siddhi,* iii. 101.
79. See Śaṁkara on *Ch. Up.* viii. I.I and *Kalpa-taru,*I. i. 20.
80. Śaṁkara on *Br. Up.* II. I. 20.
81. VS. III. Iv. 26.
82. The only other level of existence where the self can be realized according to the Upaniṣads is Brahma-loka or the world of Brahma (*Katha Up.* II. Iii. 5), the mokṣa thus achieved being designated krama-kukti as stated in the chapter on the Upaniṣads (p. 74). It results, according to the Advaita, from the combination (samuccaya) of Vedic

karma with meditation upon the saguna Brahman regarding it as the highest reality, either because the disciple does not know there is a higher one or because, knowing it, he feels himself unequal to the task of realizing it.
83. VS. IV. I. 1-2.
84. Cf. Kim tu srutyādayo anubhavādayaśca yathā-saṁbhavam iha pramāṇam anubhavāsānatvāt bhūta-vastu-viṣayatvācca brahma-jñānasya: Com. On VS. I. i. 2 See Dr. Belvalker: *op. Cit.*,p.14.
85. Apart from the question of direct revelation, the Upaniṣads also should in the last resort be regarded as recording only such intuitional knowledge of ancient sages. See Note 4 on p. 182.
86. Cf. *Paṇca-dasī,* vi. 270-8. It is interesting in this connection to refer to Śaṁkara's statement at the end of his com. On VS. IV. I. 15, which tradtition views as an allusion to his own direct experience of the ultimate truth.
87. *Isa Up.* 6.
88. xiii. 27.
89. Cf. Śaṁkara on VS. II. Iii. 48.
90. *Naiṣkarmya-siddhi,* iv. 69.
91. See e.g. SB. I. iv. 27.
92. This, as we shall see, is termed bhakti by Rāmānuja.
93. SS. P. 189.
94. The Upaniṣads were not explained by him separately and that work was left for a much later hand—Rangarāmānuja.
95. Cf. *Adhikarana-sāravalī.* Introductory stanza, 25.
96. Pratiṣṭhapita-vedāntaḥ pratikṣipta-bahirmataḥ: Bhūyāḥ traividya-mānyaḥ bhūri-kalyāṇa-bhājanam.
97. It is pointed out that if at the second apprehension the former impression is not revived, the knowledge will be only nirvikalpaka and that it will continue to be so till such revival takes place. See VAS. P.-51. (com.).
98. SB. Pp. 70-5.
99. SB. P. 71.
100. *Yatīndra-mata-dīpikā* (Ānandāśrama Series), p. 51.
101. Jñàna, though attributive to jīva or Ìšvara, is in itself regarded as a 'substance,' as will become clear later.
102. In the case of Ìšvara the dharma-bhūta-jñàna, being all-pervasive, does not contract or expand; but yet it undergoes transformations. The consequent changes of

form are what are meant by divine knowledge, divine grace, etc.

103. According to the Nyāya-Vaiśeṣika, the flame comes into being first and the particles of tejas which constitute its rays are supposed to radiate from it afterwards. Cf. SV. Pp. 842 f.

104. That such is the aim will become clear when we consider the case of Ìśvara, who by hypothesis is everywhere unlike the atomic jīva, and therefore does not stand in need of any such aid.

105. SB. Pp. 183-8.

106. Yathārtham sarva-vijñānam iti veda-vidam matam. Cf. pp. p. 32.

107. Tadeva sadrsam tasya yat taddravyaika-desa-bhak: SB. P. 184.

108. The analogy is here adduced of a small bird soaring in the sky which her that has followed its course from the moment it began to fly, is able to spot easily but not others.

109. *Br. Up.* IV. iii. 10.

110. SB. III. ii. 3.

111. SB. III. ii. 5.

112. SB. P. 187.

113. The peculiar view upheld in sat-khyāti, however, makes one thing certain. There can be no errors of commision. Here is a point of agreement between Rāmānuja's sat-khyāti and Prābhākara's akhyāti. The two are not, however, identical. Compare Vedānta Deśika's description of the former as akhyāti-samvalita-yathārtha-khyāti in SAS. Pp. 403-7.

114. *Yatīndra-mata-dīpikā,* p. 3.

115. Jñàna-phala-bhūta-pravṛtti-bādhyatvam: SB. (com.) p. 185.

116. Compare the kevala-jñàna of Jainism (p. 159).

117. Yatīndra-mata-dīpikā, p. 27.

118. See Note 2 on p. 332.

119. To all appearance, Bādarāyana is against agama. Compare Śaṁkara on VS.11.ii. 42-5.

120. This is known as the Ekāyana-sākhā. See SB (com.) P.559 (Madras Edn.,)

121. The vaikhanasāgama, which also upholds the supremacy

of Viṣṇu, seems to exhibit closer kinship with the Veda.

122. Since according to Rāmānuja inorganic matter also is ensouled, God is its self only mediately throught the jīva (see VAS. Pp. 30-1).Yet he is sometimes spoken of as being so directly. Cf. Rahasya-traya-sāra, iii.pp. 121-2 (Bangalore Edn.).

123. The Nyāya-Vaiśeṣika postulates the relation of samavaya between things that are inseparable. The Viśiṣṭādvaita discards this relation as superfluous and views inseparability itself, which it regards as the nature (svarupa) of the two relata, as apṛthak-siddhi, strictly it is not therefore a relation (see SB. 11. Ii. 12); but it is still sometimes spoken of as a sambandha. (cf. SAS. P.590.)

124. SB.11. i. 9. This intimacy of relation is expressed thus- niyamena ādheyatvam, niyamena vidheyatvam, niyamena śeṣatvam.

125. Cf.SB. p. 132 (com.): Viśiṣṭāntarbhāva eva aikyam.

126. Cf.SB.pp.75,204-5; vas. Pp. 50, 97-8.

127. SB. p. 132.

128. Some exceptions are made. See SB. Pp.205-7.

129. Aparyavasana-vṛttiḥ śabda-vyāpāraḥ. Cf. VAS.p.36.

130. SB.pp. 198-9.

131. Karma or action is explained as mere disjunction and conjunction and therefore as expressible in terms of samyoga and its opposite, Vibhāga. Jāti, as in Jainism or in the Sāṅkhya-Yoga, is only a certain disposition of the several parts constituting the thing. Abhāva is conceived positively as in the Prābhākara school.

132. Pṛthak-pratipatti-sthityanarha:SB.p.205.

133. SAS. p. 590.

134. Not all viśeṣaṇas therefore change, though whatever changes is necessarily a visesana.

135. SB.111.ii. 21.

136. SB. 11. I. 15.

137. The term guna here means'secondary' and does not bear the significance which it does in the Nyāya-Vaiśeṣika.

138. SB. P. 83.

139. See Vedānta Deśika: Rahasya-traya-sara.

140. Prof. P.N. Śrīnivasachari. Rāmānuja's Idea of the Finite Self (Longmans),p.62.

141. Prof. P. N. Śrīnivasachari: *op. Cit.*, p. 26.

142. VAS. Pp. 139-42.
143. VAS. P. 249.
144. *Yatīndra-mata-dīpīka*, p. 88.
145. II. Vii.
146. See *Rahasya-traya-sara*, v. pp. 283-4.
147. Cf. SB. II. Ii. 31. See also the discussion of this point by Raṅgarā-mānuja in his com. On *Muṇḍaka Up*. I. i. 3.
148. See Note 1 on p. 353.
149. Cf. Sneha-pūrvam anudhyānam bhaktiḥ. Quoted in SB. P. 35 (com.).
150. IP. vol. ii. p. 705.
151. SB. III. Iv. 26.
152. Cf. VAS. P. 5.
153. See *Gadya-traya*, iii.
154. Ānukūlyasya saṁkalpaḥ prātikūlyasya varjanam: Rakṣiṣyatīti viśvāsaḥ goptṛtva-varaṇam tathā: Ātma-nikṣepa-kārpaṇye ṣaḍvidhā śaraṇāgatiḥ.
155. See com. On BG. Xviii. 66.

two

INTRODUCTION TO VEDANTA PHILOSOPHY

Vedanta philosophy, based on my understanding, has two main concepts. The first is the human's real nature is divine and the second concept is that the aim of human life is to realize this divinity.

Let us try to examine each of the concepts separately. Vedanta asserts that the universe perceived by the senses is not real. This is called Maya. Unfortunately, maya has been confused to be really illusion leading to questions like, 'Wouldn't blood flow out if I slit my wrists?.' Maya just means out that the perception of a person not 'self-realized' is not real because such a person associates himself with his emotions, and his ego. Since we are unable to perceive the world as a superimposition of the One reality (which is unchanged in time and space) and thus that all beings are inter-related, the vedantist says that the world we perceive is an illusion. Thus what the vedantist implies is that the world is not unreal like the existence of an offspring of a barren woman, but the world is unreal like the mistaking of a rope to be a snake.

Having said that, it is difficult to imagine that a lotus, the marsh where it resides, and the rock nearby are all made up of identical units. But, an scientist will agree with this statement, saying that it is indeed true.

Vedanta goes on to assert that beneath this outward changing appearance lies an fundamental reality which is supreme, called Brahman. This is the 'Sat-chit-ananda (being—consciousness—bliss)' and 'the peace of god which passeth all understanding' according to the Bible. The scientist protests this contention, saying that he cannot measure this underlying reality, if any. The vedantist is not surprised, he adds that since Brahman is beyond the senses, not being able to detect an underlying reality does not prove anything. Now, we are at crossroads, we can either agree with the scientist or the Vedantist. But in order to examine the next concept carefully, we have to have to agree with the Vedantist for a moment, and come back and question him later.

The vedantist goes on to say that the purpose of human life is to realize this underlying reality. He refers to the essential nature present in every human being as Atman (which is called God Immanent). A few vedantists differ on whether that this Atman is essentially the same as Brahman. This led to many philosophies including the three main ones, Advaita, Dvaita etc.. as mentioned in the Hinduism section. Advaita philosophy says that everything is Brahman and that only maya prevents us from seeing that. The other philosophies differ from this contention. But we will not worry about that, since all of the Vedantists seem to agree that Atman and Brahman are 'related' and the aim of the human life is realization of this. A good contention is to realize this Atman for ourselves, and investigate how the Atman is related to Brahman.

We are prone to ask why do we want to realize Atman? To answer why, we have to find an alternate purpose unless one contends that life is of no real purpose. Of course there is no need to seek a new purpose if one is satisfied with his present life. Let us see what the majority do: get a education, get a job, make money, be beautiful, become strong, have children, and preferably, become famous. But, does one become satisfied with any of this ? Of course not, one always wants more since the desire is endless.Therefore desire can be satisified only by the infinite. But a common person does have periods of happiness and periods of sorrow. But is this really happiness or just pleasure ? Everyone would agree that sickness, death etc are suffering. Not getting what we want or getting what we don't want is also suffering. The only question is whether getting what we want and not getting what we don't want is also suffering. Actually, they are also suffering. Most of us when we get what we want don't really enjoy it. It is like eating a small ice-cream cone. One eats it hurriedly so that the ice cream won't melt and make a mess. The pleasure from these objects are so fleeting, yet the mind tries to repeat this experience and assumes it as happiness. When it so happens that we can't get this object, we experience sorrow and unhappiness.

Here is where saints like Sankara, Buddha and Jesus interject and say you can have HAPPINESS all the time if you let go of this cycle of joy and sorrow which you have by holding on to the unreal hoping that they bring you happiness. They even go on to say that desire is the root cause of suffering and unjust action leads to more action, and death brings a sudden end to all this. To pause and think about their statements seems unneccessary since down deep we seem to know that this indeed is the truth and we seem helpless. So, some take a high road and dismiss them as pessimists, and their teaching as escapism from the world. But some of us have achieved many of the material successes, and still have an 'empty' feeling. Some others realize that all their ambitions have failed, and there seem to be no purpose to life. A few others have lost their loved ones, their valued possessions and wonder their true purpose of life. Among these people, a few of them would like to give the benefit of doubt to these prophets. He is prone to ask these masters, 'I don't entirely believe in this

Atman, but let us assume this exists, how do I realize it ? and how am I to enjoy this everlasting bliss you all seem to be enjoying?'.

Pat comes the answer requesting you to quit thinking who you think you are but finding out and realizing who you really are. This sounds stupid, but they continue to say that who you really are is the Atman, and not the ego you associate yourself with. What exactly is this ego ? It is feeling that one is a separate unique individual, and shows whenever we boast our accomplishments, desire, or when we bemoan our failures, and fear the unknown. The Vedantist will say that this is an illusion and you are not separate. The scientist, to our surprise, will agree with the Vedantist that all objects are interrelated on all levels.

A simplistic person may ask whether this means that he should just stop believing he is an individual. But it ain't so easy. First, we have to overcome our possessive attitudes towards our action. This does not mean stop doing action but forgetting the fruits of the action. Thus, we have to stop taking credit for successes or bemoaning our failures, and be freed from these 'false' highs and lows. The vedantist goes on to say that you should work as a service and think of our body/mind as an instrument of the Atman.

A good question now is why does the Atman need our help and why we should work for it. Here, the vedantist is bound to give you a profound answer saying work is worship and the motive for worship is Love. Considering our normal ways of thinking about Love, we are bound to question this. But the Vedantist points out that this Love is perfect since now one is loving something which is perfect and everlasting. But, as usual, we are bound to feel somewhat unhappy with this answer. The Vedantist is advising us to Love something (which he claims to be perfect and permanent) but something we have never seen while loving your spouse seems to be more permanent, while we know it is not since death will separate the spouse.

The Vedantist here asks you to take up meditation, and stick with a practice of yoga. It is important, he adds, that one should drop any attachments which binds you more to this world. This can be achieved by judging every thought and every action from a standpoint of whether this action will help me freer, less egoistic, more aware of the Reality or would this action make me more attached to the world and would enlarge the illusion of separateness.

Here, some of us may view the Vedantist as a person who hates the world, or one who is an escapist. But in reality, only the self-realized persons are able to find the reality beneath all the appearances. The Vedantist is also able to serve the society more effectively than us since he has nothing to gain/lose from it and has no selfish motives and his love for the world is much more than an ordinary individual.

At this point, we come back to the original question whether this reality actually exists. The sage says it does, since he has experienced it but one cannot measure it. The prophet goes on to say that it is entirely up to us to believe him or not. But by following a set of procedures like Yoga, one is bound to realize it. So, he gives us a choice of following a path and experimenting it ourselves.

The messenger is as important as the message. When we look at Jesus, Ramana, Krishna, Ramakrishna, Buddha, we wonder whether these people were deluded or did they lie or whether they were speaking the truth. Reading their life histories, we seem to be inclined with the last option, but we can always follow their path and see for ourselves whether an underlying reality exists or not.

The saint becomes aware of the Atman residing within everyone. He also realizes this reality at all time, having no desires nor ego. This is called by Christians as the mystic union, while the Vedantist prefers the sanskrit word, which means the same, 'Samadhi'. Samadhi is beyond the three states of consciousness normally experienced, waking, dreaming, and deep sleep. However, no one can describe it but one has to experience it.

More thoughts

The vedantist is finished, he says once you are established in samadhi, all questions are answered, but we would like to investigate two questions. One, how did ego come about in the first place and the second, what happens if one fails to achieve this samadhi state in this birth.

The first question is answered usually answered with a straight face, 'Ignorance'. Having been accustomed to our college degrees and our ego, we are indeed livid with anger. We have been told to our face that we are unaware of the reality because we haven't looked for it. We have been called ignorant because we reflect the society, imitate actions like a parrot, and hardly have a thought which is unique. We don't want to agree that we are unaware of this reality and concede to the sage that only ego separates us from this experiencing this reality because without the identification with our ego, we seem unable to identify ourselves.

The answer to the question what created this ego would depend on who you are asking. Buddha will tell you that this question is irrelevant since when a house is burning, you put out the fire, not enquire who started it. Christian theology may introduce the concept of original sin, and postulate the fall of man from the divine nature. Vedanta points out that the whole universe is timeless, and endless, and the concept of creation and destroying is an illusion by itself. But, knowing how and what created this ego does not really help one in attaining samadhi, in my opinion.

The second question of what happens to someone who fails to attain samadhi is a profound one. Unlike the christian view of heaven and hell, and no more, the vedantist says that a person is reborn (reincarnated) in this world based on the fruits of the actions in this previous birth. Now, we need to introduce a much maligned word, Karma. What exactly does Karma mean ? Karma, from the sanskrit word, kri, means 'to do'. In other words, Karma is an action, work, deed. It is just not physical action, but also mental action, both conscious and sub-conscious action. Hence, Karma is generated for every action, and thought we do. The proverb, 'as you sow, so shall you reap' has profound implications. Every action and thought makes an impression on our mind (called samskaras), and this is repeated, form our habit, and character. Karma is of three types, sanchita (karma from our past lives), prarabdha (the fruits resulting from the past actions or the karma in motion) and akamya (karma generated due to the present action/thought). The last typifies free will, since a Vedantist points out that while we can not change our past actions or the fruits we enjoy because of it, we have every right to live rightly now and influence the future. He also points out that at the state of samadhi there is no karma and a person who dwells in the Atman incurs no karma and no future births. Thus, it is entirely up to us to realize this Atman and be freed from the eternal cycle of rebirths (samsara). Thus, if one fails to achieve samadhi in this birth, the deeds will be carried over to his next birth, and he will be born under favorable circumstances to achieve samadhi.

Karma is beginningless, and endless which seems to be weird to us, since the human mind can not comprehend this. But, the scientists and Vedantists, both agree that the universe is also beginningless and endless.

We seem to blame karma for all our material successes or failure. However, we fail to note that these successes and failure arises exactly to keep us in this cycle of samsara. We haven't taken a moment to be an observer and see whether this success has indeed made us closer to the

Reality or is it in fact separating us from it. We seem to proclaim that many evil people succeed, but we somehow seem lost to the idea that the success you attribute to them is material, is impermanent, and is in fact, detaches them from the Reality and engrosses one in Maya.

Thus, to avoid karma and hence rebirth, one has to perform actions selflessly, without worrying about the fruits of the action, and doing it as a service to the Divine. Let us examine the concept of sin. The Vedantic and Christainity concept of sin are not fundamentally different but there are some differences on the surface. When a Christian talks about sin, he usually refers to an act of ingratitude or a negative act towards God, the Father. A vedantist prefers to call this God, the Father, the Reality as it appears within time and space, as Ishwara and distinguishes this from the concept of Brahman and Atman. A vedantist approach towards sin would be any act which results in alienation of the Reality within us. Both these approaches has drawbacks. The christianity approach, by heightening the enormity of sin by relating to the Father, whom we have every reason to love and obey, may lead to self-loathing and despair. The vedantist approach has a major drawback since we tend to not find the offense of doing something against the Atman, since we have not realized it. Sometimes, this leads to the attitude that since one has millions of lives ahead of them, and there is no need to hurry and be engrossed in realizing the reality. But, we realize that both the concepts agree fundamentally that the act of sin is just a separation from the reality or Ishwara.

The main advantage of this approach of looking at sin, is that we come to realize that though it may appear that unrighteous people seem to be rewarded, this reward is just material, impermanent and just separates them more from realizing the reality. Now who is sinned ? Is it better to hang on a cross with the enlightenment and non-attachment of a Christ or to suffer here in the ignorance, agony and bondage of a rich man? Who is happier: Buddha or the richest man in your town? This is for an individual to decide.

The Unreal Mind

As soon as one has even a glimpse of what lies beyond [actually it is Truth revealing Itself], one realizes that one is neither the mind nor the body. The difficult part is to realize this TRUTH all the time. Frequently, the mind tells you otherwise, and the realm of maya weaves itself a seemingly inescapable web. The only way to realize is to control the mind. One has to use the mind to transcend it, akin to a ladder, only to realize that the mind never did exist in Reality.

To one who perceives the illusionary mind, there are lot of ways out to defeat this illusionary opponent, but all can be classified into five D's.. Dedication, Devotion, Discipline, Discrimination coupled with Do (action). Dedication of the fruits of the action, and the discipline of senses through various techniques including yoga, coupled with right action leads to excellent Devotion and Discrimination. All japa, dhyana, and even complicated philosophy and techniques are in fact only stepping stones to shape your mind for devotion and discrimination.

Thus there are only two ways to control the mind : One is to go to the source of thoughts and investigate 'Who am I, to whom do these thoughts occur, who is the thinker and the thought'. This is called self-inquiry or atma vichara (discrimination). The second way is complete surrender of body, mind, ego to Her (devotion). [I use Her to describe Shakti, the Divine Mother, though She is beyond gender similar to the usage of him/his above for persons of both the genders].

This surrender need not be a long drawn out process at all. The surrender should be motivated by Love for the Divinity. Faith is not a blind belief but a belief that whatever happens is God-Given and She looks after your happiness {which is not neccessarily your comforts}. This is like going to a doctor and trusting the medicines he gives without engaging in prolonged conversation of the chemical nature of the drug or how the drug enters the blood stream etc.

During the wakefulness, be a good servant to Her, and try to carry out your duties to perfection, all the while dedicating the actions to Her. Like a snake the ego raises its hood and is charmed by the music of the material world until Shakti Herself by Her Grace draws Her sword and cuts off the head of the snake and the ego withers at the magnificance of Her grace. All the struggles and sadhanas are just preparatory to the extinction of the illusionary mind and killing of the ego since once it is killed, the unreal ego never arises again since The Real does not die, and the unreal never existed.

One of the commonly asked questions is what will happen to so many things one does if one ceases to be attached to them. It is with great confidence that I say 'NOTHING'. The world is in you, you are not in the world. Do an action with good intent [since intent is important than the action itself, for example, a doctor cuts a tumor to save the life of a patient, the cutting of tumor is not ahimsa (non-violence), but the intent is] and FORGET the results of the action. Try it for a week, and see how calm you are, how happy you are when this ego is a servant of Her. Somehow many people have come to feel that they are doing the action, but in reality, it is not so, it is just the prarabdha karma working itself out.

One has to carry on the worldly affairs, but with the understanding that the body-mind has appeared of itself—no one asked for it. The atman is the witness, and the mind is operating, but the mind will tempt you to believe that you are the operator and not the witness. The apparatus of mind-body which is functioning has come upon your original essence, but you are not the apparatus.

By all means, live in this material world, just surrender your ego to Her, or apply the atma vichara at every moment of your life. The true sanyas is only an renunciation of ego. There is no need to go to some place holy and settle down. Any place can be holy, if the mind is devoid of ego, and no place can be holy with an impure mind.

Shri Ramana Maharshi says:

> 'Surrender to Him and abide by His will whether he appears or vanishes; await His pleasure. If you ask Him to do as YOU please, it is not surrender but command to Him. You can not have Him obey you and yet think you have surrendered. He knows what is best and when to do it. Leave everything entirely to Him. His is the burden; you have no longer any cares. All your cares are His. Such is surrender. This is BHAKTI. Or, enquire to whom these questions arise. Dive deep in the Heart and remain as the Self. One of these two ways is open to the aspirant.'

Be detached, allow the karma work itself out, just be devoted to Her since you do not belong in what you think is this the world, and never has this Self being a part of it.

Non-duality

If you are willing to give everything you think you are, the body/mind emotions, intellect, unconditionally to a Higher power (call it Shakti if you want) which is just another manifestation of your Atman (Self), you will know an deep and abiding peace which will fill you. You will eternally happy for apparently no reason because you don't need a reason to be happy, since your very nature is happiness. An example here would be appropriate. When your body aches, you take medicines to make the pain go away because the pain is not your real nature. Similarly, you are constantly trying to alleviate worries and unhappiness by seeking happiness. There is nothing wrong with that, only that the seeking is misplaced. No outer object can satisfy you eternally.

This happiness, bliss, tranquility depends on nothing and has no beginning or an end. It does not matter what you have done so far and what you have not done. All you have to do is surrender unconditionally, absolutely to your Self. The Self cannot abandon you, even if your mind rejects it, because you are the Self. One way to surrender is to just believe these words, or similar words from any of the saints, mystics, sages whose ever-present Grace is apparent. If you don't want to do that, you can go to the source of the thoughts of the questions you raise. To whom is this perceived unhappiness ? Who needs to be happy ? You know you exist. Start with this. Who am I ? Investigate this. This is atma vichara (self-enquiry).

Duality gives birth to the 'I' and 'non-I' concept. The seer and the seen, the seeker and the sought, the lover and the loved, the good and evil, and this endless cycle continues so long as the illusion of duality persists.

The "me" concept generates numerous misidentifications, the primary being the idea that 'I am the body/mind' and is the worst of all. In fact any identification with anything leads to a trap which creates duality and interrupts the flow of immortality. Nisargadatta puts it aptly, 'Anything that is perceived by me can not be me.' There is no escape from the dualistic world and misidentifications so long as the believer thinks he is someone else than who he really is or rather as long as one thinks he is a separate individual. Individuality is an illusion. Egoistic thoughts have to go ! All identifications with the unreal [emotions, body, mind, intellect and finally the concepts of good and evil] will have to finally cease !!

To remove this dualistic thought, one has to discard the

"Me/mine" concept and when that is discarded the "other" concept will also be automatically discarded. Only in this state in which the ego and the personality associated with it completely disappears, one truly awakens to the state of the non-duality and there is no seeker apart from the sought, no seen apart from from the seer. This is the eternal Now, without the past, future. This is the state of fullness, oneness of the universal being, the state which is beyond all identities but is the identity of all beings. This is the state which is so near and but yet seems so far.

Just as you are sure that you are awake now, you should be aware that you are neither the body or the mind and thinking is not our real nature.

Please be sure to check out my wonderful friend's page at Ego Dust, for an excellent exposition on atma vichara and advaita vedanta. If you think you are ignorant and seek to be liberated through the practice of atma vichara, read this page carefully. Go deep into the meaning of the words, meditate on them and your misunderstanding that you are ignorant will disappear. All what you are seeking, you are already That. There is nothing to be 'done' because whatever you do and identify with as a separate phenomenal entity is itself your bondage. All you need to get rid of is not ignorance but the concept of ignorance. The transcending of conceptualization does not happen by suppressing concepts but by being free from purposeful intention. This will make you spontanteous, without any binding, making you realize that you already are what you seek. Truth will reveal itself when you negate your identity as a separate entity.

May Shakti make you aware of Her ever-present grace and help you in your spiritual practice. May the Truth prevail.

three

VEDANTA BASICS

I. An Introduction to the Metaphysics of Vedanta

Our very nature is Freedom. Only our minds tell us otherwise. Therefore there's nothing positive for us to achieve, but only something negative to eliminate. And this is done by applying various techniques such as viveka, which is discriminating between the real and the unreal—that is, finding out what things in life carry permanent versus temporary fulfilment. This, as well as certain other methods are applied in due course, each of which contributes to our ability to one day successfully employ our divine weapon, being the atma vichara (path of Self-enquiry), which is a devastating process for the ego-Mind, causing it to relinquish its stronghold on the individual. Liberation results.

Over the course of a few centuries, the idea of metaphysics and what its practical study has come to imply, especially within the New Age community, is actually the polar opposite of what it was really intended to represent. Exactly how this occurred is not important beyond the fact that the accumulation of "average" people who chanced upon it misconstrued its deeper meaning, hence its popularized mutated [superficial] version.

This article is therefore an attempt to not only correctly define metaphysics, but in so doing, to hopefully succeed in transmitting its essence to whoever may pursue reading it.

Before we commence, we have to eliminate some obstacles to our understanding by way of re-evaluating and re-defining certain relevant concepts and perceptions, which strategy represents a necessary elimination of false ideas accumulated.

First, let's define metaphysics. What is commonly referred to as metaphysics would more appropriately be generally termed 'non-ordinary physics,' since only insignificant portions thereof deal with what is genuinely metaphysical. Such capabilities of the mind as telepathy, clairvoyance, prophesy, or divination (via Tarot, astrology, palmistry, etc.) as well as 'psychic' and 'thaumaturgic powers' such as psychokinesis, levitation, astral projection, etc, actually fall within the domain of physics, since they are all qualified or modified forms of energetic phenomena, and therefore have a materially quantifiable counterpart—albeit possessing the nature of unfamiliar forms—hence the term 'non-ordinary physics.'

On the other hand, metaphysics is beyond physics (as the word implies, although not actually defined as such in the dictionary—since, as mentioned, its usage has been misconstrued over time). Now, what does this signify? The answer to this is profoundly simple yet equally profoundly elusive, as we shall see.

What follows represents the culmination of three decades of comparative religious, philosophical and scientific study. During the course of this study there emerged for me [what was later realized to be] a metaphysical insight which, in turn, eventually achieved a marked level of certainty and reliability. Whereupon, the latter decade was devoted to seeking out and simultaneously discovering certain historic [scriptural] documents that again and again corroborated this insight—thereby not only further reinforcing it but, more importantly, furnishing the understanding that virtually every culture in every time arrived at the same realization. Some of these documents include: the Upanishads, Bhagavad Gita, Dhammapada, Bardo Thodol, Tao Te King, Kabala, Zend Avesta, and the Gospels of John and Thomas.

Also, the so-called New Physics (Quantum Physics) is tending toward a parallel collaboration with metaphysics (Vide: Michael Talbot's The Holographic Universe; Fritjof Capra's The Tao of Physics; Gary Zukov's The Dancing Wu Li Masters; as well as physicists Einstein, Planck, and Bohr, among numerous others, who paved the way in this direction).

Please understand that this is an abridged essay and therefore some observations made are not expounded upon insofar as addressing some pertinent and quite valid objections that may arise.

Before we begin, it's important to understand that there is nothing to achieve which you have not already in your possession. You are already fully enlightened. You already [naturally] own the very thing you're attempting to possess. The illusion that you are mortal, finite, suffering, and in bondage, is itself an illusion! That you think there are obstacles to overcome, mysteries to solve or powers to attain, are themselves the very obstacles blocking your way to the reality of what you ALREADY are. That you doubt this and believe you are yet in need of something, is, in fact, a mind-trick (fabrication), and will be attempted to be disproved by the observations that follow.

This Journey's Direction is Inward:

1. Ordinary awareness accepts at face value the idea of the condition of the self confronting the world. This is the Naive Life-Code of Reference. From it is born the entire realm of maya—from which follows ignorance, fear, desire, bondage, and suffering. From which, in turn, follows

samsara (the Wheel of Rebirth).

2. This world-appearance is immense, complex, mysterious, of unknown origin and endowed with indelible laws of physics, gross and subtle, all within the framework of space-time/Relativity.

3. What is not ordinarily attended upon is the fact that whatever is witnessed in this world is done exclusively through the only conceivable instrument capable of assessing it: the mind.

4. When this mind is studied, some hitherto unrecognized characteristics begin to surface. First and foremost, it is observed to go through phases of waking, dreaming, and deep sleeping. And, since such phases exist, we must conclude that the mind lacks continuity, especially since it is observed to be utterly non-existent in the deep sleep state. This is our first clue.

5. We are inherently compelled to seek out the truth of what, a priori, is. To accomplish this we must set up a standard for Reality. Consider: there are many characteristics that could feasibly be deemed to be integral to what the scope of Reality may actually encompass. Whatever such characteristics we may settle upon, there is one that must be indispensable and foundational to each of them, and cannot be violated under any circumstances: Existence itself. And, as we just established, Existence, by its very implication, cannot be here today and gone tomorrow; it must be permanent and omnipresent (i.e. not subject to birth and death; not found in one place over another; nor present in one creature over another). Therefore, our standard of Reality must rigidly adhere to that which is in an unchanging state of universal permanence.

6. Going back to our clue (viz. that the mind cannot be considered a permanent principle), and applying it to our standard of Reality (viz. that which is not permanent can-

not be considered real, as such), we must hence conclude the mind is not real, as such. The caveat, as such, implies that it is in fact real, yet not real as something separate or apart from its source or cause in the Absolute. This is very important to come to terms with and understand, for it addresses the essence of nonduality (being the inherent unification of all things in existence—manifest and unmanifest).

7. If the mind is not real, as such, are we to further conclude that we are not real? Yes, if we consider that we are merely the mind. However, we are not merely the mind! (For, when the mind shuts off in deep sleep, we do not lose our continuity of Self—a Johnson, going to sleep, doesn't wake up a Benson.) This is our second clue—and an important one.

8. Since the Self continues to thrive through the phases of the mind, it qualifies as a candidate for Reality, providing that it does not suffer an interruption with the advent of the death of the body and the mind. Let's investigate further.

9. To prove that there is no real death for the Self (as opposed to the ego self which is intimately bound to the mind), we must consult a law of physics, namely that "energy can neither be created nor destroyed." Now, the forms or modifications of energy do appear to change, but not their source (such as fire absorbed into an object and changing its form to heat, while the source of fire and heat is always energy). So is the mind a modification of its source, the Self. Therefore the Self, being likened to energy, was never created nor will it ever be destroyed.

Note: At this point it is necessary to reiterate the fact that the Self is really not the true source of the mind. For that would imply that It created the mind; and that would be, by definition, impossible. As pointed out earlier, its source is really shakti. Now, what is the origin of shakti? What created it? To help answer this, let's consult the axioms set down by Sri Shankaracharya:

1. Brahman is the only Reality.
2. The world is an illusion.
3. Brahman is the world.

What this apparent contradiction of ideas is saying is that the world is an illusion on its own terms, but is Reality as Brahman Itself! Moreover, it's important to understand that the world, or anything in it, is not an aspect of Brahman, but Brahman Itself. That is, every concept, object, event and perception in and of the world is AT ONCE the Entirety. An intuitive grasp is needed to comprehend this. It obviously defies logic.

Moreover, it should be understood clearly that the only condition where illusion arises is if any conceivable thought or thing in Life is believed to be a separate reality apart from its substratum source in the Absolute (Brahman). Aside from that, everything is real and is Brahman itself. As the Upanishads tell us, "All this, verily, is Brahman." So that, as alluded to above, whenever something is spoken of in these pages as not real, it is meant, not real apart from its substratum source in Brahman. The idea that the world is purely an illusion is a misconception commonly attributed to Advaita Vedanta; whereas it's really not saying that at all! It is vitally important to understand this. If not, we're propounding dualism. Advaita is telling us the entirety of what is, Manifest and Unmanifest, Immanent and Transcendental, Relative and Absolute, Phenomenal and Noumenal, Physical and Spiritual, is ONE BEING.)

10. Based on the clues provided, the first key for the journey to freedom can now be given: since the body is not real, pay no mind to it. And the second key: since the mind is not real, detach yourself from its thoughts.

There are a number of ways that this can be practically approached. The easiest is to accept that the mind is on its own journey and will generate thoughts as it pleases. In this sense you can watch them like a motion picture in a theater. They are not you yourself, nor do they represent you. For, really, who are you? If you're an ego, then they can be equally thought of as being you. But this is actually absurd to even imagine. Why?

Because self-enquiry exposes that the ego is itself merely fiction. So then, who are you? We'll explore this in item number 10.

Another approach—more difficult or less, depending on one's temperament—is to seek out the root-thought—which is the "I"—thought—and chop it down like the trunk of a tree, and all the branches of ideas and leaves of thoughts will simultaneously topple.

11. The most powerful method known as atma vichara (Self-enquiry) is applied by asking oneself "Who am I?" (i.e. What is my true nature? What is the source of the phenomenon experienced as "I"?) This can be practiced in or out of the steady state of meditation. In fact, it becomes more effective when performed during the course of normal activities, since then it has a better chance of allowing the practitioner to disengage his identification with not only the ego but the world, as well as his activities in the world.

12. As with most yogic methods, there are a number of approaches within the atma vichara. The most popular one involves a vigil kept on the mind [by asking "Who am I?"] where, as each answer comes, it is categorically denied as having anything to do with the Self. In this way each thought is indiscriminately rejected as not-Self by inwardly addressing them as "neti, neti, etc" (not this, not this, etc). And since virtually every idea or description is negated along the way, what is left over cannot therefore be in the nature of a relativistic value or property but rather is at once transcendental as well as all-pervading, and in fact is the

core Self Itself! In this way the mind—which is the thought process—is gradually weakened, undermined and eventually finally destroyed.

The only thing the mind is capable of realizing is that it hasn't the ability to realize [Reality]. Enquiry is the means for the Mind to discover this. Once it's discovered, the Mind can no longer hold its jiva captive and victimized/manipulated [as a leaf at the mercy of the wind]. And since the Mind is no longer the commander-in-chief attempting to dictate Reality, the Self (Paramatman) automatically surfaces. In the strictest sense, there is nothing (no entity) that realizes anything else (another entity). Rather the Self shines unimpeded. The fogbank of avarana (veil of ignorant distortion) is isolated in the beam of atmavichara and eventually burned away by the sun of the Self. The Self was always there, only the mysterious fog seems to block it. Yet such fog isn't in the least substantial. Here lies the paradox that would be better left forgotton, for indeed *there is no paradox* upon honest enquiry! It simply all crumbles itself into a dream of perfect void.

Yes, Brahman is all that is. Doubts are so many fictions...

13. If Self-realization is genuinely accomplished, our jouney has reached its zenith...there is no further distance to trek in the evolution of consciousness...it is the end of the road...the end of all.

four

AIM OF THE VEDĀNTA
THE DESTRUCTION OF AN INNATE ERROR

The fundamental thought of the Vedānta and its previous history; a glance at allied theories in the west.

In the, introduction which Śaṅkara prefixes (p. 5-23) to his Commentary on the Brahmasūtra's he introduces us at once to the fundamental concept of the system, declaring all empirical, physical knowledge to be ignorance (Avidyā), to which he opposes the metaphysics of the Vedānta, as knowledge (*Vidyā*). Before we approach this thought in detail, let us call to mind certain truths suited to throw light on its philosophic, meaning, and thereby on the Vedanta Bystezn of which they are the root.

The thought that the empirical view of 'nature is not able to lead as to a final solution of the being of things, meets us not only among the Indians but also in many forms in the philosophy of the west. More closely examined this thought is even the root of all metaphysics, so far as without it no metaphysics can come into being or exist. For if empirical or physical investigation were able to throw open to us the true and innermost being of nature, we should only have to continue along this path in order to come at last to an understanding of all truth; the final result would be Physics (in the broader sense, as the teaching of φυσις, nature), and there would he no ground or justification for METAPHYSICS. If, therefore, the metaphysicians of ancient and modern times, dissatisfied with empirical knowledge, went on to metaphysics, this step is only to he explained by a more or clear consciousness that all empirical investigation and knowledge amounts in the end only to a great deception grounded in the nature of our knowing faculties, to open our eyes to which is the task of metaphysics.

Thrice, so far as we know, has this knowledge reached conviction among mankind and each time, It appears, by a different way, according to conditions of time, national and individual character; once among the Indians, of which we are to speak, again in Greek philosophy, through Parmeinides. And the third time in the modern philosophy through Kant.

What drove the Elestic sage to proceed beyond the world as "το μη δν" to the investigation of "the existent, seems to have been the conception, brought into prominence by his predecessor Xenophanes, of the Unity of Being that is, the Unity of nature (by him called), the consequence of which Parmenides drew with unparalleled powers of abstraction, turning his back on nature, and for that reason also cutting off his return to nature.

To the same conviction came Kant by quite another way, since with German patience and thoroughness he subjected the cognitive faculties of mankind to a critical analysis, really or nominally only to examine whether these faculties be really the fitting inbtrumer-ta for the investigation of transcendent objects, whereby, however, he arrived at the astonishing discovery that, amongst others, three essential elements ox the world, namely, Space, Time and are nothing but three forms of perception adhering to she subject or, if this be expressed in terms of physiology, innate functions of the brain, from this he concluded, with incontestable topic that the world as it is extended in space and time, and kmit together in all its phenomena, great anti small, by the causal nexus, in this form exists only for our intellect, and is conditioned by the same,. and that (consequent, tge world reveals to us "appearances" only, and not the being of "things in themselves." What the latter are, he holds to be unknowable, regarding only external experience as the source of knowledge, so long an we are restricted to in" faculties like ours.

These methods of the Greek and German thinkers, admirable as they are, may seem external and cold, when we compare them with the way in which the Indians, as we may assume even in the present condition of research, reached the same concepts. Their pre-eminence will be intelligible when we consider that no people on earth took religion so seriously, none toiled on the way to salvation as they did. Their reward for this was to have got, if not the most scientific, yet the most inward and immediate expression of the deepest secret of being.

How the development which led them to this goal is to be conceived in detail, we cannot yet accurately determine; it seems to us specially matter of question how the historical relation between *Brahman* and *Ātman*, the two chief concepts on which Indian metaphysics grew, and which already in the Upanishad's, so far as we see, are used throughout as synonyms, is to be considered: whether the concept of *Ātman* developed itself from that of *Brahman* through a mere sharpening of the subjective lying therein, or whether we have rather to distingush between two streams, the one, more ecclesiastical, which raised Brahman to a principle; the other, more philosophical, which did the same for *Ātman*, until both, closely connected in their nature, were led into a common bed. Putting aside these questions for the present, let us briefly, by a few selected examples, indicate the steps along which the Indian genius probably raised raised itself to the conception of the world, which we are then to set forth.

1. We have already pointed out how the Indians, setting

out from the worship of personified powers of nature, recognised in that raising of the feeling above the consciousness of individual existence which occurs in prayer, that is, in the *Brahman,* the central force in all the forces of nature, the shaping and supporting principle of all Gods and all worlds; the word *Brahman* in the whole Ṛigveda never meaning anything else than this lifting and spiritualising power of prayer. (With the history of this concept may be compared that of the Logos of the Αογος) fourth Gospel, which rests on a similar abstraction and hypostasis.) From the standpoint of this apprehension of the Brahman as a cosmic potency inherent in the subject, the *Taittiriya-Brahmanam* (2,8,9,6) for example, takes up a question put in the *Ṛigveda* (X, 81, 4) and answers it as follows:—

"Where was the tree and where the wood,
From which the heaven and earth were shaped?
Musing in mind seek that, ye wise,
Whereon the bearer of them stood!" (Ṛigv. 10, 81, 4)

The Brahman was the tree, the wood,
From which the heavens and earth were shaped.
Musing in mind, I say, ye wise,
On Him the bearer of them stood!"

2. To this is joined the idea that Brahman is the innermost and noblest in all the phenomena of the world; it is, the Kāthaka-Up. (5, 1-3) expresses it, charging and deepening the sense of the verse-Ṛigv. 4, 40, 5; the sun in the firmament (*hañsah sucishad*), the God (*vasu,* the good) in the atmosphere, the Hotar at the altar, the guest at the threshold of the house, it dwells everywhere, is born everywhere.—but he only is, free from sorrow and sure of liberation, who honours it, the unborn, unassailable spirit, in "the city with eleven doors" (the body), wherein it dwells, with the powers of life round it,—

"And in the middle sits a dwarf,
Whom all the godlike Powers adore."

3. Here "in the lotus of the heart" the ! Brahman. is now nothing else than the Ātman, that is, the soul, literally "the self." We select an example from Chāndogya-Up. 3, 14.

Verily this universe is Brahman; as *Tajjalān* (in it becoming, ceasing, breathing) it is to be adored in silence. Spirit is its material, life, its body, light its form; its decree is truth, its self endlessness (literally rather); all-working is He, all-wishing, all-smelling, all-tasting[1] comprehending the All, silent, ungrieved: this is my soul (*ātman*) in the inmost heat, smaller than a grain of rice, or of barley, or of mustard-seed, or of millet's kernel;-this is my soul in the inmost heart, greater than the earth, greater than the atmosphere, greater than the heaven, greater than these worlds.The all-working, all-wishing, all-smelling, all-tasting, embracing the—All, silent, ungrieved, this is my soul in the inmost heart, this is Brahman, into him I shall enter on departing hence. He to whom this happens, he, verily, doubts no more!—Thus spoke Sadilya, Sāṇœilya?

4. The last-mentioned entering into the true Self after death presupposes the consciousness of difference between the empiric self, that is, the bodily personality, and the highest Self (*paramātman*), which is the Soul, that is, God. This differ is the subject of a lesson, which Prajāpati gives to Indra, *Chandogya-Up*. 8, 7-12, and in which he leads him up step by step to ever truer knowledge. To the question- "What is the Self'?" comes as the first answer: 1) "The Self is the body, as it is reflected in the eye, in water, in a mirror." To the objection, that then the Self is also affected by the defect and dissolution of the body, follows the second explanation: 2) "The Self is the soul, as it enjoys itself in dream." To the objection that the dreaming soul, if it does pot suffer, still believes itself to suffer, it is replied: 3) When he who has sunk to sleep has come altogether, fully, and wholly to rest, so that he beholds no dream,—that is the "Self, the undying, the fearless, the Brahman." To the objection that in this condition consciousness ceases, and that it

is like entering into nothing, Prajāpati at last answers. 4) "Mortal, verily, O Mighty one, is this body, possessed by death". It is the dwelling-place of that undying, bodiless Self. The embodied is possessed by pleasure and pain, for while he is embodied, there can be no escaping of pleasure and pain. But pleasure and pain, do not touch the bodiless one. Bodiless is the wind;—clouds, lightning, thunder are bodiless. Now as these arise from the atmosphere (in which they are bound, like the soul in the body center into the highest light, and tired appear in their own form, so also this full rest (that is, the Soul, in deep sleep)) arises from his body, enters into the highest light and reached its own form; that is the "highast Spirit."

In similar fashion the *Taittiriya-Up*. 2, 1-7 leads from the bodily self, by stripping one covering after another, off it, at last to the true Self. It distinguishes: 1) the Self consisting of food; in this, as in use case, is held 2) the Self of breath, in this the 3) Self of manas, in this 4) the Self of knowledge, in this finally as innermost 5) the Self of bliss. Verily, this is the Essence (*rasa*); he who reaches this essence, is filled with bliss; for who could breathe and who, could live, if this bliss were not in space? For he it is that causes bliss; for when one finds peace and support in this invisible, bodiless, unspeakable, unfathomable one, then has he entered into peace; but if he in this also (as in the four first) recognises a hollow, an "other," then he finds unrest; "this is the unrest of him who thinks himself wise."

5. The Self, in this sense, is, according *Chāndogya-Up*. 6, 2, 1 "the existent," "the One without a second," and, answering to this, *Bṛihadaranyaka-Up*. 2, 4, 5 refers and limits all investigation to the Self: The Self, verily, O Maitreyi, must be seen, heard, thought on, and investigated; he who sees, hears, thinks on, and investigates the Self, has understood mall this world. "These worlds, these Gods, these beings, all these are what the Self is." It is the point of union

(*eka-yanam*) for all, as the ocean for the waters, the ear for sound, the eye for forms, so on; all outside it is as devoid of being as the sound that goes out from a musical instrument; he who has laid hold on the instrument has therewith also laid hold on the sounds that spring from it (loc. cit., 2, 4, 6-11). It is, according to *Chandogya-Up.* 6, 1, 4, that from which all the world has come into being, as a mere transformation of it he who knows this One, therewith knows all, just as, oh dear "one, by a lump of clay, all that is made of clay is known; the transformation is a matter of words, a mere name; in "reality it is only clay!"

6. In conformity with this, the *Isā-Up.* 1, 6 bids us', sink the whole world in God," that is in the Self:

"Who, seeking, finds all being in the Self
For him all error fades, all sorrow ends;"

and the *Kāthaka-Up.* (4, 10-11) warns us not to admit a multiplicity, anything different (*nānā*) from the soul:

"For what is here it there, and what is there is here;
From death to death he hastes who here another knows!
In spirit shall ye know, here is no manifold;
From death to death is he ensuared who difference sees."

7. It was a simple consequence of these conceptions when the Vedānta declared the empirical concept which represents to us a manifold existing outside the Self, a world of the Object existing independently of the Subject, to be a glamour (māyā), an innate illusion (*bhrama*) resting on an illegitimate transference (adhyāsa), in virtue of which we transfer the reality, which alone belongs to the subject, to the world of the object, and, conversely, the characteristics of the objective world, *e.g.*, corporeality, to the subject, the Self, the Soul. Concerning this, let us hear Śaṅkara himself.

Analysis of Śaṅkara's *Introduction*

"Object (*vishaya*) and Subject (*vishayin*)", he says at

the beginning of his work, "having as their province the presentation of the 'Thou' (the not I) and the 'I,'[2] are of a nature as opposed as darkness and light. If it is certain that the being of the ore is incompatible with the being of the other, It follows so much the more that the qualities of the one also do not exist in the other. Hence it follows that the transfer (*adhydsa*) of the object, which has as its province the idea of the 'Thou,' and its qualities, to the pure spiritual subject, which has as its province the idea of the I, and conversely, that the transfer of the subject and its qualities to the object, is logically false. Yet in mankind this procedure resting ron false knowledge (*mithya-jñāna-nimitta*) of pairing together the true and untrue (that is subjective and objective) is inborn (*naīśārgika*), so that they transfer the being and qualities of the one to the other, not separating object and subject, although they are absolutely different (*atyanta-vivikta*) and so saying, for example: "'This am I,' 'That is mine.'"[3]

However this transference be defined, in any case it comes to this, that qualities of one thing appear in another, as when mother-of-pearl is taken for silver, or when two moons are seen instead of one. This erroneous transference of the things and relations of the objective world to the inner Soul, the Self in the strictest sense of the word, is possible because the soul also is, in a certain sense, object, namely, object of presentation to the "I," and, as our author here affirms, in no sense something transcendent, lying beyond the province of perception (*paroksham*).[4]

"This transference, thus made, the wise term IGNORANCE (*Avidyā*), and, in contradistinction to it, they call the accurate determination of the own nature of things" (vastu-svarūpam, of the being-in-itself of things, as we should say) "KNOWLEDEGE" (*vidyā*). If this be so, it follows that that to which a (similar, "false) transfer is thus made, is not in the slightest degree affected by any want or excess caused thereby".

The object of knowledge, the Soul, thus remains, as

made clear in these words, entirely unaltered, no matter whether we rightly understand it, or not. From this we must conclude that the ground of the erroneous empirical concept is to be sought for solely in the knowing subject; in this subject the avidyā, as repeatedly asserted, is innate (*naīśārgika*); its cause is a wrong perception (it is *mithyā-jñāna-nimitta*); its being is a wrong conception (*mithya-pratyaya-rupa*);—all these expressions point to the fact that the final reason of the false empirical concept is to be sought—where, however, the Vedānta did not seek it—in the nature of our cognitive faculty. An analysis of this, as Kant undertook it, would in fact give the true scientific foundation of the Vedānta system; and it is to he hoped that the Indians, whose orthodox dogmatics, holding good still at the present day, we here act forth, will accept the teachings of the Critique of Pure Reason," when it is brought to their knowledge, with grateful respect.[5]

On the soil of this natural Ignorance stands according to Śaṅkara, all human knowledge, with the exception of the metaphysics of the Vedānta; thus, not only the empirical thought, that is, thought by means of the sense-organs, of common life, but also the whole ritual canon of the Veda, with its things commanded and forbidden under promise of reward and punishment in another world.

The immediate ground on which both worldly and Vedic actions must be referred to the sphere of Ignorance, lies in this, that both; are not tree from the delusion (*abhimāna*) of,seeing the "I" in the body; for neither knowledge nor action is possible unless one considers as belonging to the Self,[6] the sense-organs and body bearing them, and the ritual part of the Veda also cannot but transfer many circumstances of the outer world erroneously to the Soul.[7]

A further ground for the inadequacy of all empirical knowledge is, that, it is: only distinguished from that of animals in degree through higher evolution (*vyutpatti*), but is in kind similar to it, so far as, like it, it is wholly subservient to egoism, which impels us to seek for what is desired and to avoid, what is not desired; and it makes no difference here whether these egoistic aims, as in the case of worldly actions, reach their realīśātion already in this life, or, as in the case of the works ordained by the Vedas, only in a future existence, thus presupposing a knowledge of it. Quite otherwise the Vedānta which, on the contrary, leaves the whole sphere of desire behind, turns its back on all differences of position in outer life (even if, as we shall see, not quite consistently), and raises itself to the knowledge that the Soul is in reality not the least involved in the circle of transmigration (samsāra).[8]

For all those, laws of empirical knowledge and action are valid for us only so long as we are influenced by the Ignorance, resting on a false transference, which nature imposets on us, of which it is said in conclusion. "Thus it stands "with this beginningless, endless, innate trans-ference, which in its essence is a false assumption, producing all the conditions of doing and enjoying for suffering) and forming the,,(natural) standpoint of all men. To remove this, the root "of the evil, and to teach the knowledge of the unity of the soul,-this is the aim of all the texts of the Vedānta."[9]

This aim the Vedānta reaches by separating from the soul (the Self, *ātman*) everything that is not soul, not Self, and is only transferred thereto falsely, thus, in a word, all Upadhi's, or individualising determinations, clothed (*upahitam*) in which the Brahman appears as individual soul. Such Upādhi's are: 1) all things and relations of the outer world, 2) the body, consisting of the gross elements, 3) the *Indriya's*, that is the five sense-organs and five organs of action of the body, represented as separate existences, 4) *Manas*, also called the inner organ (*antahkaranam*), the central organ for the sense-organs as well as for the organs of action, in the first place closely approaching what we call understanding, and in the latter almost synonymous with, what we call conscious will, the unified principle of conscious life) the *Mukhya prana* with its five offshoots, is the unified principle of unconscious life, subserving nutrition. All this, of which more in our psychological part, meta-physics cuts away, in order to retain the soul, that is, the real Self or 'I' which is, present as spectator (*sākshin*) of all individual actions, but Itself only apparently individualised by the Upādhi's, is on the contrary in reality indentical with the highest godhead, and, like this, is pure spiritual nature, pure consciousness (*caitanyam*).

And here we touch the fundamental want of the Vedānta system, which, among other things, causes the absence of its proper morality, however near this, in its purest form, lay to 'Its principle.[71] Rightly the Vedānta, recognises, as the sole source by which we may reach true knowledge, true apprehension of being-in-itself, our own "I," but it wrongly halts at the form in which it directly appeals to our consciousness, as a knower, even after it has cut away the whole intellectual apparatus, and ascribed it to the "not I," the world of phenomena, just as it has also, very rightly, indicated as the dwelling of the highest soul, not, as Descartes did, the head (about which Bṛih), but the heart.

Meanwhile, as we shall see, the spiritual (*caitanyam*) is, in our system, a potency which lies at the root of all motion and change in nature, which is therefore also ascribed, for example, to plants, and means thus rather the capacity of reaction to outer influences, a potency which, in its highest development, reveals itself as human intellect, as spirit.

> "This highest Godhead hath his seat in every being,
> And liveth though they die; who seeth him, is seeing,
> And he who everywhere this highest God hath found,
> Will not wound self through self...."

Foot Notes:

1. Otherwise Max Müller and Oldenberg (buddha, p. 31); cf. However BṚih. 1, 3, 24 and the of Xenophanes.
2. *Yushmad-asmat-pratyaya-gocara;* Banerjea translates: *"indicated by the second and first personal pronouns,"* and so p. 15, 2 *asmat-pratyayavishayatvat:* "because it (*the soul*) is the object *of the first personal pronoun*," which, however, gives us no clear meaning, for only *preserntations, not pronouns, have objects,*—The soul is therefore subject (*vishayin*), yet not (empiric) subject of knowledge as which the *ahampratyayin* (that is, the manas, to distinguish from the *ahamkartar*) figures, to which the soul again stands opposed as object (*vishaya*); cf of the passages in notes 29 and 30, and further in the course of the work (Chap. XXVII, 3).
3. By this the objective, e.g., the body, is sometimes treated as subject, sometimes as a quality of it. As explanation the following Passage May serve, p. 20, 8: 'As one is accustomed, when it goes ill or well with his "son or wife and the like, to: say, it goes ill or well with me,' and thus transfers the qualities of outer the things to the Self (soul, *ātman*) (cf. P. 689, 3 ff.), in just the same way he transfers the qualities of the body, when 'he says...I am fat, I am thin, I am white, stand, I go, I leap,' and similarly the qualities of the sense organs when he says: I am dumb, 'impotent, deaf, one-eyed, blind,' and similarly the qualities of the inner "organ (*antahkaranam = manas,* cf. 2, 3, 32) desire, wish, doubt resolution land the like;-thus also he transfers the subject presenting the 'I' (*aham-pratyayin*) to the inner soul, present solely an witness (*sakshin*) "of the personal tendencies, and conversely the witness of all, the inner soul, to the inner organ and the rest" (that is to the sense organs, the body and the objects of the outer world).
4. P. 14, 5: "Question. but how is it possible to transfer to the inder, soul, which is no object, the qualities of objects? For everyone transfer (only) to one object standing before him another object: and of the 'inner soul thou maintainest that it in cut oft from the; dea of 'Thou' (not-and-I is no object I read with Govinda: avishayatvam)?—

Answer: "Not in every sense is it non-object; for it is the object of perception of the taken strictly and according to p. 78, 6, cf. 73, 5). 672, I, not the *sakshin,* but only the *kartar,* that is, the individual soul already endowed with objectivequalities, is *ahampratyaya-vishaya*); and the (whole) assumption of an inner soul rests on this, that it is not transcendent (aparoksha). It is also not necessary "that the object, to which we transfer another object, should stand before us; as, for instance, when simple people transfer to space (ākāva), which is not an object of perception, the dark colour of the ground, and the like. In just the same way is it possible to transfer to the inner soul what is not soul."

5. Also Kant's axiom that the transcendental ideality of the world does not exclude its empiricreality, find its full analogy in the concepts of Cañkara. cf. p. 44,3, 6: 8. All empiric action is true, so long as the "knowledge of the soul is not reached, just as the actions in dream,,,before awaking occurs. As long in fact as the knowledge of unity with the true Self is not reached, one was not a consciousness of the unyreality "of the procedure connected with standards and objects knowledge and fruits of works, but every creature, under the designation of I' and mine,' takes mere transformations for the Self and for characteristics of the Self and on the other hand leaves out of consideration "their original Brahman-Selfhood; therefore before the consciousness "of identity with Brahman awakes, all worldly and Vedic actions are "justified."

6. P. 17, 2. "But how is it possible that the means of knowledge, perception and the rest, and the (ritual) books of doctrine are limited to the province of Ignorance?—Answer: Because without the delusion that "'I' and 'mine' consist in the body, sense-organs, and the like, no knower can exist, and consequently a use of the means of knowledge. —is not possible. For without calling in the aid of the sense-organs, "there can be no perception but the action of the sense-organs is not 'possible without a resting place (the body), and no action at all is "possible without transferring the being of the Self (the Soul, *ātman*) "to the body, and without all this taking place no knowledge is possible "for the soul, which is independent (reading

asangasya) (of embodied existence). But without action of knowing, no knowing is possible. 'Consequently, the means of Knowledge, perception and the rest, as well as the books of doctrine (in question) belong to the province "of Ignorance."

6. P. 20, 5: "For when is said, for example: Let the Brahman 'offer', the like ordinances rest on the fact of transferring the castes, 'Acrama's ages of life and similar differences to the soul; this transference is, as we have said, the assumption that something is where it is not."
7. The interesting passage which gives us an insight into the Indian idea of the difference between man and animals, reads in its -entirety as follows, (p. 18, 4 cf.):—"For this reason also" (worldly and Vedic knowledge belongs to the province of Ignorance), because (thereby) no 'difference is made between man and animals. For just as the animals, when, for instance, a sound strikes their ears, in case the perception of the sound is dĪśāgreeable to them, move away from it, and in case it is agreeable, move towards it,—as, when they see a man with an upraised stick before them, thinking. 'He will strike me,' they try to escape, and when they ace one a handful of fresh grass, approach him one sees that when the Indian speaks of an animal, he thinks of a cow, somewhat as we think of a dog). So men also whose knowledge is more developed (*vyutpanna-cittāh*), when they perceive strong men of terrible aspect, with drawn swords in their hands, turn away from them, and turn towards the contrary.-Thus with reference to the means and objects of knowledge, the process in men and animals is alike. Of coarse in the case of animals perception, and the like, goes on without previous judgment see viveka); but as can be seen by the resemblance, even in the case of (spiritually) developed (*vyutpattimatam*) men, perception and the like for the time (of false knowledge) is the same; and if 'according to the spiritual canon the performance of works is permitted only to one who has gained insight (*buddhi*), and not to one who has not 'recognised the connection of the soul with the other world, yet for this 'permission it is not imperative that one (should have recognised) the truth concerning the soul freed from the

Saṃsāra, to be taught by the Vedānta, "which leaves behind hunger and the other (desires), and turns away 'from the difference between Brahmans, warriors and the rest. For this 'truth is not implied in the injunction (of the work of sacrifice), but is rather in contradiction to it. And while the canon of ordinances is valid (only) for this degree of knowledge of the soul, it does not rise above the province of Ignorance."

8. Cf. for the doctrine of the Avidyā also the following passages: p. 98, 8. 112, 3. 182, 12. 185.12, 5. 205, 10. 343, 4. 360, 2. 433. 13. 452, 2. 455, 4. 473, 17. 483, 6. 507, 1. 660, 10. 680, 12. 682, 3. 689, 1. 690. 5. 692, 14. 787, 13. 804, 1. 807. 11. 837, 2. 860, 860, 15. 1056, 1. 1132, 10. 1133. 12. 1133. 15.

9. The command ("Love thy neighbour as thyself") is an immediate consequence of the fundamental concept of the Vedānta, as the following verses of the *Bhagavadgītā* (18, 27-28).

five

SURVEY OF THE VEDĀNTA SYSTEM

1. Introductory

Fundamental thought of the Vedānta.

§ 1. The fundamental thought of the Vedānta, most briefly expressed by the Vedic words: *tat tvam asi*, "That art thou" (Chānd. 6, 8, 7) and *aham brahma asmi*, "I am Brahman" (Bṛih. 4, 10), is the Identity of Brahman and the Soul; this means that *Brahman*, *i.e.*, the external principle of all Being, the power which creates, sustains and again absorbs into itself entire world, is identical with the *Ātman*, the Self or the Soul, *i.e.*, that in us which we recognise, when we see things rightly, as our very self and true essence. This soul of each one of us is not a part, an emanation of Brāhman, but wholly and absolutely the eternal, indivisible Brāhman Himself.

Contradiction by experience.

§ 2. The statement contradicts experience (*vyavahāra*), which shows us not that unity, but a plurality (*nānātvam*) an impressions of ear and eye sense-impressions) and as a part of them our own Self in the form of our created and perishable body.

Contradiction by the law of works.

§ 3. But the fundamental dogma of the Vedānta is

equally is contradiction with the canon of Vedic ritual; this is true teaches the continued existence (*vyātireka*) of the soul after the body, but it assumes a plurality of individual souls different from Brahman; they are entangled in unceasing transmigration (*saṃsāra*) and at the death of each body pass into a new body; in this process the works (*karman*) of anyone life condition inexorably the succeeding life and its nature.

Ignorance and Knowledge.

§ 4. Both experience, as a result of worldly means of cognition (*pramāṇam*)—perception (*pratyaksham*), inference (*anumānam*) etc.—and the canon of the Vedic ritual with its commmands and prohibitions, promises and threats rest on false knowledge (*mithyā-jñānam*), an innate illusion (*bhrānti*), which is called *Avidyā*, Ignorance; wht it tells us is, like the pictures of dream, only true till the awakening comes. This innate Avidyā is more accurately described by sayig that the *Ātman*, the Soul, the Self is unable to distingusish itself from the *Upādhis* or limitations (*i.e.*, the body, the psychic organs and works) with which the Soul is clad, and of which only a part—the body—is annihilated in death, the rest accompanying the Soul on its migrations.—This *Avidyā* is the contrary of *Vidyā*, knowledge, also called perfect knowledge (*samyagdarśnam*), by virtue of which the *Ātman* distinguishes itself from *Upādhis*, and recognises that they are dependent or *Avidyā*, a glamour (*māyā*) or an illusion (*abhimāna*); while it is itself identical with the one Brāhman, without a second, who comprehends all things in Himself.

Source of Knowledge.

§ 5. *Samyagdarśanam*, perfect knowledge can neither be produced by worldly means of knowledge (*pratyaksham, anumānam*, etc.), nor commaned by the canon of the Veda as a duty, because both are rooted in *Avidyā* and do not lead beyond it. The only source of Vidya is revelation, *Śruti* (which we, not quite correctly, generally term "Scripture") *i.e.*, the Veda, and of this in particular the part of knowledge (*jñāna-kāṇḍa*) which exists side by side with the part of works (*kārma-kṅḍa*); and contains texts scattered thought the Mantas and *Brāhmaṇas*, but more especially a formed in the concluding chapter of the later, the *Vedānta* (end of the Veda) known as the *Upanishads*.—The whole of the Veda without distinction, that is the whole body of Mantras (Hymns and formulas) and Brāhmaṇas (theological explanations) together with the *Upanishads* is of divine origin; it was "breathed out" by Brāhman and only "beheld" by the human authors (*ṛishis*). The world and the Gods with it pass away but the Veda is eternal; it outlasts the destruction of the world and continues to exist in the spirit of Brahman; in accordance with the words of the Veda, which contain the eternal archetypes of things, gods, men, animals, etc. are created by Brāhman at the beginning of each world period; thereupon the Veda is revealed to them by "Expiration"—the part of works as a canon of actions which have happiness (*abhyudaya*) as their object, the part of knowledge as the source of *Samyagdarśanam*, the only fruit of which is bliss (*niḥśreyasam*) *i.e.*, liberation.—Perfect knowledge is not attainable by reflection (*tarka*), and just as little by tradition or *Smṛiti* (including the Vedic Sūtras, Kāpila, Mānu, the Mahābhāratam, etc.); both of these reflection and Smṛiti, can only in a secondary sense be considered a source of truth, so far as they are directed to the Veda and serve to clear up and compile its revelation.

2. Theology

Higher and lower knowledge.

§ 6. The aim of man (*purusha-artha*) is liberation (*moksha*) *i.e.*, the cessation of transmigration (*saṃasāra*); and the release of the soul from its wanderings is brought about by man's own Self (*ātman*) being recognised as identical with the highest Self (*parama-ātman*), *i.e.*, the *Brahman*. The whole content of *Vidyā* is therefore knowledge of the *Ātman* or *Brahman* (they are interchangeable ideas).—But there are two sorts of knowledge of Brahman—the higher knowledge (*parā vidyā*); its aim is *Sāṁyāgdarśnam* and its one and only fruit is liberation; and the lower knowledge (*aparā vidyā*) which aim at the knowledge but at the worship (*upāsanā*) of Brahman; it brings as its fruit, according to the steps of this worship, in part the prospering of works (*karma-samṛiddhi),* in part happiness (*abhyudaya*, heavenly, perhaps also in the following birth), and finally in part *kramamukti*, *i.e.*, gradual liberation.—The object of the higher knowledge is the higher Brahman (*pārām brāhma*) and of the lower the lower Brāhman (*apāram brāhma*).

Higher and lower Bràhman.

§ 7. For the Scripture distinguishes two forms (*rūpe*) of Brahman; the higher, attributeless (*param, nirguṇam*) and the lower attribute-possessing (*aparam, saguṇam*) Brāhman. In the former case it is taught that Brāhman is without any attributes (*guṇa*) differences (*viśesha*) forms (*ākāra*), and limitations (*upādhi*)—in the latter, for the purpose of worship many attributes, differences, forms, and limitations are ascribed to him.

Difference between them.

§ 8. One and the same object cannot be at the same time with and without attributes, and with and without form; in Himself (*svatas*) Brahman is therefore without attributes, forms, differences, and limitations; and this higher Brahman becomes the lower when Ignorance (*avidyā*) for the purpose of worship ascribes to him the limitations or *Upādhis*. That Brahman is subject to *Upādhis* is only an illusion (*brahma*), just as much as it is an illusion to hold a crystal for red in itself because it is painted red. As the clearness of the crystal is not changed by the red colour, so the essence of Brahman is not altered by the limitations ascribed by Ignorance.

The higher Brāhman cannot be perceived.

§ 9. The higher Brahman is in his own nature attributeless (*nirguṇam*) formless (*niṛākāram*), and without differences (*nirviśesham*) and limitations (*nirupādhikam*). It is "not "coarse, and not fine, and short, and not long," etc. (Bṛih. 3, 8, 8); "not to be heard, not to be felt, not formed, imperishable (Kāṭh. 3, 15); it is "not thus and not thus" (*neti, neti*, Bṛih. 2, 3, 6); *i.e.*, no shape and no idea corresponds to its real being. Therefore it is "different from what we know, "and from what we do not know" (Kena 1, 3); "the words "and thoughts turn back from it and find it not" (Taitt. 2, 4); and the sage *Bāhva* met the question as to its essence by silence.

Essence of the higher Brahman.

§ 10. The only assertion that can be made of the attributeless Brahman is that it is not. In this sense it is "the Existent" (*sat*); but if this conception is taken in its empirical sense, Brāhman is rather "the non-Existent."—The Scripture further defines the essence of Brahman as through and through pure spirituality (intelligence, *caitanyam*) just as the lump of salt tastes salt through and through. But by this two characteristics (plurality) are not ascribed to Brahman, because both are identical, so far as the essence of Being consists in spirituality, and of spirituality of Being. Bliss, *ānanda* [attributed to Brāhman as a third predicate by the later Vedānta in the name *Sac-cid-ānanda*] is occasionally recongised as a limitation of the attributeless Brahman; it remains unmen-tioned however in the discussion of his being perhaps because it can be regarded as a merely negative quality, as painless-ness, which is ascribed to Brāhman alone, for "what is different from him is afflicted" (*ato nyad ārtam*) as the Scripture (Bṛih. 3, 4, 2) says.

Brāhman is the soul.

§ 11. That the attributeless Brahman cannot be perceived

depends on the fact that he is the inner Self (*antar-ātman*) of all; as such he is on the one hand the greatest certainty of all and cannot be denied by anyone; on the other hand He is not to be perceived because in all perception He is the Subject (*sākshin*), and can therefore never become the object.—He is however beheld by the sages in the state of *Saṃrādhanam* (perfect satisfaction), which consists in a withdrawal of the organs from all external things, and a concentration on their own inner nature. On the consciousness of being this attributeless Brāhman and on the accompanying conviction of the unreality of all plurality of names and forms depends salvation.

The lower Brāhman.

§ 12. The higher Brāhman becomes the lower Brāhman by being connected with pure (*viśuddha*) or perfect (*niratśaya*) limitations. The lower Brāhman is to be recognised wherever the Scripture ascribes limitations, attributes, forms or differences of and sort to Brāhman. This happens when the aim is not knowledge but worship (*upāsanā*), and the fruit of this worship is, like tht of works, which are to be placed in the same category, not liberation (*moksha, niḥśreyasam*) but happiness; this is, as it seems, mainly heavenly; it is however limited to the *Saṁsāra* though the heavenly lordship (*aiśvaryam*) attained after death by the path of the gods (*devayāna*) as a result of the worship of the lower Brāhman leads by means of *Krāmamuktī* or gradual liberation to perfect knowledge and therefore complete liberation. These results however does not follow immediately, because the worshippers of the lower Brāhman have not completely "burnt up" Ignorance; for it is this which ascribes the limitations to the higher Brāhman and transforms it into the lower Brāhman. The nature of Brāhman is as little changed by these limitations as (in the already mentioned simile) the clarity of the crystal by the colour with which it is painted—as the sun by its images saying in the water—as space by bodies moving or burning it i.—The richly developed ideas of the lower Brāhman may be divided into three groups, according to whether they regard Brāhman pantheistically as world soul, psychologically as principle of the individual soul, or theistically as a personal God.

The lower Brāhman as world soul.

§ 13. The most important passages of the first group are Chānd. 3, 14 which terms Brahman "all-working, all-wising, all-smelling, all-tasting [the principle of all action and sensuous perception], embracing the All, silent, ungrieved"; and Muṇḍ. according to which sun and moon are his eyes, the cardinal points his ears the wind his breath etc. We bring under the same head Brāhman as source of all light; as the light beyond the sky and in the heart; as the ether from which all things proceed, and which holds asunder names and forms; as the life from which go forth all beings, in which the whole world trembling moves; the inner ruler as the principle of the world-order; the bridge, which holds these worlds asunder that they do not blend, by which sun and moon, heaven and earth, minutes, hours, days and years are kept apart; finally as destroyer of the world, who swallows up all created things.

The lower Brāhman as individual Soul.

§ 14. With the dimensions expressed by these ideas is often contrasted the smallness which belongs to Brāhman as psychic principle; as such he dwells in the stronghold of the body, in the lotus of the heart, as a dwarf, a span large, an inch high, smaller than a grain of millet, large as the point of an awl, as principle of life as onlooker; also as the man in the eye etc.

The lower Brahman as personal God.

§ 15. These ideas which assign attribute to Brahman culminate in the conception of Him as *Īśvara*, *i.e.*, personal God. In the Upanishads this idea is relatively rare and little developed (*e.g.*, Īśa 1; Bṛih. 4, 4, 22; Kaush. 3, 8; Kāṭh. 4, 12); in the system of the Vedānta on the other hand it plays an important part; it is *Īśvara* by whose permission Saṁsāra, and by whose grace (*prasāda, anugraha*) the saving knowledge is conditioned; He decrees for the soul its works and suffering, taking into consideration in this the works of the previous life, and causing the fate in the new life to proceed from them as the rain produces the plant from the seed after its nature. The personification of Brāhman as *Īśvara*, Lord, Ruler, to whom is opposed the world as that which is to be ruled, is expressly limited to the standpoint rooted in Ignorance of worldly action, which and no reality in the highest sense.

3. Cosmology

The empirical and metaphysical standpoint.

§ 16. The dual knowledge (*aparā* and *parā vidyā*) of Theology (and as we shall see of Eschatology) has as its counterpart in the spheres of Cosmology and Psychology dual standpoint:—The empirical (*vyavahāra-avasthā*, literally, standpoint of worldly action) which teaches a creation of the world by Brāhman and a wandering of the soul rendered individual by the *Upādhis*; and the metaphysical (*paramārtha-avasthā*, literally, standpoint of the highest reality) which maintains the identity of the soul with Brāhman, and denies all plurality, and therefore the validity of the ideas of the creation and existence of the world, as well as the individuality and wanderings of the soul.—To the detriment of clarity and logic this dual standpoint in Psychology and Cosmology is not always strictly adhered to. The system takes up the metaphysical standpoint as a rule and neglects the empirical, without however, denying or being able to deny its relative right of existence, it being the indispensable presupposition for the *aparā vidyā* of Eschatology. This *aparā vidyā* treats the creation in the Cosmology very fully and regards it as real, at the same time we meet with the assertion again and again that this scriptural doctrine of the creation has only the purpose of teaching the Brāhmanhood of the world;

to support this view the idea of causality is transformed into that of identity; in Psychology the metaphysical doctrine of the identity of Brahman and the world is always in the foreground, and is defended against an opponent who generally speaking upholds the empirical standpoint indispensable for the Eschatology of the system, but also (*e.g.*, in maintaining the creation of the soul) deviates from it, so that the relative recognition and appropriation of his arguments only concerns a part of them, and a complete theory of the empirical psychology is thus wanting. Still by bringing together occasional and scattered assertions a reliable picture of this part of the system too may be obtained.

Relation of the two kinds of knowledge to the two points of view.

§17. The coherence of the system may prove to us that the *pārā vidyā* in Theology and Eschatology forms with the *paramārtha-avasthā* in Cosmology and Psychology an inseparable unity of metaphysical doctrine; and that on the other hand the *aparā vidyā* of Theology and Eschatology with the *vyavahāra-avasthā* of Cosmology and Psychology a connected picture of metaphysical viewed from the empirical standpoint of *Avidyā* (*i.e.*, innate realism) and forms a system of popular religion for all those who cannot raise themselves to the standpoint of the doctrine of identity.—And it is clear that only a lower, not a higher Brahman can be conceived as creator of the world, firstly because the act of creation, as has been repeatedly insisted on, requires a plurality of powers, which can only be ascribed to the *apārām brāhma*; and further, because the passage by which this plurality of creative powers is proved: "all-working is he, all-wishing, all smelling, all-tasting" (Chānd. 3,14,2) receives the preference as a proof of the doctrine of the lower Brahman.

World-periods.

§ 18. According to the Upanishads Brahman creates the world and then as individual soul (*anena jīvena ātmanā*) enters into it (Chānd. 6, 3, 2. Taitt. 2, 6. Bṛih. 1, 4, 7. Kaush. 4, 20). There is no question either of an existence of individual souls before the creation, or of a periodically repeated creation.—In this view the germs of the empirical and metaphysical doctrine of the Vedānta are present in an undeveloped form side by side; the metaphysical part is the identity of the soul with Brahman, the empirical the extension of the world of sense. In the Vedānta system the two are separated; metaphysically we have the identity of the soul with Brahman but neither origin, persistence, nor destruction of the world; empirically on the other hand we have a creation of the world but no identity of Brahman and the soul; on the contrary the individual soul with the *Upādhis*, which cause its individuality, has existed from all eternity and migrates (except in the case of liberation) from one body to another to all eternity; and the dogma of the creation of the world is transformed into that of a periodically alternating emanation of the world from Brāhman and reabsorption in it; these processes repeat themselves not once only but continues with times throughout eternity. Souls, like the elements, continue to exist, at the reabsorption of the world, potentially and as seed in Brāhman, and at each new creation will go forth from Him unchanged. The original sense of the doctrine of creation is thus completely abandoned; it is adhered to, in the modified from in question, simply because the Veda teaches it; In the system there is a motive not for a creation of the world, but rather for its eternal duration; in place of this (to save the authority of Scripture) we have the periodical creation and reabsorption, which however must incessantly be repeated, and are not permitted to alter the order of the world; this is to satisfy the conditions of eternal existence demanded by the system, and is as we shall see, dependent on a moral necessity.

World has no beginning.

§ 19. The fundamental idea of the empirical Cosmology and Psychology is that Saṁsāra (transmigration) has no beginning.

There exists from eternity a plurality of individual souls different from Brāhman. What distinguishes them from Brāhman (with whom they are in the metaphysical sense identical) is the *Upādhis* in which they are clothed; by *Upādhis* are understood, in addition to the works, which accompany the soul, the psychic organs (*indriyas, manas, mukhya prāṇa*), the subtle body (*sūkshmaṃ śarīram*) which bears them, and, in a more extended sense occasionally the gross body together with external objets. Only the gross body is annihilated by death; the subtle body on the other hand with the psychic organs has existed from eternity as the vestment of the soul and accompanies it on all its wanderings. And the wandering soul is further accompanied by the works (ritual and moral) performed by it during life; and it is just these which present Saṁsāra from coming to a standstill. For every deed, good and evil, demands retribution, and therefore reward and punishment, not only in the Beyond but, besides that, in the form of another existence. Without works no human life is conceivable; and therefore also no life that is not followed by another as its retribution. Very good works result in existence as a god; very bad in existence as an animal or plant; even if the soul does not works in these lives, this does not protect it from rebirth, for works of special goodness or badness demand for their retribution several successive existences. On this depends on the fact that Saṁsāra through all spheres of existence from the gods down to plants is without beginning and (if the seed of works is not "burnt up" by knowledge) without end.

Moral necessity of the creation of the world.

§20. The spātial extension of the sense-world (*nāmarūpa-prapañca*) is essentially nothing more than the fruit of works which is imposed as a burden (*adhyāropita*) on the soul; the world is, as the common formula runs, *kriyā-kāraka-phalam*, "requital of the deed on the doer;" it is bhāgyam (what is to be enjoyed) while the souls in it is *bhoktar* (enjoyer) and on the other hand *kartar* (doer); both of these of necessity and in exact agreement with its *kartṛitam* (activity) in the preceding existence. The intermediator between the works and their fruit (which includes the deeds and suffering of the succeeding existence) is not an *adrishṭam* (invisible power of the works reaching beyond life) or at least not this alone but rather the *Īśvara*, a personification of Brāhman, which is valid for the empirical standpoint alone (§ 15); the *Īśvara* decrees action and suffering for the soul in the new birth in exact correspondence to the works of the former existence. Moreover each new creation of the world after its absorption into Brāhman depends on the same necessity as the rebirth; for even when the souls are absorbed in Brahman, they still continue to exist in the from of seed together with their works, and the latter require for their retribution another creation of the world, *i.e.*, the emanation of the elements from Brahman: this process we shall now consider more closely.

Ignorganic nature (the elements).

§ 21. At the creation, *srishṭi*, which according to this word is to be conceived as an "outpouring," *i.e.*, emanation, there goes forth from Brāhman first of all the *Ākāśa*, ether, or more properly all-penetration space conceived as a very subtle form of matter; from *Ākāśa* goes froth air (*vāyu*), from this fire (*agni, tejas*), from this water (*āpas*), from this earth (*prithivī, annam*); and in this process each successive element is produced not by the elements themselves but by Brāhman in the form of the elements. In reverse order at the end of the world earth first becomes water, this fire, this air, this ether, and this Brāhman.—Ether is perceived by the sense of hearing, air by hearing and touch, fire by hearing, touch and sight, water by hearing, touch, sight and taste; and earth by hearing, touch, sight, taste and smell. These elements occurring in nature, however, are not the pure, original elements but a mixture of all with preponderance of some one of them. [There is no systematic account of theory of mixture in Śaṅkara's Commentary on the *Brahma-*

sūtras; we do not find one before the *Vedāntasāra*.]

Organic nature (souls).

§ 22. After Brāhman has created the Elements. According to the Upanishads, he enters them, according to the Upanishads, as the individual soul; *i.e.*, in our system the wandering souls, which continue to exist potentially (*śakti-ātmanā*) in Brahman even after the destruction of the world, awake from this state, itself a part of the glamour [of empirical reality], of very deep sleep (*māyāmayī mahāsushuptiḥ*, and assume divine, human, animal or plant bodies according to their works in the previous existence. This comes about by the seed of the elements, carried by the soul with it on its wanderings in the form of the subtle body, becoming the gross body by the addition of homogeneous particles from the coarse elements which surround it; at the same time it unfolds the psychic organs (*mukhya prāṇa, manas, indriyas*) which during the wandering were rolled together (*sampiṇḍita*). (What becomes in the case of the organs of plant souls remains in discussed; it may be assumed that they remain rolled up.) The body is nāmarūpakṛita-kārya-karaṇa-saṅghāta, "the complex of "the organs of work formed of names and shapes" [*i.e.*, from the elements], and the soul is lord (*svāmin*) of this complex. The growth of the body takes places from the elements, in which gross, middle and fine are distinguished; correspondingly faeces, flesh, and Manas are developed from earth; urine, blood, and Prāṇa from water; and bones, marrow, and speech from fire;—as however according to the system the soul already has with it its psychic organs, and among them Manas, Prāṇa, and speech, we must either see a contradiction here, or assume that the growing Manas, Prāṇa and speech are related to the similarly named organs which the soul always has with it, as the coarse body is to the subtle. The absorption of this material from food is rendered possible by the fact that (v. § 21) every natural body contains all the original elements.—According to their origin organisms are divided into those born from germs (plants), hose born from moisture (vermin), the oviparous, and the viviparous; procreation consists in the soul of the child, which has entered into the father as food and sojourned in him as a guest, passing by means of the sperm into the body of the mother and from her blood developing the subtle into the coarse body. Death is the separation of the soul (with its organs and the subtle body), from the material body; if the organism is destroyed the soul wanders forth. The duration of life is not accidental but is predestined exactly according to the quantum of works to be atoned for, just as the nature of the life is by their quality. On the other hand again we find works, which cease to be, not all at once, but only after repeated rebirths; only in this way can we explain why *e.g.* transmigration does not come to a standstill when the soul enters into a plant. As every plant is an embodied soul, and every incarnation only serves the end of atonement, the system is quite logical in attributing sensation to plants also.—While the duration of life of plant, animal, and human souls is short, those souls which, in consequence of exceptional performances in the previous life, are born as gods, are immortal, *i.e.*, they continue to exist till the next destruction of the world; then they again enter the cycle of Saṃsāra; and the laces of Indra etc. can be occupied by another soul in the next period.

No world from the metaphysical point view.

§ 23. Just as all clay vessels are in reality only clay, since the conversion of the clay into vessels is "a mere name, dependent on words" (*vācārambhaṇam vikāro, nāmadheyam*, Chānd. 6, 1, 4 cf. Parmenides' saying: "□ τ ψ παντονομεοτι ν,υσσφβροτοικατευεντο,πεποτυοτε;ει ναιαληθη), so also existence beyond Brahman (*brahma-vyatirekena*); there is nothing different from Brahman (*na iha nānā asti kiñcana*, Bṛih. 4, 4, 19). But here our system goes further than the Veda. The whole extension of names and forms (*nāmarūpa-prapañca*), the whole plurality of phenomena (*rūpa-bheda*) is, from the standpoint of highest reality, caused, produced and laid as a burden [upon the soul] by Ignorance (*avidyā-kalpita, avidyā-pratyupasthāpita, avidyā-adhyāropita*), arises from false knowledge (*mithyājñāna-vijṛim-bihta*), is a mere illusion (*abhimana*), which is refuted by perfect knowledge (*Samyagdarśnam*);—just as the illusion that there is a snake, where there is only a rope, a man where there is only a tee trunk, or a sheet of water where there is only a mirage, is refuted by closer examination and deceives no longer. The whole world is only an illusion (*māyā*) which Brāhman projects (*prasārayati*) from himself like a magician is by the magic he creates; or, to change the image, Brāhman owing to Ignorance appears as multiplex (*vibhāvyate*) just as the magician does owing to the illusion; he is the cause of the continued existence (*sthiti-kāraṇam*) of the world, as the magician is of the magical scene he projects, and of the absorption of the world into his own Self (*sva-ātmani eva upasaṃhāra-kāraṇam*), just as the earth withdraws living beings into itself; the action of plurality (*bheda-vyav-ahāra*) during the existence of the world and the force of plurality (*bheda-śakti*) before and after both depend on Ignorance or false knowledge. As to this idea of *avidyā, mithyājñānam*, all further enquiry is at a loss; of the origin o this Ignorance, innate in all of us, we learn nothing; we penetrate deepest by the repeatedly employed image of the person with diseased eyes, who sees two moons, where in reality there is only one. However the non-existence of the world is only relative: the plurality of phenomena, fames and forms, and Māyā are *tativa-anyatvābhyām anirvacanīya*, *i.e.*, "one cannot say that they "are Brahman (*tat*), nor yet that they are different from Him." They are like the figures in a dream, true (*satya*), so long as the dream lasts, and are so no longer when the awakening (*prabodha*) comes.—This idealism, of which we see the dawn only in the Upanishads, the Vedānta tries to bring into unison with the Vedic doctrine of creation by maintaining that by creation is only meant the identity (*ananyatvam, tādātmyam*) of the world and Brahman; the world is the effect, Brahman is the cause; and effect and cause are identical; for the proof of this proposition the persistence of mater through changing states serves as the main argument.

4. Psychology

The soul alone is real.

§ 24. While we recognise in all Beings around us, in all the names and forms, of which the world consists, a deception, a mere illusion dependent on Ignorance and comparable to a dream, there is one point in the Universe when these considerations have no application; this point is our soul, *i.e.*, our own Self (*ātman*). This Self cannot be demonstrated because it is the basis of every proof, but it cannot be denied either, because anyone who denies it presupposes its existence. Of what nature is there this sole foundation of all certainty, the soul or inner Self? How is it related to Brahman, who includes all Beings in Himself?

Identity the soul with Brahman

§ 25. The soul can (I) not be different from Brahman because there is nothing "Existent" outside Brāhman; but it is (2) not to be regarded as a transformation of Brāhman either, for Brahman is unchanging; it is (3) just as little a part of Brahman, for He has no parts.—Therefore it only remains that the soul is identical with Brahman, and that each of us is the whole, indivisible, changeless Brāhman who comprehenes all Being in Himself.

The soul from the metaphysical standpoint.

§ 26. From this follows that all that is established of the Brāhman who is without differences, is also true of the soul; like Brahman the Soul is essentially pure spirituality (*caitan-yam*), and to it are applicable all those negative characteristics whose purpose is to secure the conception of Brahman from all ideas by which His Being might seem to be limited. Therefore the soul is, like Brahman (1) omnipresent (*vibhu, sarvagata*),or, as we should say, spaceless, (2) omniscient and omnipotent, (3) neither agent (*kartar*) nor enjoyer (or sufferer as the case may be, *bhoktar*).

The soul from the empirical standpoint.

§ 27. If the true nature of the soul lies in these characteristics, it follows that all which contradicts them is "ascribed" to it only by Ignorance. These ascribed limitations or *Upādhis* have their foundation only in false knowledge and to them as we saw all which conditions bodily existnece belongs; on them depends the fact that the soul in the state of Saṁsāra is (1) not all-pervading and omnipresent but dwells in the heart, its size being limited to that of the *Manas*, (2) is also not omniscient and omnipotent; for its natural omniscience and omnipotence become latent through the Upādhis, just as the light and heat of fire in wood in which it is hidden and slumbers; (3) finally the soul by its connection with the *Upādhis* becomes an agent and enjoyer (*kartar* and *bhoktar*) and by these latter qualities its entanglement in Saṃsāra is conditioned; for the works of one life must be recompensed by enjoyment and works in the following existence: the works however which form one part of the requital demand a further requital and so on *ad infinitum*.

The *Upādhis*.

§ 28. This beginningless and endless Saṁsāra depends only on the soul's true nature being hidden from it by the *Upādhis* due to *Avidyā*. They make Brahman the individual, active and enjoying soul; in addition to all outward things and relations and including the "gross body" which belongs to them and at death returns into the elements, they are the following: (1) the *Manas* and *Indriyas*; (2) the *Mukhya Prāṇa*; (3) the *Sūkshmaṃ Śariram*; and with this unchanging psychic apparatus, with which the soul has been clothed from eternity and remains clothed till liberation, is associated (4) a changeable element which we shall term moral determination. We have now to consider these *Upādhis* individually.

***Manas* and *Indriyas*.**

§ 29. Wile the gross body (*deha, kārya-karaṇa-saṅghāta*) and its organs (*karaṇam*), such as eye, ear, hands, feet etc. perish at death, their functions (*vṛitti*) regarded as separate entities remain united with the soul for all time. These organs and the *Indriyas* (the powerful ones) which the soul puts forth like feelers and withdraws at death. On these depend the two sides of conscious life, perception on the one hand and action on the other. Answering to this the soul has five faculties of perception (*jñāna-indriyas*)—sight, hearing, smell, taste, and touch, and five faculties of action (*karma-indriyas*) grasping, moving, speaking, procreating, and evacuating. These ten *Indriyas* commonly named after the corresponding organs of the gross body, are directed by a central organ, the Manas, which on the one hand works up the data of perception into ideas (*mansā hi eva paśyati, manasā śṛiṇoti*, Bṛih. 1, 5, 3), and on the other by the faculties of action causes what is willed to the executed; it is therefore at once what we call understanding and conscious volition. While the *Indriyas* pervade the whole body, the *Manas* "large as the point of an awl" dwells in the heart, and in the *Manas*, filling it completely, dwells the soul in the closet connection with it, broken only by liberation: only by the organs to which Ignorance chains is does the soul become an agent and enjoyer; it is itself as regards the activity of the organs a passive onlooker (*sakshit*) pure apperception (*upalabdhi*) so that in spite of its frometion in worldly actions is remains in its essence untouched by it.

***Mukhya Prāṇa*.**

§ 30. 'With the *Mukhya Prāṇa* the soul seems to be

less intimately connected that with *Manas* and the *Indriyas*, this term still has in the Upanishads the meaning of "breath in the mouth," but in the system it has come to denote "chief breath of life." Just as *Manas* and the *Indriyas* are the functions of perception and action hypostatised into separate entities, the *Mukhya Prāṇa* on which they all depend is a hypostasis of empirical life itself, which its five branches—*Prāṇa, Apāna, Vyāna, Samāna*, and *Udāna* condition. Of these *Prāṇa* causes exhalation, *Apāna* inhalation; *Vyāna* is what supports life when breathing is momentarily suspended; Samāna is the principle of digestion; just as these four sustain life, *Udāna* brings about its termination, leading the soul out of the body at death by one of the 101 principal arteries. By the same road withdraw *Mānas*, the *Indriyas* and *Mukhya Prāṇa*; just as during life they are the forces that rule the organs of the body, they are after the death of the body the seed from which at each rebirth the bodily organs arise.

Ikehmaṃ Śarivam

§ 31. Just as the soul carries with it the seed of the bodily organs in the *Iṅdrīyaā*, it bear with it the seed of the body itself in the form of the "subtle body" *sūkshmaṃ śarīram*, or as it is paraphrased repeatedly by Śaṅkara, *deha-vījāni bhūta-sūkshmāṇi*, *i.e.*, "the subtle parts of the elements which form the seed of the body" [and, according to Śaṅkara the impure elemnts]. How these subtle parts are related to the coarse elements is not further explained. The subtle body formed of them is material (*tanutvam*) but transparent (*svacchatvam*); therefore it is not seen at the withdrawal of the soul. On it depends animal heat; the corpse grows cold because the subtle body has left it to accompany the soul on its wanderings along with the other organs.

Moral determination.

§ 32. With this psychic organism (*manas, indriyas,*

mukhya prāṇa, sūkshmam śariram) which is attached to the soul in life and death at all times, and appears completely unchanging, is associated further as companion in the migrations a changing Upādhi; this is moral determination consisting the treausre of works (*karma-āśaya*) collected during life; side by side with the physical substratum (*bhūta-āśraya*) *i.e.*, the subtle body, it departs with the soul as a moral substratum (*karma-āśraya*) and inexorably determines the nature of the future existences in respect of enjoyment and suffering as well as of works.

Special State of the soul.

§ 33. There are four states of the wandering soul—waking, dreaming, deep sleep, and death. In the waking state the soul sojouring in the heart in association with Mānas rules over the whole body, perceiving and working through *Mānas* and the *Iṅdrīyās*. In dream sleep the *Iṅdrīyās* enter into rest while the *Mānas* remains active; and the soul, surrounded by *Manas* into which have withdrawn the *Indriyas*, pervades the body in the veins and in doing so beholds the dreams "fitted together" from waking impressions (*vāsanā*). In deep sleep the union of the soul with the *Mānas* is dissolved; *Manas* and the *Indriyas*, entering into rest, go into the veins or the pericardium and then into *Mukhya Prāṇa*, whose activity continues in deep sleep also; meanwhile the soul, temporarily freed from all the *Upādhīs*, enters into Brahman man in the ether of the heart; as the soul without the *Upādhīs* is Brahman, this entrance into Brāhman is only another way of expressing the complete deliverance from the *Upādhīs*. From this temporary identification with Brāhman the soul on waking issues with all its individual characteristics, the same that it was before.

5. Transmigration

The passing of the soul from the body.

§ 34. At death the *Iṅdrīyās* first of all enter into the

Mānas, this into the *Mukhya Prāṇa*, this into the soul affected by moral determination, and lastly the soul into the *Sūkshmaṃ Śariram*. After all these are assembled in the heart, its tip glows to illuminate the way and the *Udāna* leads the soul, together with the *Upādhīs* mentioned, out of the body. The soul of him who has acquired (lower) knowledge passages by the artery of the head (*mūrdhanyā nāḍi*, later termed *sushumnā*); those who have not knowledge depart by 100 remaining main arteries of the body. (He who has acquired the higher knowledge does not, as we shall see later, depart at all.) From this point the roads branch; the Ignorant who has performed works follows the *Pitriyāna* or way of the fathers; he who has the lower knowledge the *Devayāna* or way of the gods; he who has neither knowledge nor works; *i.e.*, the wicked man, is excluded from both these roads.

Fate of the doers of works (*Pitṛiyāna*).

§. 35. The *Pitṛiyāna*, intended for those who have neither the higher not the lower knowledge of Brāhman but have performed good works, leads the soul up to the moon to be recompensed. The stages on this road are the following—(1) smoke, (2) night, (3) the half of the month in which the moon wanes, (4) the half of the year in which the days grow shorter, (5) the world of the fathers, (6) the ether, and (7) the moon. In the luminous realm of the moon the souls enjoy converse with the gods as a reward for their works, and that until no more works remain. Only a part of the works however is recompensed on the moon. Another part forms a residue (*anuśaya*) and find its recompense in the next birth. Which works are to be understood in each case in a question that is not cleared up. After the woks which find their reward on the moon are consumed the soul descends again; on the return journey the stages are—(1) the ether, (2) the air, (3) smoke, (4) the cloud, (5) rain, (6) the plant, (7) the male semen, and (8) the mother's womb. In all the soul sojourns merely as a guest and is to be distinguished from the elements and souls it traverses. After it has finally reached a womb corresponding to the merit of its works it again passes out to another life on earth.

Fate of the wicked (Hell and the third place).

§ 36. The wicked who have neither knowledge nor works do not ascend to the moon; their fate is not clearly developed, for Śaṅkara refers on the one hand to punishment in the seven hells of Yama, and on the other to the "third place," in which they are born again as lower animals, but the connection between the two is not made clear. Though the wicked remain excluded from life on the moon, among those who return from the moon there is a further difference made between those of good conduct who are reborn I one of the three higher castes and those of evil conduct who enter the bodies of Caṇḍālas or animals. A combination of these ideas to a connected whole, easily possible by the distinction of various steps the good and evil works to be atoned for, is not found in the work from which we draw our facts.

Fate of the wicked (Hall and the third places).

§ 37. From those who do good works (§ 35) and adhere to the old Vedic cult of sacrifice are to be distinguished those who retain the Brahman doctrine but are unable to rise to the perfect knowledge of the doctrine of identity; and who therefore regard Brahman not as the soul in themselves but as God outside themselves and worship him accordingly. These possessors of the lower knowledge (*aparā vidyā*), *i.e.*, the worshippers of the lower, attribute-possessing (*aparam, saguṇam*) Brahman, all enter, (with the exception of such as have worshipped Brahman under a symbol, *pratīkam*), after death by the *Devayāna* into the lower Brāhman. The stages of this road are variously given in the different accounts, and Śaṅkara weaves them into a whole. According to Chānd. [Bṛih., Kaush.] the soul of him who possesses the lower knowledge, after leaving the body by the artery of the head, traverses the following regions—(1) Flame [= *Agniloka*], (2) the day, (3) the half of the month when the moon waxes, (4) the half of the yer when the days grow longer, (5) the year [(6) *Devaloka*, (7) *Vāyukoka*], (8) the sun, (9) the moon, and (1) lightning. These stages are neither to be regarded as signposts, nor as places of enjoyment for the soul, but as guides which it needs, because it cannot use its own organs as they are rolled up. While therefore by those already mentioned we are to understand divine, quasi-human guides of the soul, the soul after its entrance into the lightning is received by a "man, who is not as a human being" (*pursusho 'mānavaḥ*) and conducted to Brahman [through (11) *Varuṇa-loka*, (12 *Indraloka*, and (13) *Prajāpatiloka*]. By Brāhman however the lower, attribute-possessing Brahman is here to be understood, who has himself originated (*kāryam*) and therefore perishes at the destruction of the world. In the world of this Brahman the souls enjoy *aiśvaryam*, lordship, which consists in a quasi-divine but limited omnipotence and includes the fulfilment of all wishes. The *Mānas* serves as organ of enjoyment; whether the soul can also make use of the accompanying *Iṅdrīyās* is doubtful. Among other powers of the soul is that of animating several bodies at once, among which the soul distributes itself by dividing its *Upādhīs*.—Though this *aiśvarayam* of those who have entered into the lower Brāhman by the Devayāna has an end and only lasts till the destruction of the world, the scripture says of them: For such there is no return." We must therefore assume that the higher knowledge of *Samyagdarśnam* is communicated to them in the Brahman-world, and that thus at the destruction of the world, when the lower Brāhman also perishes, they enter with Him into the "eternal, perfect *Nirvāṇa*." This way of entering Brāhman is termed *Kramamukti* "progressive liberation" because it is conditioned by a progression, or "liberation by steps" because it is brought about by the intermediate step of heavenly lordship. To be distinguished from it is the immediate liberation of those who possess knowledge and this we shall now consider.

6. Liberation

"From knowledge comes release."

§ 38. The question of the possibility of a release from individual existence which forms the cornerstone of the Vedānta as of other Indian systems presupposes the pessimistic view that all individual existence is a misery. This view is occasionally put forward both in the Veda (Bṛih. 3, 4, 2 *ato 'nyad ārtam*, "what is different from him is afflicted;" Bṛih 4, 4, 11, *anandā nāme te lokaḥ*, "yea joyless are these worlds" cf. Kāṭh. 1, 3. Īśa 3) and in the system but is not emphasised to anything like the extent we should expect.—How is liberation (*moksha*) from the bond (*bandha*) of existence possible?—Not by works; for they, good and evil alike, demand their recompense, condition a new existence and are the cause of the continuance of *Saṃsāra*; but not by a (moral) purification (*saṁskāra*) either; for this can only take place in an object capable of change; but the Ātman, the sol, whose liberation is in question, is unchangeable. Therefore liberation cannot consist in a process either of becoming or of doing something but only in the knowledge of something, already present, that is hidden by Ignorance: "from knowledge liberation" (*jñānān mokshaḥ*). After the Brahmanhood of the soul is recognised liberation follows at once ("that thou art" is the phrase not "that thou wilt be,"; simultaneously with the attainment of the knowledge of the identity with Brāhman the soul becomes the soul of the universe.

Knowledge brought about by the grace of God.

§ 39. The Ātman, in the knowledge of which consists liberation, is nought else than the subject of knowledge in us. For this reason it is not recognisable by natural means: "thou canst no see the seer of seeing" *etc.* (Bṛih. 3, 4, 2); it cannot be sought for and looked at as an object; knowledge of it cannot be obtained at will, and even research in the scriptures does not produce a knowledge of it at once: this only serves to clear away the obstacles in the way. Whether the Ātman is known depends like the knowledge of every object on whether it shows itself to us, and therefore on itself. For this reason in the lower knowledge, which contrasts the Ātman to ourselves and worships him as a personal God, knowledge appears as dependent on the grace of God; but in the higher knowledge, as the Ātman is in reality not an object, we cannot enquire further after the cause which makes it known to us.

Auxiliary means of acquiring knowledge.

§ 40. Religious practice however knows certain means (*sādhanam*), by which the acquisition of knowledge of the Ātman is furthered. Thus from those who are called to knowledge is demanded the study of the Veda and the four requirements (1) Discrimination between eternal and non-eternal substance. (2) Renunciation of the enjoyment of reward here and in the other world, (3) the attainment of the six means-tranquillity, self-restraint, renunciation, resignation, concentration, belief, (4) desire for release).—In a more general sense and apart from this enumeration customary in instruction there are two means of furthering knowledge—work and meditation. (1) Work cannot, it is true, produce knowledge but are auxiliary (*sahakārin*) to the attainment of it, and that by destroying the obstacles that stand in the way; as obstacles are reckoned the affections (*kleśa*) such as (passion ate (love, hate, etc. Works have therefore in the plan of salvation not a meritorious but as ascetic rôle). Works which serve as a means of knowledge are auxiliary in part "outside" (*vāhya*) in part "closer" (*pratyā-sanna*). As these "outside" means are reckoned—the study "of the Veda, sacrifice, alms, penance, fasting" (Bṛih. 4, 4, 22); these are to be employed only till knowledge is gained. In contrast to these the "closer" means continue to exist even when knowledge is attained: they are "tranquillity, restraint, "renunciation, resignation concentration" (Bṛih. 4, 4, 23).—(2) Side by side with works pious meditation (*upāsanā*) serves as a means of knowledge. It consists in the devout consideration of the words of scripture, e.g., the saving *tat tvam asi,* and is, like threshing, to be repeated till knowledge appears as its fruit; this requires a longer or shorter time according as a person is mentally limited or afflicted by doubts. With the attainment of the higher knowledge meditation becomes unnecesary, for it has served its purpose. (The meditation o the other hand which is a part of the service of works, and that which is usual in the lower knowledge are to be practised till death, for the thoughts in the hour of death are of importance in determining the fate in the life beyond.) The posture is indifferent in the case of meditation serving the purpose of the higher knowledge. (So too for meditation as part of the service of works; the meditation necessary for the lower knowledge must be practised sitting, not standing or lying down.)

Destruction of works.

§ 41. Knowledge consists in the immediate intuition (*anubhva*) of the identity of the soul with Brahman. The works of Him who has attained this and with it the conviction of the unreality of the world of plurality and transmigration, are annihilated and in the future cleave to him no more. This annihilation refers just as much to good as to evil works, for both demand retribution and therefore do not lead beyond Saṃsāra. He on the other hand who has attained knowledge has won this conviction—"that Brāhman the nature of which is opposed to the nature, previously considered by me to be true, of agent and enjoyer, which is in its own nature in all time past, present and future non-agent and non-enjoyer, that Brahman am I; therefore I never was agent and enjoyer, and I am not one now, nor shall I ever be". With the unrelaity of activity the unreality of the body which exists as the fruit of works is recognised;

therefore he who has attained knowledge is as little affected by the sufferings of his own body as by the sufferings of another; and he who still feels pain, has verily not yet attained full knowledge.

Abolition of all duties.

§ 42. Even as for the man who has attained knowledge there is no longer a world, a body, or suffering, there is also no longer prescribed action. But he will not therefore do evil; for that which is the presupposition of all action, good and evil,—illusion—has been annihilated. It is a matter of indifference if he does works or not; whether he does them or not they are not his works and cleave to him no more. (However natural it would have been to desire from the described position of him who knows himself as souls of the world a positive moral disposition which shows itself in works of justice and love, this consequence is not drawn in Śaṅkara but only in the Bhagavadgītā.

Why the body of the liberated continues to exist.

§ 43. Knowledge burns the seed of works so that no material is at hand to cause a rebirth. On the other hand knowledge cannot annihilate works, the seed of which has already germinate, *i.e.*, those from which the present life is put together. This is why the body, even after the awaking (*prabodha*) is complete, continues to exist for a while, just as the potter's wheel goes on revolving even when the vessel which it supported is completed. This continuance is however a mere appearance; the possessor of knowledge cannot destory it, but it cannot deceive him any more either; just so the man with diseased eyes sees two moons but knows that in reality thee is only one there.

Absorption of the possessor of knowledge in Brāhman.

§ 44. After the works whose fruit has not yet begun to appear have been destroyed by knowledge, and after those, the fruit of which is the present existence, have by completion of this present life come to an end, with the moment of death full and eternal liberation comes to him who possesses knowledge; "his vital spirits withdraw not; Brahman is he, and into Brahman he is resolved."

"As rivers run and in the deep
Lose name and form and disappear
So goes, from name and form released.
The wise man to the Deity."

six

THE CULTURAL VALUE OF THE VEDĀNTA: A RETROSPECT

If philosophy, as we believe, is a matter of illumination or *darsanam*, a world-view or *Weltanschauung*, its importance as a factor in general culture can hardly be overestimated. What forces this fact into a well-deserved prominence is Max Müller's description of the Vedānta as 'the native philosophy of India'—a description that may, in all fairness, be said to form the keynote of this course of lectures. Nothing could be a more accurate description of the Vedānta philosophy, philosophy, being in ultimate analysis, only life brought to the focus of self-consciousness. In appraising the net values of these world-views or philosophies, one must, however, remember that the 'views of the world which proceed from the spirits of different ages, as products of the general development of culture, are not so much thoughts as rhythms in thinking, not theories but modes of intuition saturated with feelings of worth.' Accordingly, a systematic survey of these world-views as they appear in their historical succession, or to put it briefly, a history of philosophy has to avoid two extremes; that of a rigid panlogism, such as that of Hegel, proceeding from an over-emphasis on the logical factor, and secondly, that of lawless individualism following upon an undue stressing of the individual or personal factor in the framing of these. Proceeding on the assurance that the different systems of philosophy are not merely a 'motley collection of opinions of various learned gentleman's but the limited process in which the categories have successively attained distinct consciousness and the form of consciousness, Hegel ends by making the whole procession of these world-views appear as 'the unearthly ballet of bloodless categories.' But what Hegel forgot to reckon in preparing his balance-sheet is that it is the whole man that philosophizes, not his understanding merely, and that at the back of the logical factor there stand certain invisible, and therefore all the more invincible, forces—psychical and historical—which though alogical in the main are nevertheless stronger than all logic. Life, as the standing refutation of the law of formal logic that we cannot go beyond the premises, always vindicates its character as something more than logic. In truth the historical movement of philosophy "depends not solely upon the thinking of 'humanity' or even the '*Weltgeist*', but just as truly upon the reflections, the needs of mind and heart, the presaging thought and sudden flashes of insight, of philosophising individuals." The one essential aberration of Hegel's analysis—fundamentally correct as it is—consists in the unwarrantable assumption that the chronological order in which the categories have presented themselves in the historical systems of philosophy must necessarily correspond to the logical order in which the same categories should appear as 'elements of truth', which is in the keeping of a final system of philisophy—of course, his own. Not inaptly, therefore, does Bradley observe that a 'true philosophy cannot justify its own apotheosis. Nay, from the other side the metaphysician might lament his own destiny. His pursuit condemns him he may complain, himself to herd with unreal essences and to live an outcast from life. It is three times more blessed, he may well repeat, to be than to think. But in such a mood the man would so far fall away from philosophy. A true philosophy must accept and justify every side of human nature, including itself.'[1] No less risky is the accentuation of the personal or alogical factor, which tends to inaugurate the reign of lawless individualism in the domain of philosophical thought. We are not introduction here to a haphazard collection of opinions and random statements but to an all-embracing world-view of that great Individual, the *Grand Etre* of Humanity. This is not, however, within the easy reach of a European side-view of Humanity,—such as we have, for example, in Windelband who announces under the palpable influence of a characteristic *idolum tribus*-that the 'History of Philosophy is the process in which European humanity has embodied in scientific conception its views of the world and its judgments of life.'[2] It might, however, be pleaded in defence that the two epithets 'European' and 'scientific' are mutually convertible terms, and, as such, in a statement of fact, there can be no insinuation of an invidious distinction within Humanity. But, then, the alleged fact may not itself be an accredited fact, and it may eventually turn out to be a discredited fact. The equation in question, arbitrary as it is, is still open to question, and one can pertinently ask. 'Who shall arbitrate'? Now, it is in the recognition of a *tertium quid*—the cultural factor—that there is provided a bulwark against the aberrations of a panlogism and individualism in the reading of the views of the world. Uniting, as it does, the complementary half-truths in these one-sided methods, it has the efficacy of stressing the all-important truth that the development of philosophy is not the only aim of the world-process but a part of the universal aim operative therein. Viewed in this light, the individual philosopher appears to be as much the product as the creator of the age he lives in, and thus is justified the claim both of the logical and the alogical factor. As shaping forces in the history of civilisation, these world-views are to be regarded not so much as doctrines or results of reflection, as postulates or vital reactions. On that understanding the 'Greek view of the world is as classic as the plastic art of Phidias and the epic of Homer; the Christian, as eternally valid as the architecture of the Middle Ages; the modern, as irrefutable as Goethe's poetry and the music of Beethoven.'[3]

Accordingly, misled essentially are those who swear by a 'disinterested intellectual curiosity' as the sole inspirer of philosophic pursuits, and charge Indian philosophy, all and sundry, with a betrayal of intellectual trust so far as it represents philosophical activities in an instrumental relation to *Moksha* or redemption from all the miseries of existence as the highest good of man. Indeed, subserviency to interests other than strictly theoretical must needs be judged a serious disqualification on the part of a philosophical inquirer. But, then, a true philosophy, as Bradley reminds us so often, can not, without shamefully abandoning the charge committed to its care, make an apotheosis of the purely theoretical impulse. It is called upon to justify every side of human nature and thus to substantiate the pledge initially held out. Well might those that espouse the forlorn cause of Indian philosophy, and of Vedānta in particular claim, in the language of Śaṃkara, that this is its very individuality, or peculiar excellence, if you please (अलंकारो न्ह्मयमस्माक यदब्रन्ह्मवगतौ मव्यां सव्वेकर्न्तव्यतान्हानिः कृतकृत्वता वेति), that all the values of life, theoretical or practical are grounded in one consummate value (परभपुरुषर्थः). All the systems of Indian philosophy, whatever their respective persuasions, acknowledge the supremacy of one such intrinsic value, and present the whole set of values in a graded hierarchy terminatating in the supreme. Without such a systematisation or co-ordination of the values, a philosophical system forfeits its title to that appellation. Indeed, for better or for worse, system-building has ever been in the blood of Indian thinkers, and as a rule Indian philosophy has been either a system or nothing at all. After all, it is quite in the fitness of things that the logical Idea along with the passion for a theoretical consistency and disinterested intellectual curiousity should be acclaimed the sovereign master in the realm of intellectual achievements. While it is proper to insist on the virtues of a disinterested intellectual curiousity or love of truth for its own sake, it is well to remember that it can easily be overdone or made a fetish of. This 'disinterested intellectual curiousity.' be it further remembered, is itself an interest, akin to the Platonic *epws*, and unless provided with safeguards, it is too apt to degenerate into an obsession. Nowhere does this fixation reveal itself in a more unalloyed and concetrated form than in 'a free man's worship' which, according to Mr. Bertrand Russell, should draw its inspiration from what he terms with the force of an opigram 'the gospel of unyielding despair.' Now, whatever we may choose to think of its merits as a philosophical dissertation, there is no gain-saying the point that it is destined to rank, by the sheer force of its 'austere beauty' and stylistic charm, if not, also, in respect of its philosophic depth or vigour, as one of the masterpieces of English literature, and, as surely, as one of the philosophical classics of our age. These, combined with the contagious passion for passionlessness,– an emotional frigidity or apathy, as the very quintessence of Stoic wisdom–account for the hypnotic spell cast on every reader of this philosophical essay. But the discerning and self–possessed student can hardly fail to notice that the passion for disinterested intellectual curiosity and a standardised theoretical consistency appears in *excelsis* and is, so to speak, running riot here. We may or may not subscribe to Bradley's contention that the demand for theoretical consistency, which mutilates the substance of religion, starts from error in principle and leads, in the result to practical discord or sterility.[4] But there is absolutely no justification for that sorry exhibition, and that in the name of intellectual probity and scientific disinterestedness, of that spirit of bravado and 'sham heroism' that lie on the surface of the 'gospel of unyielding despair.' There is evidently more wisdom in the sage counsel: "Because thou must not dream, thou needst not then despair!" The emancipation of the intellect from 'desire,' its 'last prison-house,' is, admittedly, a salutary advice so far as it goes, but one has to see that it does not go too far, and end by throwing away the see that it does not go too far, and end by throwing away the babe along with the bath. A relentless rejection of all petty, private interest, and the cultivation of a temper of judicial neutrality must undoubtedly be put in the forefront as being an essential pre-requisite of the pursuit of truth; for these alone have the efficacy of purifying the intellect and predisposing it in such a way as to make it a fit recipient of truth. But in carrying out this purificatory rite, one stands in danger of making a broadcaust of the abiding or permanent interests, in a word, the values along with the changing or ephemeral interesteds of life, and thus carrying the process beyond the saturation-point of a total indifferentism. There is surely heroism in renouncing things which a man has no right to renounce; nor is there any–moral grandeur–and, if there be one got up, it is a fictitious one-about a martyrdom that is as gratuitous as it is foot-hardy. "It is vain" as Kant reminds us, "to profess indifference to those questions to which the mind of man can never really be indifferent." Indeed, there is such a thing as 'ostentatious poverty'—the classic prototype of which we have in the meeting of Diogenes the Cynic with Plato the intellectual aristocrat. When, the *nil admirari* cynic visited Plato in the latter's house, he is said to have called out to the latter to the following effect: "Look here, Plato; thus do I tread on your carpet". "But not without a pride" was the smart reply of the other who is reported to have followed it up with the remark: "I see into your pride through the holes in your jacket". Now, whose was the victory?—Of the aggressive, world-renouncing cynic, or of the unostentatious philosopher-king? The verdict of history has not left it a dubious issue. The anecdote is, however, not without a moral for us. If, we care to read between the lines of 'a free man's worship'—without allowing ourselves to be carried away by its insidious rhetoric—we should detect in it a morbid passion for passionlessness, a sentimental yearning for martyrdom for its own sake which has neither sanity nor seemliness about it. 'But if martyrdom is to be proclaiumed as a gospel for man, if must be more than courageous; it must be in the best sense wise and profitable.'[5] Such is the inevitable response to Mr. Russll's delusive gospe of renunciation that 'for man....it remains only to cherish, ere yet the blow falls, the lofty thoughts that ennoble his little day;... proudly defiant of the irresistible forces that tolerate, for a moment, his knowledge and his condemnation, to sustain alone, a weary but unyielding Atlas, the world that his own ideals have fashioned despite the trampling march of unconscious power.' This is unmistakably one of those typical passages which mark him out as a consummate artist, whose appeal lies not so much in any lure of intellectualism, but in the esthetic effect produced by words of ehiselled beauty and vivid imagery. While, therefore, we feel unconvinced by his logic, Mr. Russell impresses us with a peculiar persuasiveness that defies analysis into reasons. Indeed, it is only by straining the resources of language,—of the words 'gospel' and 'worship'—that the 'gospel of unyielding despair' can be made to serve as the keynote of a 'free man's worship.' Truly, it is neither deserving of the name of 'worship' nor that of a 'free man'. On the one hand, the 'proud defiance' inherent herein is at the farthest remove from the attitude of worship; on the other, a stupefying admiration for, and a craven submission or resignation to an 'unconscious power' trampling on our cherished ideals give the lie direct to the spirit of worship, and that of a 'free man'. The 'gospel of unyielding despair' is not the gospel of a 'free man', but of a bondslave, enchained like Prometheus to the bed-rock of naturalism, unrelieved by the Promethean spark of the Ideal. 'Fear of the Lord' it has been well said 'is the beginning of all wisdom.' But it is, be it remembered, only the beginning—and neither the end nor the essence of wisdom. Thus, the fear of relentless matter rolling along—and, as the psychologist will assert, the proud defiance is but the paralysing fear turned inside out—may mark the beginning of an intellectual curiosity, but it is, in the end, conducive neither to intellectual uplift, nor religious edification. The cult of spiritual worship must necessarily be in a minor key, where worship thrives by the working upon the instinct of fear, and man sinks into the comparative insignificant position of a mere 'tooth in the wheel', forfeiting eventually the right to record his approval or disapproval of the ways of this unconscious power. This attitude might readily fall in with the modernist craze for the 'Reenaissance of instinct' with its gospel of *la bete humaine*, but it lacks the essentially human \note of that elevating trust in the spiritual dignity of man, which is the best ministration to religious worship. Summarily speaking, the sense of being thus overwhelmed and awed into submission by an unconscious, albeit stupendous, power, and the sense of defeatism born of despair, and the consequent deification of the natural or the actual give the lie direct to the attitude of worship.

The ingrained intellectualism of Mr. Russell's standpoint has been, as we know, steadily on the increase, and, in his latest writings, it shows itself to be on the verge of bankruptcy, and stultifying itself by a veritable *reductio ad absurdum*. It appeared *in excelsis* in the course of lectures he delivered, under the auspices of the British Philosophical Institute during the Lent term of 1928. The course was entitled 'Philosophy of Physics,' and although some portion of it has been incorporated in his *Analysis of Matter*, the course was of a more sketchy character, and therefore too intellectual to be intelligible to the ordinary student uninitiated into the intricacies of mathematical logic. At the conclusion of one of these evening discoursees (which I had been regularly attending)—and this was on the nature of Substance–one elderly gentleman, an artist by profession took the lead during the question-time and made the telling remark: "I have followed with rapt attention the frame-work of the Physical universe which the lecturer this evening has unscrolled before our admiring eyes. But when I am told in the name of a Philosophy of Physics to believe that my wife sitting next to me is a mere'formula' representing a group of events in the series—$x+f_1(x)\, dt + f_2(x)\, dt^2 + \ldots$ $f_1(x)$ being continuous function of time, it sends a thrill of horror through my blood." The whole house burst into a peal of laughter but the redoubtable Mr. Russell rose equal to the occasion and replied with a characteristic smile: "I cannot help it: such is in the abstract the character of the universe, and I was not consulted at the time of its creation."

Apart from the humour of the situation, there is a candid confession in Mr. Russell's retort here, as to the real character of intellectualism. In his vocabulary the intellectual, or the scientific method, for the matter of that, is the method of anaysis and abstraction. And it is in the sense of a vicious abstractionism that the charge of intellectualism has been, curiously enough, pressed against the *Upanishads* and the *Advaita-Vedānta* in general. Thus, there is a *volte face,* a complete change of front, so far as it is maintained that here at least one system of Indian philosophical thought lays exclusive emphasis upon contemplation, or *θειυρια,* without making the intellectual impulse subservient to some other end,—as all the other systems do as a rule. What these some-what contradictory rulings plainly reveal is the hollowness of the indictment on both the counts—of anti-intellectualism and intellectualism—as pressed against Indian philosophy. Does not this procedure on the part of critics lend countenance to the suspicion that any stick is good enough to beat a dog with? Admitting, under protest, the force of the contention that Indian philosophy has not always lived up to the ideal of theoretical consistency or intellectual curiosity, one may yet reply that the charge cannot be maintained at least against Sriharsha's *Khandanakhanda Khadyam*, or in a wider reference, against the thinkers of the Neo-logical (*Navya Nyaya*) school in the face of their dialectical *finesse* wherein the urge of intellectual curiosity has been pursued rigorously—perhaps with a vengeance.

After all, it must be admitted that the main drift of Indian philosophy has been in the direction of a subordination of the logical values, along with others, to one Supreme Good, and decisively against the absolute authority or paramount claims of the intellectual ideal. In the West, however, this has never been the case—with the exception, however of one brief interlude of philosophical thinking. But in India at least philosophical thought has never been in intellectual pastime merely, cut off front the moorings of all other values of life. Free thinking in the sense of an unchartered freedom to indulge in polemics foir their own sake has seldom found favour with the Indian mind. This is a fact that has to be accepted as such, and let not the judgment be surreptitiously converted into a judgment upon fact. Just as there can be no disputing about tastes, so also there can be no comparative evaluation in this matter.

No less confusing, on this very score, is the uncritical application to Indian philosophy, of the technique of philosophical thought and critical evaluation obtaining in the West. While an exaggerated sense of, and scrupulous regard for, the individuality of Indian thought and culture that defies comparison with all else is, to say the least of it, dogmatic and unphilosophical, it is no less reprehensible to make an off-hand use of such epithets as 'rationalistic,' 'intellectual' or 'anti-intellectualistic' in the matter of describing the position of India thinkers. Quite apart from the fact that philosophical labels are essentially misleading, the chances of misdirection on the part of these labels become all the greater when the canons of criticism are exotic in origin, and, therefore, must needs undergo some transformation in meaning as taken out of their proper context. It is a commonplace,—amounting almost to a truism—of all comparative studies, but it is more honoured in the breach than in the observance. Accordingly, when we have recourse to such descriptive phrases as 'Śaṃkara is a rationalist' or 'a revelationist in the service of orthodoxy' or even 'a scholastic expounding theological dogmatics' and the like, seldom do we pause to consider whether we are not sometimes straining the resources of language beyond their breaking-point. The enormity of this procedure reaches its climax when, in appraising an old system of thought, we conveniently forget the interval of time that separates it from us, and apply our standards and canons of criticism to it. Following this questionable method, critics have not infrequently tabooed the philosophical system of Śaṃkara as 'uncritical' or even as 'unphilosophical.' It is, however, sheer perversity to apply a standardised method of evaluation all through, and on such application brand a system as 'uncritical', simply because it does not fall in with the current standard of critical thinking. No one, even with a modicum of historic sense, would make the preposterous claim that our standard of critical evaluation should be applicable *in toto* to a system dating twelve centuries back. Apart from a glaring historical anachronism involved in such a procedure, the claim itself is, on the very face of it, arbitrary and irrational. In reckoning his claims to be called a philosophical thinker, Śaṃkara must be placed in his proper' historical setting and judged accordingly. Here, as elsewhere the supreme or crucial test is 'how strive you?' and whatever we may choose to call him, 'the sin of unlit lamp and the ungirt loin,' in the matter of critical thinking, can by no means be imputed to him. His frequent insistence on *jijnasa* (a sifting enquiry), *vicāra* (ratiocination) and *mimāmsā* (critical investigation) surely admits him into the rank of philosophical inquirers of all ages and of all climes. What, however, decides once for all his claims to be reckoned a critical thinker, in the modern sense of the term, is an epoch-making pronouncement of his with regard to the status and function of *vicara* or rational criticism in the matter of attaining unto the highest bliss of manking. Entrenched, as he was, in a rigid orthodoxy, Śaṃkara had yet the hardihood to assert with all the emphasis he could command that a man who somehow espouses a creed without a prior discussion or critical reflextion is debarred from beatitude and incurs evil.[6] For an orthodox thinker of Śaṃkara's eminence, this must be pronounced to be a remarkable verdict—which is, however, hardly ever given the prominence it deserves. In thus formulating the rights of private judgment in the face of *Śruti* or *Āgama*, that is, Authority, Śaṃkara may be said to have shuffled off the antiquated badge of mediaevalism and taken on that of modernism. His critical apparatus or dialectical machinery may not have approximated the modern standard, but it is the rational mood or temper that prompted this verdict of his which is to be regarded the sole arbiter of his claims. Hence the apologetic strain in which we sometimes speak of the claims of Śaṃkara as a philosophic thinker is altogether uncalled for and unjust.

Now, we are in a position to take stock of our findings, from the cultural standpoint of the Vedānta, in our retrospective review of the foregoing lectures. The first lecture started with the admission of what seems to be of central importance in the Vedānta—namely, the message of a full-fledged autonomy of the Spirit which, although brooding on us perpetually like 'a presence which is not to be put by', is only the legacy of the privileged few who have realised in their own experience the oneness of their being with the spirit behind the mightly frame of nature, symbolised by that dynamical sublime, the *Pushan* or Sun-god in the sky. Accordingly, the well-known invocation to Sun-God in the *Iśopanishad*[7]—"O thou all-sustaining, solitary, all-controlling Sun, descended from the Lord of all creatures, do thou restrain and centralise all the streaks of light that I may envisage thy blissful countenance; forsooth, I am the very Being that abides in thee"—may be taken as symptomatic of the Vedānta as a whole, and the cult of spiritual worship it has prescribed. It is the realisation of this oneness of spirit that alone can afford a sense of security and peace that man is ever hankering after. So runs the testimony of the *Brhadaranyaka Upanishad*[8] among many others: 'अभयं

वै जनक पगापगोऽसि' But no man in his senses would claim that this realisation of oneness of Being,—this priceless legacy of the ancient world—sprang perfect into existence, like Juno from the head of Jupiter, and could be found in a full-fledged from in Hymns of the Rgveda, which, by common consent, mark the germinal beginnings of Vedāntic thought and culture. While fully subscribing to the principle that the Vedānta, and in particular its essence, Advaitism, is implanted in the Veda, (वेदे वेदान्तः भुप्रतिष्ठितः) one need not and indeed must not, construe the principle with a literalness that strikes at the very root of all notion of development. In fact, it is not possible within the meaning of the law of development, to have the flower along with the fruit, for the simple reason that the decay of the flower is the condition of the appearance of the fruit. The attempt, on the part of these well-meaning apologists of Rgvedic thought, is symptomatic of the absolutist's Absolute, which, on Bradley's own showing 'has no seasons, but all at once bears its leaves, fruit and blossom.' But the question of a steady development of thought from the Rgveda to the Upanishads, as we may conveniently note here, may itself be challenged and repudiated as being only a favourite dogma of the modernist. Indeed, it has been seriously maintained that the trend of reflective thought from the Ṛgveda to the Upanishads exhibits a steady degeneration, rather than an evolution in respect of 'the sacredness and secrecy of self-knowledge and the true knowledge of the gods.' The plea is, therefore, rotted out for an occultist treatment of the hymns of the Rgveda as in the case of 'the historical Eleusinian and Orphic mysteries' of ancient Greece. To seek to stem the tide of approved scholarship and widespread acceptance is sure to be laughed out as mid-summer madness on the part of its author. But the sponsor of this peculiar hypothesis stands in a class apart, and his name is a sufficient guarantee against summary rejection or any other disrespectful treatment. But the superior claim that he has upon our regard gives him no immunity from criticism when he enters the arena of polemics and pleads, in a confessedly rational manner, for a preferential treatment of things that are supposed to be above and beyond reason in its normal functioning. Such an esotericism or aristocratism to say the least of it, is fundamentally at variance with the native absolutism of the human intellect which squares, paradoxically enough, with the democratic temper of our age. Indeed, the effort to take shelter behind a supra-rational Authority is a discredited relic of Mediaevalism and psendo-mysticism, and is unquestionably a glaring instance of historical anachronism in this age of rationalism and free thinking. Without reverting to discussion on the thorny problem of Authority *vs* freethinking, it may be safely laid down that the endeavour of the mystery-mongers and high-browed esoterics fails to uphold the cause of either—to command authority in the one case and induce conviction in the other. It is too late in the day to learn that truth is one organic whole, just as reason, as the only availing guide in our search after truth, is also unitary in character, and that, therefore in the republic of the Vedānta we can acknowledge no other authority except that of reason. It is undoubtedly, a question of principle, and not merely one of modernism or spirit of the times (*Zeitgeist*). For, it is preposterous to suggest that truth is to be obtained by a counting of heads. Truth does not, and most certainly did not, as the history of human civilisation clearly shows, depend on a majority of votes to enforce its acceptance. It rules everywhere by its own inherent right. When the historic martyr to truth stood up, like another *Athanasius contra mundum*, in defiance of the universally accepted creed and the impending persecution staring at him, and exclaimed: "still it moves" (*eppur si muove*), the principle was amply vindicated. Nor is this radical brreach in the nature of reason—from which alone the distinction between the esoteric and exoteric truth derives all its plausibility—conducive to the best interests of the 'spiritual and psychological knowledge of the race' which the scholar-mystic holds a brief for. If this so-called sacred and secret knowledge had to thrive upon this breach in human nature and had no other *locus standi* to count upon, it would have stood upon a precarious foundation indeed. If truth be really what it is represented to be, then reason and unreason cannot equal abide therein; for, unreason in aught is unreason in all. If reason in its analytic function is pressed, as it needs must be, into the service of this mystical knowledge, it must be all in all or never be at all. For, the spectre of reflective thought once summoned to our aid can not conveniently be laid in its grave. Indeed, those who seek to gain a Pyrrhic victory for the cause of esoteric or mystical knowledge by thus antagonising it to the clear deliverances of reason seem to be hardly conscious of the dangerous precedent they are thereby creating. For, such a procedure has its inevitable Nemesis in that common rain which awaits all the hard-won findings of an occult or mysterious organ of the soul. In point of fact, mysticism does not enjoy such a precarious eminence. Anti-intellectualism or anti-rationalism is the plea of the pseudo-mystic only. It is in reference to these psendo-mystics that Plato made the remarks in the *Phaedo*: 'Many are the thyrsus—bearers, but few are the mystics'. The mystic, forsooth, is one 'who believes in spiritual apprehension of truths beyond the understanding.' The name μνοτης would originally be given to to 'one initiated' or to a priest of secret rites of divine worship. This affords an instructive comparison with the radical meaning of the term '*Upanishad'*, which, as derived from the root 'सद्', ('sad'=to sit) with the prefixes of सप. ('Upa') and ('ni'), means—Samkara's interpretation, not withstanding—'that which is imparted to the (initiated) disciple when he sits close to his preceptor;—hence, a 'secret doctrine or mystery' (गुदाऽर्थाः, रन्हस्वम् परा विदाा) (and so forth). The word μνδτηριον is, again, cognate with μνειν which literally means 'closing of lips or eyes'—perhaps as being symbolic, and suggestive of withdrawal of the senses from the scene of their operation and concentration within the soul. It is strikingly similar to the literal as well as symbolic meaning of (आहन्तचक्षः) (avrttacakshuh) or 'closed eyes' that occur in the opening verse of the second chapter of *Kathopanishad,* which, again, in its turn is strongly reminiscent of the 'averted eye' of the Pythagoreans. There is undeniably in man's nature a haunting passion for a Beyond, a twilight region, or a realm beyond the senses—figuring more or less as the outlying penumbra of the known. It is from this region, as Bradley would have us believe, that 'philosophy as a satisfaction of what may be called the mystical side of our nature" derives its constant inspiration: only "when the sense of mystery and enchantment no longer draws the mind to wander aimlessly and to love it knows not what; when, in short, twilight has no charm—then metaphysics will be worthless'.[9] This is one, perhaps the only one, way of ensuring the satisfaction of the mystical side of our being—through an intellectual effort to understand the universe; and with certain persons, among whom Bradley is one, it is a principal way of experiencing the Deity'. But when it is claimed that 'the Vedic hymns were conceived and constructed' in such a way as to convey 'a spiritual sense for the elect' and the 'initiate', terminating eventually in 'self-knowledge and the true knowledge of the gods', it is instructive to note, as Bradley clearly affirms, that 'there is no calling or pursuit which is a private road to the Deity', and that 'there is no sin' 'which philosophy can justify so little as spiritual pride'. Granted that the intitiate are privy to this sacred and secret knowledge from which the vulgar and the profane are shut out, and like Browning's musicians it is they that can say: 'it is we mystics know'. But that knowledge from which reason is debarred on pain of profanation has not even that redeeming grace of letting down the ladder for the vulgar and the uninitiate, which entitles it to the name of 'knowledge'. When all is said and done, one feels that there is a peculiar persuasiveness inherent in the claim thus advanced on behalf of the hymns of the Ṛgveda. At the same time there is some pathos attaching to this forlorn endeavour to espouse a dying cause and stick to it unto the last. But whatever the nature of the appeal, the truth-claim of this hypothesis cannot reasonably be endorsed by any systematic study of the kind to which this course of lectures stands pledged. What is, however, instructive to note in regard to the question of a continuous development from Ṛgveda to the upanishads is, in the luminous phraseology of the late Prof. Wallace, that 'all development is by breaks and yet makes for continuity'.

The conceptual formulation of the Hymns of the Rgveda by way of three recognised strata of naturalistic polytheism, spiritualistic monotheism, and speculative (or agnostic) monism hardly does justice to Ṛgvedic thought and culture as a whole. There may, roughly speaking, be distinguished six stages in the history of human culture and civilisation, and it is usual to reckon six stages in the development of a philosophical doctrine or thought-type, the second half recapitulating the first half on a higher plane and thus constituting what has been aptly called the method of spiral progress.[10] The first in the first half is the Magic stage which invariably expresses itself in social instincts and postulates expressed in rituals. The second is the Myth stage in which the ingrained mythopoeic activity of the race bursts forth in the form of myth, folklore, beast fables etc. The third is the Symbol stage which evinces a growing maturity in symbolization and sublimation of myth and ritual. Now, the fourth stage in the series (which is but the reproduction of the first on a higher ploane in this spiral of progress), is the stage of Dogma manifesting itself in varying degrees of conceptual abstraction—in pictorial imagination, in *vortsellung*, as the *alterum idem* of the thing, and in creed. The fifth is the stage of Rationalisation proper with its elaboration and perfection of the conceptual apparatus in the form of Critique and Dialectic—of *Pūrvapaksha, Uttarapaksha* and *Siddhānta*. The sixth and the final stage in the series is the stage not of θεωρια merely, but of μραξις, of *sadhana* or realisation. Applying this formula to the famous doctrine of Karma and its evolution in Indian Culture history we have the following series. The first stage is that of *Yajna karma* as ritual drawing its inspiration from the instinct of continued personal existence or will to live and expressing itself in ritualistic performances for heaven (*svarga*), and from the instinct of race-preservation and manifesting itself in rituals for fertilization, fecundity, or race-multiplication. The germinal beginning of this law of Karma makes itself felt also, in this very first stage, as certain *samskaras*, family and tribal customs, as sacraments and the like. The second is the stage of myth formation which crystallizes as the myth of the double path of *prayana* (outward journey) and of *punaravrtti* (return journey), of Heaven and hell and the like—pointing unmistakably to what is known as the doctrine of the transmigration of souls or metempsychosis. The third stage in the evolution of the law of Karma is that of symbolization or sublimation of *Yajnas, Tapas, Samskaras*, as rituals—such as we have in the different Upanishads and the Gita. The fourth stage which marks the beginning of conceptual formulation naturally expresses itself in the Dogma of Karma conceived as a Law along with the entire para-phernalia of *samcita* and *Prārabdha Karma* together with the idea of a cyclical existence. The fifth stage is that of Moral causation and its dialectic revealing itself in a code of injunctions and prohibitions (*vidhinishedha*), *niyoga* being the ground of Karma. It is on this stage that a rational enquiry into the relation between *Karma* as Law and free of will of man and *Karma* and *Iśvara* or the Moral Governor of the universe is fully envisaged. The sixth and the final stage in the development of the law of Karma is the emergence of the notion of value (*purushārtha*), intrinsic and instrumental, of μραχος and *sadhana* or disciplines, and of the relation of the way of *Karma (karmamārga)* to *Paramapurushartha,* the *Summum Benum* and *Moksha* or redemption as a final release from the domination of the Law of Karma.

Similarly, reviewing the various states in the development of the thought-types or categories in religious philosophy among the early Vedantic teachers, we find *Kasakrtsna*[11] employing the category of absolute identity in conceiving the relation between the individual and the universal self, *Asmarathya*[12] and *Sandilya* teaching an identity-in-difference, *Audulemi* inculcating difference before absorption,[13] and finally, *Kasyapa* insisting on a fundamental difference between the two. Our interest in these early conceptual formulations of one of the main problems of the Vedānta is that they are the distinct anticipations of a more articulate and dialectical defence of these in Śaṃkara-Vedānta, Rāmānuja, Nimvārka (and Bhāskara), and Madhvacaryya—comparing not unfavour-ably with the so-called 'review-course' (*Repetitionkursus*) in contemporary German thought of the phases of the Kantian movement in the well-recognised movements of Neo-Kantianism, Neo-Fichteanism, Neo-Hegelianism and Neo-Romanticism.

Now, what is the net result, it will be asked, of our findings with regard to the Vedānta from the standpoint of an all-round culture? Deussen thinks that 'the New Testament and the Upanishads, these two nobles products of the religious consciousness of manking, are found when we sound their deeper meaning to be nowhere in irreconcilable contradiction, but in a manner, the most attractive, serve to elucidate and complete one another"[14] The supplementation in question, according to Deussen, appears in relation to the central teaching of each. " 'Thou shalt love thy neighbour as thyself' is the requirement of the Bible" and this injunction remains inexplicable and unauthoritative, until the Vedānta adds by way of explanation the reason therefor: "Because thy neighbour is in truth thy very self, and what separates you from him is mere illusion."[15] Apart from the fact that Deussen has not sustained this position all through his book, the comparison in question is altogether inapt and unsatisfactory. The Upanishads might not unreasonably suffer under the pressure of this somewhat embarrassing charity displayed in paying to them a compliment they do not go in for. Whatever may be the point of comparison between the 'Sermon on the Mount' and the Upanishads, the latter do neither claim to be, nor are in point of fact, sermons or injunctions figuring as so many copy-book headings for the guidance of our lives. What the Upanishads profess to do is not to lay down rules for the betterment of our daily lives, but to enlighten us as to the spirit in which our lives are to be lived. Indeed, having, as it does, in view a good, higher than that of action, the good or blessedness of a *vita contemplativa*, the Upanishads conceive their main function to be the creation of a spiritual atmosphere and not the formulation of an ethical code. In their functioning, the Upanishads emulate that all-pervading ether which works invisibly and unceasingly, but does not vibrate into light. The ineptitude of the comparison should not have escaped the notice of a scholar of Deussen's eminence. What has some semblance of justification is their comparison with the first maxim of Pure Practical Reason as formulated by Immanuel Kant viz. "So act that the principle of thy action can be consistently universalised." The point of the comparison consists in their respective answers to the question of the spirit in which our lives are to be lived—in the enunciation, in short, of an a *priori* maxim of universal applicability. Both acquiesce, on the whole, in the same merits and demerits. The barren formalism of a princple of universal legislaıion which fails to give us a concrete code of maxims, or a guidance in the practical concerns of life, must naturally and necessarily provoke its own Nemesis in the entire set of casuistical literature that has followed in the wake of both. The criticism may not be relished by the Vedāntists, but it is none the less true. It is undeniable that Kant sought to obviate the empty formalism of his teachings in the proposal to make Humanity always the end of action, and never a means only—that is to say, the happiness of humanity, represented in your neighbour, always the end of our action. Whether the cult of the love of one's neighbour' has failed or not is writ large across the face of history which, if Croce is right, is but contemporary history. But that is not the point of philosophical importance in this connection. It is just when Kant was warning up to the idea of a 'unity of our lives as a systematic whole, as a 'Kingdom of Ends', he was moved, by reason of a hampering prejudice and fatal dualism, to neutralise the force of this fruitful conception with a characteristically Kantian 'as if.' The saving clause 'as if' does not save but damns for ever the Kingdom of Ends which, we are told, on its authority, has a mere heuristic or regulative validity but lacks a constitutive one. Thus punctuated and sterilised, the Kingdom of Ends—which could have developed far more fruitfully than what Kant could have intended it to do—becomes in the end one of those 'floating air-bubbles, gay in the sunshine and broken by the passing wind'. Is not in all conscience, the injunction of (सभदर्शनं) that we have in the Gita, although backed by the metaphysical oneness of being of the Śaṃkara-Vedānta, confronted with the same deadlock in practice, and pursued by the same aftermath of casuistry that the other draws in its wake? Indeed, we must look for the cultural significance of the Vedānta elsewhere–not in any positive prescripts that it might have unconsciously enforced, but in the very abstention therefrom, because its function is with a negation which appears to many as a fall from the sublime to the ridiculous—an anti-climax: "enjoy but do not covet any other man's wealth"; but it is, in fact, no bathos, nothing of the kind. No high-flown idealism can afford, without prejudice to its own safety, to neglect making sure of the *terra firma* of the elementary Levitical morals on which it has to stand. Summarily, speaking, Vedantism stands for the cult of *'no-cult.'* Although it is of the nature of a paradox, that appears to be the exact transcript mainly limitative or prohibitive. When there is even the remotest suspicion of its acquiring a positive signification, the upanishadic thinker hastens at once to correct that misdirection. That is why the high-pitched key on which the *Ishabasyopanishad* begins thus:

"ईशवास्वमिदं सर्व्वं यत् किंच जगत्वां जगत्
तेन त्यक्तेन भुच्चौथाः"

i.e. "whatever is active in this world is to be known as permeated by the Lord and to be enjoyed as provided by Him"—and is in the very next line saddled of its attitude towards the universe. It presents the impressive spectacle of the spirit of Humanity passing under review all the distracting cults of human existence, demanding divided allegiance from them, and giving the redemptive warning. It is in bitter earnest with the 'Everlasting Nay' which, in its view, must be pressed to its ultimate limit before 'the Everlasting Yea' of a blessed life symbolised by '*Aum*' can make itself felt to us; for it is grounded in the belief that in spiritual things 'the greatness of the price we pay has much to do with the value of the good that we acquire.' In thus carrying out its life-giving mission it strongly reminds the discerning mind of the much persecuted preacher of Galilee, drawing men away from the delusive worship of earthly gods with the perpetual reminder: "My kingdom is not of this world!" This *via negativa* is no more the last word in the one case than it is in the other. It does not land us, as is sometimes apprehended, in sheer emptiness or negation. If the negative prescript were to terminate in pure negation or blank, would it (in all propriety) be called the true of the true, as asks Śaṃkara most significantly?[16]

Thus is revealed ultimately the source of abiding inspiration for the Vedantist. It is the spirit of the Whole, which does not allow us to half at any half-way house,but bids us march past till the goal is reached. This, the underlying and informing spirit of the Whole, may best be indicated, in the words of Bradley, as 'Justice in the name of the whole to each aspect of the world according to its special place and proper rank—Reality everywhere through self-restriction in claim and in denial.' Well might the Vedantist declare in

Bradley's own words: "Everywhere on behalf of the real Absolute I have been warning [*all*] against that false absolutism which in philosophy is to me another name for error...as against such absolutism, the very soul of the Absolute which I defend is its insistence and emphasis on an all-pervasive relativism." Accordingly, 'one main work of philosophy,' for the Vedantist as much for Bradley 'is to show that, where there is isolation and abstraction, there is everywhere, so far as this abstraction forgets itself, unreality and error.'[17] Critics there will be who would repudiate this version of the Vedānta as unorthodox, and as being fundamentally at variance with the ingranined 'Oriental despotism' that has never respected the rights of minority and which makes its appearance in philosophy as absolutism in its objectionable sense. But instead of submitting to this parrot's training, constantly dinned into our ears, we should bring an unprejudiced mind to bear on the situation and see if we have not in the epistemological rendering of the doctrine of *'adhikaribheda'*, a full substantiation of the case for the Absolute as presented by Bradley. It is under the perennial inspiration of that spirit of the Whole, that the Vedantist passes by the cult of family, society, nationalism, or even internationalism, with the characteristic anathema—(भेदं यदिदमुपायतै). Such other-worldliness may not be quite in tune with the spirit of modernism, but it is there and must make itself heard. "The roots of modern philosophy", so writes one European Historian of Philosophy, "are sunk deep in the fruitful soil of nationality, while the top of the tree spreads itself far beyond national limitations. It is national and cosmopolitan together; it is international as the common property of the various peoples which exchange their philosophical gifts through an active commerce of ideas."[18] Nothing could be a truer description of the cult of internationalism that has its root struck deep in the soil of nationality! Ah, there is the rub! Mischief, they say, always lies about the root. A Parliament or Federation of Mankind, must forever remain an idle dream, and a League of Nations is too apt to degenerate into a clique of nations, until and unless the making of the international mind is an accomplished fact; and this has the greatest chance of materialising under the perpectual inspiration of the Vedantic cult of 'no-cult', or what is the same thing, the inspiration of a Church Invisible. The method of working from bottom upwards has been tried and found wanting. Why not try the other—namely, of working from above downwards. That is why the Upanishadic sage, with unerring prophetic vision, declares that this ancient holy fig tree (symbolising the Infinite and the Eternal, the भुमा) has its roots in heaven and its branches spreading downwards (उर्ड्ढ्भुलोऽतोक्शख एषोऽश्वत्थः समातमः). This is however, no mere dream of some future possibility, of some 'far-off divine event', no mere vague aspiration of the Futurist, but is verily the Everlasting Real, dwelling in us, 'nearer than our hands and feet'. It is easy to deride the notion and take to the blunt Johnsonian method of refuting an ideal by kicking against it. If, in short, it is contended that such a vision of perfect unity or human solidarity is too good to be true, the Vedantist can meet that contingency by saying that the vision is too good *not* to be true. It is no mere remote theological mystery, but God be thanked, it is inwoven with the very texture of our experience. Accordingly, for the Vedānta *Brahman* or *Bhùmà* the Infinite, is the Alpha and Omega, the beginning and the end, the first and last of all things. It starts on its career with ब्रन्ह्मजिज्ञासा, enquiry into Brahman, a the supreme good of man, sustain our interest therein by perpetual reminder that it is the *Bhuma* that alone is to be enquired into (भुमात्वेव विजिज्ञासितव्यः), and closes on the high-pitched key:—"Do thou enquire into that. Verily that is Brahman."(तहिजिज्ञासख। तन्हन्ह्मेति)।

Foot Notes

1. *Essays on Truth and Reality,* pp. 13-14.
2. A *History of Philosophy,* p. 9.
3. Falckenberg, *History of Philosophy* (Eng. Trans.) *Introduction.*
4. *Essays on Truth and Reality,* p. 432.
5. Perry, *Present Philosophical Tendencies,* p. 346.
6. तत्राविचार्य्य यत्किच्चित प्रतिपदामानो निःरेयसात् प्रतिन्हन्यत्नर्थझेयात्—Com. On V.S.I.1.I.
7. पुषन्नेकर्षे यभ भुर्य्य प्राजापत्यव्युन्ह रश्भोन् सभुन्ह तेजो यन्ते रुपं कल्यान्वतमं तते पश्यामि योऽसावसौ पुरुषः सोऽन्हसस्मि।
8. Chap. IV. Brahmana ii. 4.
9. *Appearance and Reality,* Introduction.
10. Vide Dr. B. N. seal and his illuminating notes on this point in his "Syllabus of Lectures."
11. e.g. in the V. S. अवस्यितेरिति काशकृत्स्न—I. 4. Xxii.
12. e.g. in V. S. प्रतिशसिद्धेर्लिंगमाश्मरथ्यः—I. 4. Xx.
13. e.g. in V. S.उत्कभिष्यत एवम्मावादित्यौडुलोमिः—I. 4. Xxi.
14. *The Philosophy of the Upanishads,* p. 49.
15. *Loc. Cit.*
16. अभावावसामे तु प्रतिषेधे किं सत्यस्य सत्यमित्युच्येत—Com. On V. S. III. 2. Xxii.
17. *Essays on Truth and Reality,* Conclusion.
18. Falckenberg, *History of Modern Philosophy.* Introduction.

seven

VEDĀNTA AND INDIAN PHILOSOPHY[1]

"आनौत वांतस्वघया तदेकम्, तस्माद्धान्यन्नपरः किच्चनास।।

Anitavacam Svadhaya tat ekam,
casmat ha anyat na parah kimehana Asa"

—*Rig Veda.*

(That one breathed breathlessly by itself,
other than it there nothing since has been).

Though there is a strong religious vein running through the six systems of philosophy, they belong to a phase of thought in which not only has the belief in the many Vedic Gods long been superseded by a belief in a Supreme Deity, but this phase also has been left behind to make room or a faith in a Supreme Power or in the Godhead, which has no same but Brahman or Sat, 'I am what I am.

Some of the systems of philosophy, though atheistic, are nevertheless treated as permissible doctrines, because they acknowledge the authority of the Vedas.

Atheism with Indian philosophers means something very different from what it means in the west. It means a denial of an active, busy, personal or humanised God only, who is called Ishwara the Lord. But behind him and above him, Hindu philosophers recognized a higher power, whether they called it Brahman or Paramatman or Purusha. It was the denial of that reality which constituted a Nastika, a real heretic, one who could say of this invisible, yet omnipresent Being, *Na Asti,* 'He is not.' Buddha therefore, as well as Brihaspati, the Charvaka, was a Nastika, while both the Yoga and the Sankhya, the former Sesvara, the other Anisvara, the one Theistic, the other Atheistic, could be recognized as Orthodox or Vedic.

The Hindus themselves are fully aware that some of their systems of philosophy stood higher than the others. Saṅkara looked upon the Vedanta as the best of all philosophies, provided he was allowed to interpret the sutras of Badarayana, according to the principles of his own unyielding Monism.

Badarayana called also Vyasa Dwaipayana or Krishna Dwaipayana is the reputed author of the Brahmasutras, called also Uttara Mimansa sutras or Vyasa sutras.

Vedanta is clearly the native philosophy of India. It is the only system of philosophy that can now be said to be living in India. In Vedanta philosophy human speculation seems to have reached its very acme. It is indeed the principal of all doctrines; any other doctrine is but a complement of it, and therefore it alone is to be reverenced by all, who wish for liberation and the according to the interpretation of the venerable Saṅkara.

The Vedanta philosophy, as interpreted by Saṅkara, if not the only true one, is still the best of all philosophies.

According to the Vedantist, who is a Monist, All that exists is taken as One, because if the existence of anything besides the absolute One or the Supreme Being were admitted, whatever the second by the side of the One might be, it would constitute a limit to what was postulated as limitless and would have made the concept of the One self-contradictory. But then came the question for Indian philosophers to solve, how it was possible, if there was but the One, that there should be multiplicity in the experience. They knew that the one absolute and undetermined essence, what they called

Brahman, could have received no impulse to change either from itself, for it was perfect, nor from others, for it was secondless.

Then, what is the philosopher to say to this manifold and ever-changing world? There is one thing only that he can say, namely, that it is not, cannot be real, but must be accepted as the result of nescience or Avidya, not only of individual ignorance, but of ignorance as inseparable from human nature. That ignorance, though unreal in the highest sense, exists, but it can be destroyed by Vidya, knowledge, *i.e.,* the knowledge conveyed by the Vedanta, and as nothing that can at any time be annihilated has a right to be considered as real it follows that this Cosmic ignorance also must be looked upon as not real, but temporary only. It cannot be said to exist, nor can it be said not to exist, just as our own ordinary ignorance, though we suffer from it for a time, can never claim absolute reality and perpetuity. It is impossible to define Avidya as little as it is possible to define Brahman, with this difference however, that the former can be annihilated, the latter never. The phenomenal world, which, according to the Vedanta, is called forth, like the mirage in a desert, has its reality in Brahman alone. Only it must be remembered that what we perceive can never be the absolute. Brahman, but a perverted picture only, just as the moon which we see manifold and tremulous in its ever changing reflections on the waving surface of the ocean, is not the real Moon, though deriving its phenomenal character from the real moon which remains unaffected in its unapproachable remoteness. Such is the Vedantic view of the Cosmos, which include ourselves quite as much as what we call the objective world.

The One Real Being is there, the Brahman; only it is not visible, nor perceptible in its true character by any of the senses, but without it, nothing that exists in our knowledge could exist, neither our Self, nor what is our knowledge is not our Self.

The fundamental doctrine of the Vedantins is that Brahman is true, the world is false, the Soul is Brahman and nothing else. We have another and still shorter abstract of the Vedanta in the words *Tattvam Asi*=Thou art that. The Tat is what we saw shadowed forth in the Upanishads as the Brahman, as the cause of the world, the Tvam is the Atman, the Self in its various meanings from the ordinary I to the divine Soul or Self, recognised in Man; and it is the highest aim of the Vedanta to show that these two are in reality one. This fearless synthesis, em-bodied in the simple words *Tat tvam Asi* seems to be the boldest and the truest synthesis in the whole history of philosophy. In the West, such a synthesis of the subjective with the objective Self would even now rouse the strongest theological, if not, philosophical protests, whereas the theologians of Indian discuss it with perfect equanimity, and see in it the truest solution of the riddle of the world. In order fully to understand it, we must try to place ourselves firmly on the standpoint of the vedanta philosophers forgetting all our own inherited theological misgivings. Their idea of the supreme cause of the Universe went far beyond what is meant by God, the creator and ruler of the world.

That being was to them a manifestation only of the supreme cause or Brahman, it was Brahman as phenomenal, and it followed that as Brahman, as they held, was indeed the cause of every thing, the All in All, man also could be nothing but a phenomenon of Brahman. The idea therefore that it would be blasphemy to make the creature equal to the creator so far as their substance was concerned, never presented itself to their minds. Their Tat was something behind above the purely personal Creator, it was the absolute divine essence, the God manifested in a subjective and personal Creator, and present likewise in all its phenomenal manifestations, including Gods and men. Even their God beyond all Gods did not satisfy them any longer; and though they might have shrunk from identifying Gods and men with that personal divine Being, Prajapati, the Lord of all Creation, they saw nothing but truth in the doctrine that man in his true nature was the same with Brahman, that he shares in the nature of Brahman, or in the spirit of God.

They saw in fact that God is hardly a name that can be used for that supreme Brahman, the absolute Cause of the Universe and the absolute Cause of Prajapati, also, when taken as the Creature God. This lifting up of the Tvam into the Tat means from the vedanta point of view real identity real recognition of the original divine nature of man, however much hidden and disfigured for a time by Avidya, or ignorance, and all its consequence. In the West unfortunately such questions can hardly be discussed in a calm philosophical spirit, because theology steps in and protests against them as irreligious and blasphemous. The teachers of the Vedanta, while striving to resuscitate in man the consciousness of the identity of the Tat, and the Tvam, and though indirectly of man and God, seem to be moving in the most serene atmosphere of thought and they work out these mighty problems with unfaltering love of truth and in an unimpassioned and truly philosophic spirit.

The fundamental doctrine of Saṅkara is that there is Brahman and nothing else. The individual Soul is no doubt Brahman for the simple reason that there is nothing but Brahman, but Brahman is not the individual soul, which in its present state is personal, that is, conditioned and phenomenal. All we may prelicate of that highest Brahman is that it is one, never changing, never in contact with anything, devoid of all from, eternally pure, intelligent and free.

Creation with Badarayana, would be nothing but the result Nescience, and yet Brahman is again and again represented as the cause of the world, and not only as the efficient, but as the material cause as well. It is easy to say that the created world is the effect, that Brahman is the cause. But the Vedantists have elaborated their own theory of cause and effect. According to them, cause and effect are really the same thing looked at from two points of view, and the effect is always supposed to be latent in the cause. Hence if Brahman is everything and nothing exists besides Brahman, the substance of the world can be nothing but Brahman. It would be therefore a quite legitimate inference to draw, that the universe with all its sins and miseries must have existed latent, in Brahman, just as steam existed latent in water before it was heated, though it does not become evident as vapour till fire is brought near to water.

The Vedantists stand for Karya-Karana-abheda, the non-difference or substantial identity of cause and effect. In the Vedanta, we read in so many words, *Tada nanyatvam,* that is, they cause and effect, are not other, are not different from each other. On this, as a general principle rests their dogma of the substantial identity of Brahman and the phenomenal world. Nor does Saṅkara support this principle by passages from the Veda only, but he appeals likewise to observation. He says –only when a cause exists, is an effect observed to exist, not when it does not exist. The non-difference of the two (cause and effect) is perceived, for instance, in an aggregate of threads, when we do not perceive the thing which we call cloth in addition to the threads, but merely threads running lengthways and crossways. In the threads again we perceive finer threads, and in these again still finer threads and so on. On this ground we conclude that the very finest parts which we can perceive are ultimately identical with their causes, *viz.,* red, white and black, these again with air, the air with ether, and at last, the ether with Brahman, which is without a second and the ultimate Cause of the whole world. Once again we look at a tree and ask what it is when we see through its leaves and fruits, its bark and wood, and ask again what it is, the answer comes that it would be nothing if it were not Brahman, that it lives through Brahman, that it exists through Brahman, that it would not be at all but for Brahman. Even so recent a poet as Tennyson is reported to have said, "Perhaps this earth and all that is in it –storms, mountains, cataracts, the Sun and the skies, are the Almighty in fact, such is our petty nature. We cannot see Him, but we see His shadow, as it were, a distorted shadow." Is not this pure Vedanta? Only that Vedantists hold that a cause by its very nature, can never become the object of perception, while what Tennyson calls the distorted shadow would come very near to the Avidya of Saṅkara. The Veda has declared that what is posterior in time, *i.e.,* the effect, has its being, previous to its actual beginning, in the nature of the cause; and Saṅkara adds that, even in cases where the continued existence of the cause (in the effect is not perceived, as, for instance, in the case of seeds of the fig-tree from which spring sprouts and new trees, the term birth, as applied to the sprout, means only that the causal substances, *viz.,* the seed becomes visible by becoming a sprout through the continued accretion of similar particles, while the term death means no more than that through the succession of these particles, the cause passes again beyond the sphere of visibility. According to the Karya-Karana-abheda (identity of cause and effect) no real effect would be possible without the continuance of its cause. Though different in appearance or phenomenally, both are the same substantially. An effect is not something newly produced or created, it is a new manifestation only, the cause being never destroyed but rendered invisible only. The doctrine that every effect pre-exists and is the effect of something real is called the Sat-Karya-Vāda, which is often illustrated by the very popular simile of the rope, which is mistaken for a snake, but which, even in its mistaken character, has the very real effect of frightening those who step into it. There is more in this often quoted simile that at first sight appears. It is meant to show that as the rope is to the snake, so Brahman is to the world. There is no idea of claiming for the rope a real change into a snake, and in the same way no real change can be claimed for Brahman, when perceived as the world.

Brahman presents itself as the world and apart from Brahman, the world would be simply nothing. If therefore Brahman is called the material cause of the world, this is not meant in the sense in which the clay is the material cause of a jar. Even the apparent and illusory existence of a material world requires a real substratum, which is Brahman, just as the appearance of the snake in the simile requires the real substratum of a rope. If we once see this clearly, we shall also see that Nescience may quite as well be called the material cause of the world as Brahman, the fact being that, strictly speaking, there is with the Vedantists no matter at all, in the Western sense of the word.

If must be clear to any one who has once mastered the framework of the true Vedanta-philosophy that there is really but little room in it for psychology or cosmology, nay even for Ethics. The soul and the world both belong to the realm of things which are not real, and have little, if anything, to do with the true Vedanta in its highest and truest form. This consists in the complete surrender of all we are and know. It rests chiefly on the tremendous synthesis of subject and object, the identification of cause and effect, of the I and the It. This constitutes the unique character of the Vedanta, unique as compared with every other philosophy of the world, which has not been influenced by it, directly or indirectly. If we have once grasped that synthesis, we know the Vedanta. All its other teaching naturally flows from this fundamental doctrine; and though its carefully thought out and worked out details are full of interest, contain no thoughts so entirely new at the time when they were uttered, as this identity of subject and object, or this complete absorption of the object by the subject.

To sum up, the Vedanta teaches that in the highest sense Creation is but self-forgetfulness, and Eternal Life, remembrance or self-consciousness. And while to us such high abstractions may seem useless for the many, it is all the more surprising that, with the Hindus, the fundamental ideas of the Vedanta have pervaded the whole of their literature, have leavened the whole of their language; and form to the present day, the common property of the people at large. No doubt, these ideas assume in the streets a different garment from what they mean among the learned in the Asramas or the forests of the country.

After all, it is not everybody who is called upon to take an active part, whether in defending or ruling a country, in amassing wealth, or in breaking stones; and for fitting men to lead contemplative and quiet lives, there is no better preparation than the Vedanta. They may be called useless by the busy and toiling portion of humanity: but if it is true that "those also serve who only stand and wait" then may we not hope that even the quiet in the land are not so entirely useless as they appear to be.

May, even among the learned, few stand up for the complete Adwaita or Monism as represented by Saṅkara!

"Brahman is both the material and the efficient cause of the Universe."—*Saṅkara.*

"Whatever is Material and whatever is Spiritual is the eternal essence, Brahman itself."—*Vallabha.*

To the sacred literature of the Brahmans in the strict sense of the term *i.e.,* to the Veda, there belongs a certain number of complementary works, without whose assistance the student is according to Hindu notions unable to do more than commit the sacred texts to memory. The task of taking a comprehensive view of the contents of the Vedic writings as a whole, of systematizing what they present in an unsystematical form, of showing the mutual co-ordination or subordination of single passages and sections and of reconciling contradictions—which, according to the view of the orthodox commentators, can be apparent only—is allotted to a separate sastra or body of doctrine which is termed the Mimamsa, *i.e.,* the investigation of enquiry, *viz.,* the enquiry into the connected meaning of the sacred texts.

Of this Mimamsa, the so-called earlier (purva) Mimamsa systematises the Karma-Kanda. The latter (uttara) Mimamsa deals with the Gnana Kanda of the Vedas *including Upanishads.* Its subject is not action, but knowledge, *viz.,* the knowledge of Brahman.

There exists a vast literature connected with the two branches of the Mimamsa. We have on the one hand, all those works which constitute the Purva Mimamsa-Sastra or as it is often shortly but no accurately termed the Mimamsa-Sastra—and on the other hand, all those works which are commonly comprised under the name Vedanta-Sastra. At the head of this extensive literature there stand the collections of Sutras, whose reputed authors are Jaimini and Badarayana.

Vedanta means the end of the Veda, whether we take it in the sense of the final portion or the final object of the Vedas. The Vedanta philosophy thus recognizes by its very name its dependence on the Veda and the oneness of Religion and Philosophy.

The Veda consists of three portions, the *Sankitas* or collections of metrical prayers and hymns of praise, the *Brahmanas* or prose treatises on the sacrifices and the *Aranyakas,* books intended for the dwellers in the forest, the most important portion of which is formed by the Upanishads. These Upanishads are philosophical treatises and their fundamental principle might seem to be subversive of all religion. In these Upanishads the whole ritual and sacrificial system of the Veda is not only ignored by directly rejected as useless, nay as mischievous. The ancient gods of the Veda are no longer recognized. And yet the Upanishads are looked upon as perfectly orthodox, nay as the highest consummation of Brahmatic Religion.

In the Upanishads not only are all sacrificial duties rejected, but the very gods to whom the ancient prayers of the Veda were addressed, are put aside to make room for the one supreme Being, called Brahman.

The same Upanishads had then to explain the true relation between that Brahman, the Supreme Being and the Soul of man. The soul of man was called Atman, literally the Self, also Jivatman, the living self; and after the substantial unity of the living or individual self with the Supreme Being or Brahman had been discovered, that Brahman was called the Highest Self or Paramatman. The word Atman asserts nothing beyond existence or self-existence.

The name Upanishad means estymological "sitting near a person" and these Upanishads may represent to us the outcome of "sittings" or "gatherings" which took place under the shelter of mighty trees in the forests where old sages and their disciples met together and poured out what they had gathered during days and nights spent in quiet solitude and meditation.

In India the forest near the village was like a happy retreat, cool and silent, with flowers and birds with bowers and huts. Think what their life must have been in these forests with few cares and fewer ambitions, what should they think and talk about, if not how they came to be when they were and what they were and what they would be hereafter.

Upanishads mean also "esoteric knowledge or esoteric doctrine," that knowledge which tears asunder the veil of ignorance and makes one realise and approach Brahman.

Religious thought in India began with a most natural faith in invisible powers or agents behind the startling drama of nature and ending with a belief in one great Power, the unknown or rather the unseen God. It was this treasure of ancient religious thought which the sages of the Upanishads inherited from their forefathers and we shall now see what use they made of it and how they discovered at last the true relation between the Divine or the Infinite as seen objectively in Nature and the Divine or the infinite as seen objectively in Nature and the Divine or the Infinite as perceived subjectively in the soul of man. We shall then understand how they erected on this ancient foundation what was at the same time the most sublime philosophy and the most satisfying religion, the Vedanta.

The most extraordinary feature of this Vedanta philosophy consists in its being an independent system of philosophy, yet entirely dependent on the Upanishads, a part of the Veda, nay, chiefly occupied with proving that all its doctrine to the very minutest points, are derived from the revealed doctrines of the Upanishads, if only properly understood, that they are in perfect harmony with revelation and there are no contradictions whatever between the various Upanishads themselves.

Speaking of the Upanishads, Scopenhauer says,:—"In the whole world, there is no study so beneficial and so elevating as that of the Upanishads. It has been the solace of my life, it will be the solace of my death."

Upanishads are the philosophical treatises which constitute the gnana-kanda the knowledge portion as opposed to the karma-kanda, the work or ceremonial portion of the Veda.

The principal Upanishads to which Saṅkara appeals in his great Commentary on the Vedanta Sutras are:—

(1) Chandogya. (2) Kena.
(3) Aitraeya. (4) Mandukya.
(5) Isa. (6) Katha.
(7) Mundaka. (8) Taitreyaka.
(9) Brihadaranyaka. (10) Swetasvatara.
(11) Prasna.

These eleven Upanishads of the four Vedas have sometimes been called the old and genuine Upanishads. They are the eleven classical Upanishads or the fundamental Upanishads of the Vedanta philosophy.

The unity of the infinite in man and the infinite in nature was not fully declared in the Sanhita portion of the Veda, but in the Upanishads. The Brahmmana portion of the Veda did not also go much further than the Mantra portion, for there also we do not find the absolute identity of the two so fully established as in the Aranyaka or the Upanishad portion. The Sanhita or Mantra portion of the Veda chiefly concerns itself with prayer and praise. The Brahmanas deal with rites and rituals.' But at the end of each Brahmana is an Aranyaka or a forest portion which is to be studied in the forest, after one fhas left his house and retired from active life. Attached to or sometimes included in these Aranyakas are the Upanishads.

Upanishads are many in number. From the 10 or 12 principal ones, we have now as many as 52, 108, 235 and according to some Hindu writers who assign an Upanishad to each Sakha of the Veda, as many as 1,180.

Even in ancient India, persons were known not to have been wanting, who denied the authority of the Upanishads, for we find Sutra of Jaimini, the author of the Purva Mimamsa, to the effect that as the purport of the Veda is action, those passages, whose purport is not action are purportless, meaning thereby that the Upanishads which purport to give information about an existing entity like Brahman are either purportless, or are subordinate to those texts of the Veda which deal with sacrificial action. The reply of Vyasa and his commentator Saṅkara, in the Brahma-sutras, was that the Veda has a meaning in so far only as it conduces to the highest end of man, *viz.,* freedom from samsara and unity with Brahman and that such passages of it as give information about existing entities like Brahman and point out the means for its attainment, instead of being purportless, serve the highest end of man.

The Upanishads are the final authority for all disputed

doctrines of the Vedanta and are appealed to by philosophers who hold such divergent views, as Saṅkara, the apostle of absolute Advaitism, Ramanuja, the teacher of Advaitism with a qualification and Madvacharya, the apostle of Dvaitism. Each of these finds texts in them to support his views, but it is absolute unity which alone finds the most support from these treatises.

Before closing this section, we shall briefly explain the scope of the six systems of Indian Philosophy.

(1) *Saṇkhya of Kapila.*—The creative force of the universe is Prakriti (nature) or Avyakta (the unmanifest) from which everything except purusha or spirit is evolved. The Purusha is a mere witness or spectator, but being linked with nature till his final release he believes himself to be an agent and enjoyer of the fruit of action. In reality it is the prakriti which binds herself by herself, though the purusha appears to be bound. When however, the latter realises that he is different from the Prakriti and its various modifications, that he is one thing and the Prakriti another, when he comes to know that I am not, nought is mine, nor do I exist, then his emancipation is complete. Prakriti then ceases to act and thenceforward there is no motive for its evolution. Sankhya denies the idea of a Supreme Deity (Iswara) and posits a plurality of souls. It stops short at tracing the origin of things to nature and finds no universal soul or atman behind.

(2) *Yoga of Patañjali*—is the sankhya with the addition of an Iswara or God, who is a particular soul untouched by distraction (Klesha), action (Karma), its fruit (Vepaka) and its resulting impression (Vasna). He is eternally omnimscient, the instructor of all, and unlimited by time.

(3) *Nyāya of Gautama*—believes in a personal creator and plurality of souls and holds that through the favor of God each soul works its own way to release. Eternal bliss in the form of complete cessation of pain is possible only

after a knowledge of truth.

(4) *Vaisesheka of Kanāda*—is a supplement of the Nyaya and its cardinal principle is that all material substances are aggregates of atoms, which are eternal in themselves, but not eternal as aggregates. These atoms are organised and are set in motion by a Personal God. The Sunimum Bonum is achieved by entire devoltion to God, when the series of miseries inherent in the soul is annihilated once and for all.

(5) *Purva Mimamsa of Jaimini*—is one of the two orthodox schools of philosophy which follow the Vedas. It is a school of ceremonial and interpretation and places the Summum Bonum in literally carrying out all Vedic injunctions. According to Saṅkara, it is atheistic and God is not deducible from it.

(6) *Uttara Mimamsa*—is the last school of philosophical thought which has largely influenced all subsequent religious and philosophical movements in India.

Foot Notes:

1. From Max Müller's "Six systems of Indian Philosophy." Speaking of the Hindus and the Hindu Philosophy, Max Muller says:—Hindu Philosophy is a long neglected mine of Philosophical thought. It is among real philosophers that I claim the place of honor for the representatives of Indian Philosophy. If hitherto non one would have called himself a philosopers who had not read and studied the works of Plato, and Aristotle, of Descartes and Spinoza, of Locke, Hume and Kant in the original, I hope that the time will come, when no one will claim that name who is not acquainted with the systems of ancient Indian philosophy the most prominent of which is the Vedanta. The place of Indian philosophic thinkers such as Badarayana, is by the side of the leading philosophers of Greece, Rome, Germany, France, Italy and England. Among the Hindus, all material interests are thrown into the shade. They form a society in which spiritual interests preduminate, a world of thinkers, a nation of philosophers.

   I am well aware that the view of the world, of God and of the son, as propounded by the Vedantists has often been declared strange and fanciful, and unworthy of the name of philosophy, at all events utterly unsuited to the west, whatever may have been its value in the East. But I maintain that Vedantism represents a phase of philosophic thought which no student of philosophy can afford to ignore, and which in no country can be studied to greater advantage than in India. I quite admit that as a popular philosophy, the Vedanta would have its dangers, that it would fail to call out and strengthen the manly qualities required for the practical side of life, and that it might raise the human mind to a height from which the most essential virtues of social and political life might dwindle away into mere phantoms. At the same time I make no secret that all my life I have been very fond of Vedanta. Nay, I can fully agree with schopenhauer, and quite understand what he meant when he said "In the whole world there is no study except that of the Upanishads, so beneficial and so elevating as that of the Upanishads. It has been the solace of my life, it will be the solace of my death."

Noets:—Besides Sankara's Monistic interpretation of the Vedanta-philosophy, there are other interpretations, which are not absolutely Monistic, or which are dualistic. Of one of such interpretations, namely that of Ramanuja, Max Muller says:—There are Schools of Vedanta who try to explain the Sutras of Badarayana in a far more human spirit. The best known is the School of Ramanuja. Ramanuja's commentary of Badarayana's Vedanta Sutras represents a more ancient and more faithful interpretation of Badarayana's Sutras while Sankara's philosophy in its unflinching Monism is his own, rather than Badarayana's. In India, instead of one Vedanta-philosophy, we have really two, springing from the same root, but extending its branches, in two very different directions that of Saṅkara being kept for unflinching reasoners. Who supported by an unwavering faith in Monism do not shrink from any of its consequences; another, that of Ramanuja, trying hard to reconcile their Monism with the demands of the human heart that required and always will require a personal God as the last cause of all that is, and an eternal Soul that yearns for as approach to or a re-union with that Being.

In treating of the Vedanta, I have generally followed the guidance of Saṅkara, as he seems to me to carry the Vedanta doctrine to the highest point, but I feel bound to say that Ramanuja is on many points the more faithful interpreter of the Vedanta-Sutras. Saṅkara is the more philosophical head, while Ramanjua has become the successful founder of one of the most popular religious sects, chiefly, it seems, because he did not carry the Vedanta to its last consequences, and because he managed to reconcile his more metaphysical speculations with the religious worship of certain popular deities. From a purely logical point of view, Sankara's position seems to be impregnable and when so rigorous a logician as Scopenhauer declares his complete submission to Sankara's arguments, there is no fear of their being upset by other logicians.

eight

DVAITISM OR DUALISM

The task that we proposed to ourselves in the preceding section becomes more difficult when we treat of the philosophy of Madhvacharya, for the general notion is that Advaitism and Dvaitism are quite opposed to each other. That there[1] is however a hope of reconciling the two systems of philosophy is clear from the following passage of Annie Besant:—

She says "The three sub-schools of the Vedanta would be regarded as successive steps[2] rather than as antagonistic theories; all assert the Divine Existence as the source of the Universe, but the Dwaita teaching alleges an internal division between God and Man, they remain eternally distinct. The Vishishtadwaita goes a step further asserting duality but merging it into a final unity. The Adwaita insists on the fundamental unity."

The following passages are from Professor Wilson's "Hindu Religions" a book published by the society for the resuscitation of Indian Literature, which speaking of the work approvingly says that in it, "Readers will find minute and faithful accounts of various systems and sects of the Hindu religion". "The essential dogma of this sect, like that of the Vaishnavas (Visishtad waitins) in general, is the identification of Vishnu with the Supreme Spirit, as the pre-existent cause of the universe, from whose substance the world was made. This primeval Vishnu they also affirmed to be endowed with real attributes, most excellent, although indefinable and independent. As there is one independent, however, there is also one independent, and this doctrine is the characteristic dogma of the sect, distinguishing its followers from the followers of Ramanuja as well as Saṅkara, or those who maintain the qualified or absolute unity of the deity. The creed of the Madhvas is Dwaita or duality. It is not, however, that they discriminate between the principles of good and evil or even the difference between spirit and matter, which is the duality known to other sects of the Hindus. Their distinction is of a more subtle character, and separates the Jivatma from the Paramatma, or the principle of life from the Supreme Being. Life, they say, is one and eternal, dependent upon the Supreme, and indissolutely connected with, but not the same with him. An important consequence of this doctrine is the denial of Moksha, in its more generally received sense, or that of absorption into the universal spirit and loss of independent existence after death. The Yoga of the Saivas, and Sayujyam of the Vaishnavas, they hold to be impracticable."

"The Supreme Being resides in Vaikuntha, invested with ineffiable splendour, and with garb, ornaments and perfumes of celestial origin, being the husband also of Lakshmi, or glory, Bhumi, the earth, and Nila, understood to mean Devi, or Durga or personified matter. In his primary form no known qualities can be predicted of him; but when he pleases to associate with Maya, which is properly his desire or wish, the three attributes of purity, passion, or ignorance, or the Sattwa, Rajas, and Tamasguna are manifested as Vishnu, Brahma and Siva, for the creation, protection, and destruction of the world. These deities again perform their respective functions through their union with the same delusive principle to which they owed their individual manifestation."

This account is clearly allegorical, although the want of some tangible objects of worship has converted the shadows into realities, and the allegory, when adapted to the apprehensions of ordinary intellect, has been converted into the legend of the supreme begetting the Hindu triad by Maya, and her subsequent union with her sons."

"It seems not improbable that the founder of the Madhwa sect was originally a Saiva priest, and although he became a convert to the Vaishnava faith, he encouraged an attempt to form a kind of compromise or alliance between the Saivas and Vaishnavas. Madhwa was first initiated into the faith of Siva at Ananteswar, the shrine of a Linga and one of his names Ananda Tirtha indicates his belonging to the class of Dasnami Gosains, who were instituted by Sankaracharya; one of his first acts was to establish a Salgram, a type of Vishnu, at the shrine of Subrahmanya, the warrior son of Siva, and as observed above, the images of Siva are allowed to partake, in the Madhwa temples of the worship offered to Vishnu.

The following passages are from "Dvaita Catechism[3] by P Srinavasa Rao and Col. Olcott:—

Q.—How can you hold that Jada and Jiva are different and separate from God, seeing that God is all-pervading, according to your own doctrine.

A.—It is quite true that god is all pervading, and that there is nothing in which God is not. God is *united* with everything else, but is not the *same* with everything else.

Q.—How can that be? Whatever is united can be disunited. Can Jiva be dissociated from God?

A.—No, you must understand that there are two kinds of unions. One union is of that kind which exists between an individual and his garment. This union has had a beginning and can be brought to an end, at any time, without destroying the nature of the individual or the garment. This is not the sort of union, that exists between God and Jiva. Their union is insperable, like that which exists between the tree and the sap; a connection which has existed always; which was not brought about at any intermediate period, and which can never cease, without destroying the nature of the tree. Thus there is no absolute unity of God and Jiva; but there is a conjunction. The conjunction between them is indissoluble but they are not the same. They are in union, but not one.

Q. How do you reconcile this with those passages in the Sashtras which favour the doctrine of absolute non-duality.

A. The Sashtras which profess to teach non-duality do not mean one absolutely, but two in one. If you closely analyse the examples given in the books in respect of the relation of God to Jiva such as, tree and sap, man and energy, water and salt, and so on, you will clearly see that there is no absolute unity; but that there is an indissoluble union of two in one. It is in this sense that the Sashtras proclaim the non-duality.

Q. If God is void of qualities of Prakriti (matter) how did He create mankind and the universe?

A. The word creation is a misnomer. God did not create anything, that is, He did not bring into existence anything that was not already existing. God evolved the whole universe, including man, out of the existing materials. We do not believe that something can come or be made, out of nothing.

Q. If so, there must have been something co-eternal with God?

A. Yes, we hold that Jada (matter) and Jiva (individual soul) and some others are co-eternal with Paramatma (supreme soul); but that they are subordinate to Paramatma in every respect.

Q. Then how do you say that God is the Cause of the universe?

A. Listen ! That which is generally known as the cause is two fold. Take the common example of the goldsmith making a bracelet with gold. Here the bracelet is the effect, while the gold and the goldsmith constitute the double cause. That gold which forms the matter of the jewel, is called the material cause (Upadana-Karana) and the goldsmith, who, like an instrument, works on gold, is called the instrumental cause (Nimitta Karana) for He does not create gold but only acts upon the already existing gold. Now applying this illustration to the universe you will find that the manufacture of the universe is like wise an effect and must have two causes also. The Jada-Prakriti, which furnished the matter is the material cause and God, who in the form of Purusha, entered Jada-Prakriti as it were and agitated it—thereby giving rise to various forms of visible creation—is the instrumental or efficient cause. But as Jada-Prakriti is incapable of evolving the universe without the help of the agitating Principle, God, the latter is recognized as the cause, the supreme cause, of the universe.

Q. When did creation take place?

A. At the beginning of each Brahma-kalpa, all that had till then remained in a dormant condition is evolved and manifested, and at the end of each Brahma-kalpa, they are all merged into the unmanifested condition, to be re-manifested at the beginning of the next Brahma-kalpa. The evolution, dissolution and re-evolution proceed alternately in determinate succession. They have had no beginning, and will have no end. Innumerable Brahma-kalpas have passed away, and innumerable ones must come after such is the wonderful revolution of the wheel of Time.

We cannot close the article better than in the words of the author of: "God, the Universe and the Hindu Trinity," a work published under the auspices of the Theosophical Publishing Company:—

"It is only when we enter into the question whether Purusha and Prakriti are principles like Brahma or the ephemeral aspects of the non-dual principle that there arises "the apple of discord" between the different religious sects of Southern India. When pralaya sets in, are these two merged into the bosom of Parabrahm as one or do they yet preserve a distinct individuality of their own? The Adwaitins contend that there is a Sayujjya or Laya state when nought else is, but the one Principle. They say that this universe of dualities is merged as one into its noumenon of Parabrahm and that it is not real, since it ever changes name and form. Dwaitins contend that the two principles, Purusha and Prakriti are as real as Parabrahm and are co-eternal with it. But Vishistadvaitins take a middling course. According to the illustration given by H.P. Blavatsky shall we take Oxygen and Hydrogen; when they combine together as water to be yet existing as two in the state of solution or as one. Water can be said to be one in its liquid condition or *in esse* but to be two *in posse,* since it can again be decomposed into two. This is merely a metaphysical difficulty which it is not worth our while to be ever fighting about, as the three sects in Southern India are always doing. Even these difficulties can be set at rest by holding that they are only different stand points from which each observer looks at the question while they tend towards the same end. They present but the three aspects of the one truth, wherein the universe is first in its latent state, secondly, in that transition stage when the latent becomes patent and thirdly in its patent state."[4]

In the words of a Sankrit writer accepted by the Hindus.

Ekam Tatvam Surayaha
Tatvathrayamathi Rishayaha
Tatvattrayamathi Acharyaha.[5]

Foot Notes:

1. This Theosophical reconciliation is not accepted by the orthodox Hindus who say that the three schools of philosophy are not reconciliable.

2. It is curious to note that Saṅkara the founder of Advaita, was born first (in 799 according to the best authorities). Ramanuja, the founder of Visishtradvaitism next and Madhwa at the founder of Dvaitism last.

3. The authors say in the Preface:—"In this work the gist of the Dwaita Sidhanta as taught by Sriman Madvachariar and as we learn from other works left by himself and his followers and others is given—The book in not to be regarded as explaining their personal beliefs. When setting forth the tenets of any particular sect, they write as would one of its own votaries; for the research of truth can never be promoted by resort to interested misrepresentation". The book is certified too as approved by some pandits of the Madhwa sects.

4. This theosophical explanation is not accepted by the Orthodox Hindus.

5. Meaning:—All is one according to God. They are two according to Rishis. They are three according to Acharyas.

nine

ADVAITIC VEDĀNTISM OR INDIAN MONISM

What in Sankara's opinion the Upanishads teach, is shortly as follows:—

> Whatever is, is in reality one; there truly exists only one universal Being called Brahman or Paramatman, the highest self. This being is of an absolutely homogeneous nature,[1] it is pure Being, or which comes to the same, pure intelligence or thought (chaitanya, jñāna). Intelligence or thought is not to be predicated of Brahman is not a thinking Being, but thought itself. It is absolutely destitute of qualities; whatever qualities or attributes are conceivable, can only be denied of it. But if nothing exists but one absolutely simple Being, whence the appearance of the world by which we ourselves exists as individual beings?— Brahman, the anser runs, is associated with a certain power called Maya[2] or avidya to which the appearance of this entire world is due. This power cannot be called Being (sat) for Being is only Brahman; nor can it be called non-being (asat) in the strict sense, for it at any rate produces the appearance of this world. It is in fact a principle of illusion; the undefinable cause owing to which there seems to exist a material world comprehending distinct individual existences. Being associated with this principle of illusion. Brahman is enabled to project the appearance of the world, in the same way as a magician

is enabled by his incomprehensible magical power to produce illusory appearance of animate or inanimate beings. Maya thus constitutes the Upadana, the material cause of the world; or if we wish to call attention to the circumstance that Maya belongs to Brahman as a Sakti—we may say that the material cause of the world is Brahman in so far as it is associated with Maya. In this latter quality Brahman is more properly called Isvara, the Lord.

Maya, under the guidance of the Lord, modifies itself by a progressive evolution into all the individual existences (bheda), distinguished by speçial names and forms, of which the world consists; from it there spring in due succession the different material elements and the whole bodily apparatus belonging to sentient beings. In all these apparently individual forms of existence, the one indivisible Brahman is present, but, owing to the particular adjuncts into which Maya has specialised itself, it appears to be broken up—it is broken up, as it were—into a multiplicity of intellectual or sentient principles, the so-called Jivas (individuals or personal souls). What is real in each Jiva is only the universal Brahman itself; the whole aggregate of individualizing bodily organs and mental functions, which in our ordinary experience separate and distinguish one Jiva from another in the offspring of Maya and as such unreal.

The phenomenal world or world of ordinary experience (Vyavahara) thus consists of a number of individual souls, engaged in specific cognitions, volitions and so on and of the external material objects with which those cognitions and volitions are concerned. Neither the specific cognitions nor their objects are real in the true sense of the word. For both are altogether due to Maya. But at the same time, we have to reject the idealist doctrine of certain Baudha Schools, according to which nothing whatever truly exists, but certain trains of cognitional acts or ideas to which no external objects correspond, for external objects, although not real in the strict sense of the word, enjoy at any rate as much reality as the specific cognitional acts whose objects they are.

The Non-enlightened soul is unable to look through and beyond Maya which, like a veil, hides from it its true nature. Instead of recognizing itself to be Brahman, it blindly identifies itself with its adjunct (upadhi), the fictitious offspring of Maya, and thus looks for its true self in the body, the sense organs and the internal organ (manas) *i.e.,* the organ of specific cognition. The soul, which, in reality, is pure intelligence, non-active, infinite. Thus becomes limited in extent, as it were, limited in knowledge and power, an agent and enjoyer. Through its actions it burdens itself with merit and demerit, the consequences of which it has to bear or enjoy in series of future embodied existences, the Lord, as a retributor and dispensor, allotting to each soul that form of embodiment to which it is entitled by its previous actions. At the end of each of the great world periods, called Kalpas, the Lord retracts the whole world, *i.e.,* the whole material world is dissolved and merged into non-distinct Maya while the individual souls, free for the time from actual connexion with upadhis, lie in deep slumber as it were. But as the consequences of their former deeds are not yet exhausted, they have again to enter on embodied existence, as soon as the Lord sends forth a new material world, and the old round of birth, action, death begins anew to last to all eternity, as it has lasted from all eternity.

The means of escaping from this endless Samsara, the way out of which can never be found by the non-enlightened soul, are furnished by the Veda. The Karmakanda indeed, whose purport it is to enjoin certain actions, cannot lead to final release, for even the most meritorious works necessarily lead to new forms of embodied existence. And in the Gnanakanda of the Veda also two different

> parts have to be distinguished, *viz.,* firstly, those chapters and passages which treat of Brahman in so far as related to the world and hence characterized by various attributes, *i.e.* of Isvara or the Lower Brahman, and secondly, those tests which set forth the nature of the highest Brahman transcending all qualities and the fundamental identity of the individual soul with that highest Brahman. Devout meditation on Brahman as suggested by passages of the former kind does not directly lead to final emencipation; the pious worshipper passes on his death into the world of the lower Brahman only, where he continues to exist as a distinct individual soul—although in the enjoyment of great power and knowledge, until at last he reaches the highest knowledge and through it, final release.
>
> That student of the Veda, on the other hand, whose soul has been enlightened by the texts embodying the higher knowledge of Brahman, whom passages such as the great saying: "That art thou" have taught that there is no difference between his true self and the highest self, obtains at the moment of death immediate final release, *i.e.,* withdraws altogether from the influence of Maya, and asserts himself in his true nature, which is nothing else but the absolute highest Brahman.

The following remarks on Saṅkara Vedānta will be of interest:—

> Saṅkara Vedānta, (though a "less faithful interpretation of the Vedānta Sutras") is more capable of amalgamating heterogeneous material than other systems and its fundamental doctrines are in greater harmony with the essential teaching of the Upanishads than those of other Vedanta systems.

The philosophy of Saṅkara stands on the whole nearer to the teaching of the Upanishads than the Sutras of Badarayana. Saṅkara Vedanta marks a strictly orthodox reaction against all combinations of non-Vedic elements of belief and doctrine with the teaching of the Upanishads. But, although this form of doctrine has ever since Sankara's time been the one most generally accepted by Brahman students of philosophy, it has never had any wide reaching influence on the masses of India. It is too little in sympathy with the wants of the human heart, which, after all are not so very different in India from what they are elsewhere. Comparatively few even in India are those who rejoice in the idea of a universal non-personal essence in which their own individuality is to be merged and lost for ever, who think it sweet "to be wrecked on the ocean of the Infinite." The only forms of Vedanta which are and can at any time have been really popular are those in which the Brahman of the Upanishads has somehow transformed itself into a Being, between which and the devotee there can exist a personal relation, love and faith on the part of man, Justice, tempered by mercy, on the part of the divinity.

We shall close this section with a few remarks on the Metaphors and similes used in Vedanta philosophy:—

> In the earliest period of Philosophic thought, they were satisfied with prophetic visions and these were often expressed in pregnant Metaphors only. The phenomenal world was to them like the mirage of the desert, visible, but unreal, exciting thirst, but never quenching it. The terror of the world was like the fright occasioned by what seemed a snake in the dark, but in the light of day or of truth, proved to be a rope only. If asked why the Infinite should be perceived by us as qualified, they answered, Look at the air in the Sky, it is not blue. Yet we cannot help seeing it as blue. If asked how the one Infinite being, the one without a second, could appear as many in this world, they said 'Look at the waves of the sea and the ripples in the rivers and the lakes; in every one there is the sun reflected a thousandfold—yet, we know that there is but one sun, though our eyes cannot bear its great glory and its dazzling light.

Saṅkara however guards carefully against the abuse of Meta-phorical illustration. An illustrative simile, he says, very truly, is meant to illustrate one point only, not all. Otherwise, it would not be a simile. He goes on to remark that the comparison of Brahman or the highest self, as reflected in the variety of this universe, with the sun or moon, as reflected in the water may seem not quite admissible, because the sun has a certain form and comes in contact with the water, which is different from it and at a distance from it. Here we can understand that there should be an image of the sun in the water. But the Atman or the Highest self has no form and as it is present everywhere and all is identical with it, there are no limiting conditions different from it. But he continues, if therefore fit should be objected that the two instances are not parallel, we answer:—

> The parallel instance (of the sun's reflection in the water) holds good, since *one* common feature with reference to which alone the comparison is instituted-does exist; whenever two things are compared, they are thought to have in common. Entire equality between two things can never be demonstrated. Indeed if it could be there will be an end of that particular relation which gives rise to a comparison. He then adds that the special feature on the which the comparison rests is only the participation in the increase and decrease. What he means is that the reflected image of the sun expands, when the surface of the water expands and contracts when the water contracts; that is trembles when the water trembles, and divides when the water is divided. It thus participates in all the attributes and conditions of the water, while the real sun remains all the time the same. Similarly the Brahman the Supreme Being, although in reality uniform and never-changing, participates as it were, in the attributes and states of the body and the other limiting conditions or Upadhies, within which it

abides; it grow with them as it were, decreases with them as it were, and so on.

This will show that however poetical and sometimes chaotic the language of the Upanishads may be, Saṅkara, the author of the great commentray on the Vedanta Sutras, knows how to reason accurately and logically and would be able to hold his own against any oppenent, whether Indian or Europeon.

There is another will-known simile in the Upanishads intended to illustrate the doctrine, that *Brahman is both the Material and the efficient cause of the world,* that the world is made not only by God, but also of God. How can that be? The pupil, asks and his teacher answers! "Look at the spider, who with the utmost intelligence draws the threads of its wonderful net out of its own body." What he meant was of course no more than an illustration that should help his pupil to understand what was meant by Brahman being at the same time the material and the efficient cause of the web of the created world.

Comparisons are dangerous things, unless they are used cautiously, and though the Upanishads abound with poetical metaphors, we see that no one could have availed himself of these philosophical similes with greater caution than Saṅkara, the author of the classical work on the Vedanta philosophy.

Foot Notes:

1. Sri Ramakrishna Paramahamsa says:—"As the shell, the pith, the kernel and the seed of a fruit are all produced from one seed, one cause, so from one God, is produced the whole creation of animate and inanimate, spiritual and material objects.
2. Saṅkara's doctrine of Maya is the most misunderstood. Saṅkara only says that the universe is not as eternal as the Brahman and not real apart from Brahman, the one Absolute Reality. He is generally misunderstood as denying the universe altogether. Many think that when Saṅkara calls the universe Maya, he denies the reality of the world. They interpret Maya to mean illusion, a non-existent something, which appears as existence. But Saṅkara means by calling the universe Maya that the knowledge of it is an obstacle to the realisation of Brahman or the self. Maya is that which prevents the realisation of Atma by itself. Let us take for example the oft-quoted illustration of the serpent in the rope. What he means thereby is that as the knowledge of the serpent in the rope (unrealised) is an obstacle to the realisation of it, so is the knowledge of the universe an impediment to the realisation of Atma. He does not say anything more about the universe. He does not say that the universe is false or an illusion. He means simply that the knowledge of it must be got, rid of for the attainment of the goal. And in this sense and this only, does he call the world Maya. This doctrine of the Advaitins when paraphrased into the philosophical language of the west would run thus:—The absolute alone exists and mind and matter are its periodical manifestations (*Theosophic Thinker*). Of Maya, Max Muller says:—"According to the Advaitin, All that exists is taken as one, because if the existence of anything besides the Absolute one or the Supreme Being were admitted, whatever the second by the side of the one might be it would constitute a limit to that which was postulated as limitless and would have made the concept of the one self contradictory. But then came the question for Indian philosophers to solve, now it was possible, if there was but the one, that there should be multiplicity in the world and that there should

be constant change in our experience. Then, what is the philosopher to say to this manifold and ever-changing world? There is one thing only that he can say namely that it is not, cannot be real, but must be accepted as the result of nescience or Avidya not only of individual ignorance, but of ignorance as inseparable from human nature. That ignorance, though unreal in the highest sense, exists, but it can be destroyed by Vidya, knowledge, *i.e.,* the knowledge conveyed by the Vedanta and as nothing that can at any time be annihilated has a right to be considered as real it follows that this cosmic ignorance also must be looked upon as not real, but temporary only. It cannot be said to exist, nor can it be said not to exist, just as our own ordinary ignorance though we suffer from it for a time, can never claim absolute reality and perpetuity. The phenomenal world which, according to the Advaitin is called forth like the mirage in a desert, has its reality in Brahman alone. Only it must be remembered that what we perceive can never be the absolute Brahman, but a perverted picture only, just as the moon which we see manifold and tremulous in its ever-changing reflections on the wavering surface of the ocean, is not the real Moon, though deriving its phenomenal character from the real Moon which remains unaffected in its unapproachable remoteness". *Swami Abhedananda* says that the Vedanta does not teach that the whole visible universe is an illusion, as some people misunderstand the spirit of this philosophy through not knowing the real meaning of Maya. Its true meaning is relative, conditional or phenomenal existence and not illusion. Speaking of Maya, Blavatsky says:— 'We see in the universe the only universal and eternal reality casting a periodical reflection of itself on the infinite spetial depths. This reflection which you regard as the objective material universe, we consider as a temporary illusion, and nothing else. That alone which is eternal is real. You and I too are illusions, we are illusions as flirting personalities, to day one person, tomorrow another we are. Would you call the sudden flashes of the Aurora Borealis, the Northern Lights, a Reality, though it is as real as can be, while you look at it. Certainly not. It is the cause that produces it, if permanent and eternal which is the only reality, while the other is but a passing illusion of Maya. Annie Besant F. T. S. says:—"Mays is illusion, all that is changing, transitory, in contrast to the permanent Reality, the one Life. Therefore it is the root of matter, matter being that which takes form and adapts itself to the impulses of the life it clothes. Avidya, absence of knowledge, is another name for it." With reference to Maya, Sri Ramakrishna Paramahamsa says:—"The relation between the Maya and the Brahman is that between the snake in motion and the snake at rest. The force that is kinetic is the Maya and the force that is potential is the Brahman. As the water of the ocean is at one time calm and at another time agitated into waves so are the Brahman and Maya. The ocean in its tranquillity is the Brahman and in its waves is the Maya."

This view of Saṅkara about Maya is criticized by Vallabhacharya, the founder of shuddadwitism or Pure Monism, whose fundamental tenet is "All the material and the spiritual is Brahman. Brahman is real and eternal and its form is the phenomenal seen about us. All that exists is Brahman and matter is intelligence as transformed. *Whatever is Material and whatever is Spiritual is the eternal essence—Brahman itself*" (Cf. "*Brahman is both the material and the efficient cause of the world" Vedanta Sutras of Saṅkara*). In the words of the author of "Hinduism, Ancient and Modem" (an Advaitic Vedantic) "The old question of how and why the Absolute becomes the relative can scarcely be said to have been solved either by Saṅkara or Vallabhacharya or by any other Vedantin and we must for ever remain ignorant of how and why the unchangeable Absolute became changed into the relative and the conditioned."

ten

VISISHTADWAITISM OR QUALIFIED DWAITISM OR MONISM

In conclusion we propose to see if the forms of Vedanta other than Adwaitism, *i.e.*, vishisthtadwairism and Dwaitism can be reconciled with Science, as Adwaitism or Hindu Monism was attempted to be reconciled in the preceding articles. From the very etymology of the word Visishtadaitism it will appear that Vishist adwaitins are those who reconcile Monism and Dualism in India. That this is so evident from the following passages taken from a pamphlet entitled "Life and Teachings of Ramanuja or Spirit of Vishishtadwaitism"" published by a Vashnavite scholar.

Like every other system of philosophy outer (Visishtadwaitism) has an outer veil. It is necessary to remove it before we can learn to appreciate its contents. The doctrine of dualism may be repugnant to the students of Monism in as much as it teaches us the separateness of jivatma from Paramatma. But we assure our readers that a careful consideration of our (Visishtadwatic) philosophy is what is required to arrive at conclusion consonant to occult theories. Saṅkara and Ramanuja start from different points in the same line and work in the same direction to reach the same goal. Visishtadwaities never affirm that Jivatma differes from Paramatma in essence.

Occult doctrine teaches that the light of logos is differentiated into separate human monads and egos during the process of evolution, and this is the point from which Ramanuja proceeds to prove that human monads are infinite in number, co-eternal and co-existent with Parabrahman.

Exoteric Budhism has done no particular good to India. But we have the highest veneration of Buddha or his esoteric philosophy, because he is one with Ramanuja in all important questions affecting the spiritual welfare of human monad.

The description of the person of Parama Prurush and Vaikunta the alleged abode of the Supreme spirit given in Visishtadwaita literature is so far enshrouded by mysticism that by interpretation we may attempt to impose upon it will only lead to scientifically absurd and extraordinary ideas of divinity.

Ramanuja mastered the occult interpretation of our ancient epic, Ramayana, and he clearly understood that all vedas, Upanishad, Smrutis, Itihasas, Puranasand Tantras had their own esoteric interpretation. He clearly saw that sound, scientific philosophical Theism lay behind the veils of Hindu Mythology and that Aryan symbolical worship had a scientific foundation.

The Vedandha Sangraha is a philosophical dissertation of Ramanuja which appears to be reconciliation between Vedantic and Puranic literature.

In the Puranas a great deal of irrelevant matter was purposely introduced into the midst of esoteric doctrine containing lofty spiritual teaching, with a view to test the discerning powers of the student who must get into the intelligent way of separating husk from grain. Portions of our puranas are highly philosophical while others deplorably nonsensical.

The samhita portions of the Rig and Yajur Vedas convey double meaning. Outwardly they speak of certain sacrifices, their modus operandi, and various other minute details that bear upon the apparatus used during Vedic sacrifices and the construction of sheds and altars wherein sacrifices are offered to celestial gods. Moreover, they contain invocations to the five elements and numerous celestial gods and prescribe different sacrifices to gods by men who desire different things.. Esoterically interpreted, they are no more than a continued discourse on divine matters such as theories of Cosmogony, Universal Evolution and Dissolution, the origin of man, his future destiny, nature of god-head, &c.

Taitreya Upanishad declares the Supreme Being thus' "He from whom, these animate and inanimate existence emanate, and in whom they live and have their being and to whom they finally return, is the Lord of the Universe" Ramanuja in his gloss adds that god is both the efficient and the Material Cause of the Universe as the Veda declares that "god creates and destroys this Universe as a spider creates and absorbs his web." With Ramanuja the cause of Universe and the Universe (effect) are identical. He lays down that the Universal soul in whom matter and animal souls are inherent is the cause and the universe a development of matter, is the effect.

The figure of personification is so profusely used in our religious literature,, that it, instead of giving a concrete shape to an abstract essence, and presenting a vivid image to the eyes of uninitiated, creates an infinite number of distinct personalities or individualised divine existences about the person or form or anything that really exists, of the one unattainable Principle with reference to the infinite spiritual forces, of which the eternal reality is a conglomeration. The study of the infinite forces, that spring up from this common center with their essence and nature was the great pains in analysing the nature of the forces, and appropriately personifying and naming them.

This is a subject very difficult in its nature and very little understood by people who have not probed to the bottom of our ancient arcane science. An adequate discussion of the personality attributed to prabharahman in our philosophy, a clear explanation of the three wives that adorn the divine personality, an attempt to let our readers know what arcane science claims to know of divine weapons and divine ornaments and of Nitya Suris (angles that move about and have their being in Para Brahman) will not only take us to the root of all occult science, but also launch us on the still unexplored shore of mystic thought.

"The logos (Srinivas or the abode of celestial light who possess a transcendental form of which even the highest initiates cannot form an adequate conception and which is composed of panchopanishads) is encircled by five outer lines. This forms the first circumference that encircles the logos. Laskhmi and others form the second circumrferential line or boundary. The there lokas form the third and the five weapons of the Deity, the fourth outer-line by which the logos is encircled. It is the essence that exists within these four circumferential lines that is called Parabrahman. None other".

The Upnishad and the above sloka are clue to the mystic doctrine of Visisthadwaities.

The logos has no form in partiuclar, but assumes one to become a fit obeject for the contemplation of the spiritually minded.

This is the essence of Ramanuja's philosophical teaching. We now purpose to explain his popular teaching.

Ramanuja permits his men to perform Pancgnaratragama rites, if they choose, and enjoy the fruits of such performances in the hope that they will be incentive to their further spiritual exertion. But it shall clearly be understood that, with Ramanuja performance of ceremonies and rites is more optional than compulsory

When Srivashnavas or devotees are seated in the presence of the Idol, they must repeat the Dwayam and prostrate themseleves before the Idol. Dwayam is a mystic formula taught in the Kathavath Upanishad. It treats of the unity of Universl Material and Spiritul principles of active and passive sides of Universal energy.

Every one of us capable of destroying the inexplicable system of our symbolical worship, but not one of us can pretend to explain the symbolism to the satisfaction of the Savantas of the Modern world. Ramanuja was an initiate like Sankaracharya and was well versed in the science of symbolical worship taught in Panchartragama and was a staunch believer in the oneness of God. He knew why the highest religious authories of the land, our Rishis, upheld the system of symbolical worship long before vyasa wrote his Vedanta Sutra and long before parasara made an attempt in the Vishnu Puran to throw light on the mystic form of the deity, its ornaments and weapons.

"Oh God! Wise men declare that your disc indicates,mind, sword knowledge, scabbard ignorance, your garland Vaijayanti the five elemtns, your conch egotism, your bow egotism your arrows the ten senses, your diamond Kaustabha the sentient soul, your mark of identification, *i.e.*, Srivatsa indicates indiscrete matter and your club, the developed matter"—Vishnu Purana

The symbolism is explained away as follows:—

The crown of the Idol represents that God is the king of kings and cause of causes

The four hands of the Deity show his omnipotence. The three eyes of the Deity indicate his omniscience.

The Weapons of the Deity show God's readiness in the protection of his creatures

The ornaments of the same tell us that he is above all wants.

Its fixed position in a fixed place shows God's determination not to leave us till the lost one of us was saved. The assuming hand of the Idol assures us, poor sinners, that we need not care for temporal mishaps, and that we would be saved.

The features of the Idol indicate God's solicitude for the welfare of his devotees. Moreover Parasara reveals to us, that weapons and ornaments with which "Pancharatragama' decorates its parama purusha indicate the twenty four tatwas.

God is an embodiment of infinite moral attributes, and the 108 Vedic Idols we see fixed in India are in themselves embodiments of a few of divine attributes individually. Esoteric doctrine teaches that the number of Idols (set up by Rishis) was regulated by the number of Upanishads and Pancharatna occult divine energy, stand for 108 Brahman Vidyas taught in the upnishads.

It must therefore be understood that pancharatragama form of Idol worship, encouraged by the Visishtadwaitic adepts, had a scientific basis to stand upon, although its exponents are scarcely to be found now-a-days.

A scientific image of God bears the same relation to God as the word God itself bears to God. Words are the vehicles for the conveyance of ideas, so also images.

As to the objection that our worship is simply become mechanical, we must affirm that it was not the purpose of our sages that our form of worship should become mechanical. Flowers of nature are not acceptable to the all-pervading Being. A devotee must possess eight flowers to worship his eternal Father with. The flowers are 1. Tolerance 2. Control over senses 3. Philanthropy 4. Forbearance 5. Knowledge 6. Devotion 7. Contemplation and 8. Truthfullness.

As to the practice of drinking water in which the feet of devotees are washed (Sripathathirthum), the magnetic aura of an adept is very pure. The occult process of washing the feet, infuses the adept's pure magnetism into water, and this magnetised waster is belived to do goods to chelas both physically and psychically.

Ramanuja holds that we should not worship idols, where such worship cannot be literally understood and appreciated and this indisputability and conclusively show, that, if we could put our faith in the sayings and doings of such a saint as Ramanuja, there is a higher philosophy in the Idol-worship of our Vaishnava temples, for which he manfully stood as an advocate, than is know to us, men of poor and limited understanding.

The generality of our community do not think of the existence of Esoteric doctrine in our Sanskrit and Dravidian literature although our Purvacharayas threw out nuemerous hints in their words that such a doctrine exists and wrote elaborate commentaries called "swapdesa Vyakhyanams" on many sanskrit and Dravidian works.

Pillalokachariyar who lived the life of an ascetic exclamied in distinct and loud tones in the third chapter of Tatwatraya that we know absolutely nothing of incarnationas of the Deity of which Sri Vishnu and other Puranas speak. He says " The incarnatiuon of Upendra, Thrivikrama, Dadhibhakta, Hayagriva, Nara, Narayana, Hari, Krishna, Mathsaya, Kurma, Varaha and others are mysterious and beyond comprehension. Their arms, weapons bodily colour, actions and places of abode are equally mysterious and above comprehension. We do not therefore reveal our knowledge concerning them" This is a serious and important passage for reflection. Hear what one of our old sages says: He denounces the exoteric interpretaion of our Puranas, which treat of Divine Incarnations are above the apprehension of men of limited faculties. He declares that when Chapter X of Sri Bhagavatha says that Krishna was born with four arms, we should not give credence to the saying Sri Vishnu Purana, that Krishna carred Sankha Chakra etc.., wherever he went. He dissuades us from believing that Krishna was black in physical appearance and committed theft and adultery and lastly he assures us that how he was born, effected his union with Gopis and played on his flute is not understood. He teaches us the other incarnations of Deity like that of Krishna, do not possess either the physical appearances or the moral attributes, which our Puranas allegorically imputed to them. He with a large heart and noble philanthropy, feeling that our Puranas written in mystical language, did Humanity more harm than good, exploded the exoteric theories and plainly informed us in unmistakable and unambiguous terms, that there was a higher philosophy in the arms, weapons physical appearances, actions and places of abode which puranas ascribe to divine incarnations, than in vouchsafed to us. He happily tells us that he has purposely withheld this knowledge of the mustery of the Divine. Incarnations for the two reasons that men are gereally wanting in intellectual capacity to understand the mystery and moral aptitutde to received the Secrete Doctrine. He purposely wrote the passage under comment for the combined purpose of the vindication of the doctrine of Divine Incarnations and the creation of an impression on the popular mind as to the existence of knowledge worth striving for in our puranic literature. If Pillalokacharyar, the like of whom never adorned the southern India, were incorrect in this remarks about incarnations and if our historical allegories have no hidden meanings, our religious system is not worth having even for a day. The sooner it is done away with, the better. It cannot but be an admitted fact that our conception of Krishna is not consistent with our notion of Deity. Nor is Krishna's life (as it is interpreted) consistent with his teaching, which enjoins purity of thought and purity of deed on men and the admission of such sages as Vyasa, Bhishma, Udhistira and Vidura who looked upon him as an incarnation of God and surrendered their souls to him. Such venerable personage as vedantachariya, with unbounded knowledge of Divine matters, would not have been foolish to look up to Krishna for the salvation of their souls and offered their life-long homage to him in the firm conviction that Krishna's flute and his crown of peacock feathers would present themselves to their inner visions when their earthy lives about to close. It remains to be seen whether Krishna is man or god in human form, Let us assume that Krishna is man and try to explain the incidents connected with his life, granting that they are facts. It is stated that Krishna was present in the houses of sixteen thousand gopies at one and the same time. This accomplishment, so long as it is attributed to man is not a physical possibility. It is clear absurdity, which any amount of sophistry cannot satisfactorily explain away. It therefore naturally follows that Krishna is not man. Now to think of his being an incarnation, adultery and theft are not the moral attributes of perfection which Vedas attribute to Divinity,—one who is possessed of qualities which are considered to be mean and degrading even in an uncivilized community cannot be declared of God as the embodiment of all moral attributes of perfection. That Krishna must not therefore neither man nor god. If he is neither man nor god what else is he? It is asserted by the highest initiates that the potentiality of the preserving power of the deity was never exhibited in such plenitude as in the avatar of Krishna, and we have got Krishna's own testimony to know what he is. In the Bhaghavadgita he says "To save the righteous and damn the unrighteous and to give a moral law to Humanity I am born in every planetory period and whoever can dive deep into the fathomless mystery of my incarnation and my divine actions, does not, after death return to the material plane. He obtains me i.e. eternal bliss." And he again declares: Whenever I assume human form for the salvation of mankind and incarnate myself, the ignorance of man makes him disregard me, while, I am no less step further, and see what acts, Paranas attribute to Krishna. The lifting up of the Govardhana Hill, the assumption of many forms of shepherds and cows are attributed to the author of Gita. Well, if we take our Puranas as authorities and if we judge of the divine nature or otherwise of the Deities that are presented to us therein, by the adoption of a literal interpretation handed down to us we must come to the conclusion that licentious Krishna lifted up the Govardhana Hill. Licentiousness of whatever form is not a quality which even savages ascribe to God while our common sense tells us that lifting up of Govardhana hill is not possible for man. According to the literal interpretations of our Puranas, Krishna is a strange commixtute of the highest form of Divinity and the lowest type of humanity. Our sincere conviction is that our Rishis whose knowledge of things in general was boundless, would not have stooped to the meanness of paying spiritual homage to Krishna, if he happened to be as dissolute and licentious, as he is ignorantly supposed to be. And further we are at a loss to know why our ancient sages could not have pitched upon another, who is now represented to have been more godly and saintly than Sri Krishna, and deified him in Krishna's place. Were our ancients, foolish to entrust their souls to an adulterer? Dear countrymen, reflect. Did Suka who imparted Divine knowledge to Parikshit, succeed in procuring salvation for his disciples by the inculcation of theories which ascribed heinous crimes to Divinity? We are prepared to give in answer a decided No. The immortal teaching contained in Gita, the upholding of Rishis of Krishna as a divine incarnation, the superhuman actions which Puranas ascribe to Krishna, our knowledge of the fact that our ancients kept esoteric knowledge under cover, the repeated assertions of many authors that knowledge of the mystery of the theory of Divine incarnation leads to one's eternal beatitude and Krishna's own testimony that his incarnation and actions are mysterious, indisputably prove that Pillalokachariyar was justified in declaring that our knowledge of our popular divine Avatars is positively nil. We must therefore understand that the popular conception of our Avatars, in far from correct and productive of many evil consequences and that the spiritual leaders of our society and the custodions of our Mutts so long as they are incapable of diffusing correct ideas of divinity, conformably to the theory of Pillalokachariyar, must be looked upon as a band of impostors, bent on the sole ruin of ignorant multitudes, whom custom has entrusted to their cruel charge.

We must frankly admit that our heart aches, whenever we think that our Puranas are destined to be productive of evil, while Vyasa and other sages intended them to be the means of benefitting humanity and it is not out of place to mention that we feel ashamed that we are not able to check the evil producing tendencies of our Puranic dogmas, in spite of the innumerable advantages, which we have reaped from Occidental and oriental systems of education jointly.

We thus see that our Vedas, Upanishads, Ithihasas, Puranas, Pancharatragama, Dravidian Prabandhams and other works are to a great extent allegorical representations of sacred religious truths.

eleven

EXPONENTS OF MAJOR SCHOOLS OF VEDĀNTA

GAUḌAPĀDA

To Gauḍapāda, the first historic philosopher of the system of Vedānta and the expounder of its nondualistic aspect, no definite date can be assigned. There is a tradition that Śaṁkara, who lived in the seventh century A.D.[1] met Gauḍapāda and received his blessing. Śaṁkara in his commentary on the Māndūkya Upaniṣad, makes obeisance to Gauḍapāda as his guru's guru. Thence arose the belief of many scholars that Gauḍapāda and Śaṁkara were contemporaries, Other scholars, on the contrary,, consider that Gauḍapāda lived many centuries before Śaṁkara, perhaps even before Buddha. And contention is that the tradition ofŚaṁkara's meeting with Gaudapāda is true, but that they met each other on the yogic plane, where, the spiritual eye of the aspirant being opened, a direct communion with the great souls of the past may be obtained. Śaṁkara is also said to have met Vyāsa, author of the Māhabhārata; if so, he must have met him too on the yogic plane, for undoubtedly Vyāsa lived many centuries before Śaṁkara. Gauḍapāda's being saluted by Śaṁkara as his guru's guru might be due to the fact he was one of the most important of the early teachers of the Vedāntic order. Scholars quote another tradition to the effect that Gauḍapda was a disciple of Suka and therefore a contemporary of the Māhabhārata.

Some Western scholars claim Gauḍapāda as a Buddhist saint main argument being that at the beginning of the fourth chapter of his philosophical treatise, the Kārikā. he adores the 'superman' whom they identify with Buddha. But the word superman had been used in the Māhābhārata and the Pūraṇas, even before the advent of Buddha, to denote one who has known Brahman, and also to denote God conceived in human form—Narayana: and according to tradition Gauḍapāda also used the word superman to denote Indian yaṇa. Ānandagiri, a disciple of Śaṁkara, mentions that Gauḍapāda practised austerities and meditation in Badarikasrama,[2] and that Nārāyaṇa, God in human form, appeared before him and revealed to him the highest truth of Vedānta.

Whatever may have been the period in which Gauḍapāda lived, he is regarded by Indian authorities as the first Vedantic philosopher and one of the greatest seers of all the ages.

The Kārikā

The advaita Vedānta (Vedānta in its nondualistic aspect) is as old as the Upaniṣads, for, however variously the ancient scriptures have been interpreted, and however much they have supplied the foundations for varying schools, it is the consensus of opinion that their final truth consists in the identification of the Self with Brahman and the absolute reality ot one and only one existence. Of the Upaniṣads, the Māndūkya most emphatically declares the turth of advaita. Gauḍapāda made himself famous by writing the Kārikā, a commentary Upon this single Upaniṣad. Sarhkara, who wrote commentaries on the Kārikā ot Gauḍapāda, very trulv remarked, 'The Māndūkya Upaniṣad, with the Kārikā, embodies in itself the quintessence of all the Upaniṣads or Vedānta.'

The Kārikā is divided into four chapters. The first, the āgama (scripture), glosses the verses of the Māndūkya Upaniṣad. The second, the vaitathya (the nature of sense experience), through an elaborate argument explains the relative and phenomenal nature of the objective universe. The third, the advaita (nondualism), establishes by means of logic and reason the truth of nondualism. The final chapter, the alātaśānti (the quenching of the fire-brand), further establishes the sole reality of the Ātman and the relative nature of our experiences in the ordinary states of consciousness.

The Philosohy of Experience

To arrive at the ultimate truth, philosophy must consider not only our experiences in the waking state but those in other states of Consciousness, such as dream and dreamless sleep, and co-ordinate them all by extending its inquiry to the possible source of all consciousness. Gauḍapāda, as well as the Upaniṣadic rsis, meets this requirement. V. Subrahmanya Iyer rightly remarks of Gauḍapāda:

'His distinction lies in the emphasis he lays on the impossibility of reaching the highest truth unless the *totality of* human experience or knowledge be taken into consideration.[3] This totality Gauḍapāda himself investigates.

"Western philosophy, in contrast, seems to have run into a blind alley, not only because it fails to recognize transcendental consciousness, but also because it does not attempt to *co-ordinate* the three other states of consciousness. Says Mr lyer:

'Philosophy, according to Gauḍapāda and Śankara, is an interpretation of the totality of human experience or of the *whole* of life from the standpoint of truth. Philosophy, therefore, is the whole, of which Religion, Mysticism (Yoga), Theology, Scholasticism, Speculation, Art and Science are but parts. Such philosophy or Vedānta as ignoresany part or parts is no Vedānta...And the object sought by philosophy, as these two pre-eminent Hindu philosophers say, is the happiness (*siikham*) and welfare (*hitam*) of all beings (*sarva sattwa*) in this world (*ihaiva*)[4]

In analysing the three states of consciousness, waking; dreaming, and dreamless sleep, Gauḍapāda discovers as the witness behind them an unchangeable reality. For in all these states there is the Self ever-present, though remaining unknown. It is the experiencer of all actions and thoughts in all the three states, but it is never affected by them. It forever remains pure, free, perfect.

Through our ignorance, however, the Self becomes identified with experience and appears to be changing, as when it appears first happy and then miserable, or to be born and then to die. But the appearance has no absolute reality. The Self remains unaltered, and when we rise above and beyond the three states to turīya. Pure Consciousness, its absolute oneness with all things, the absolute nonduality, is at last clearly revealed.

It is true that in deep sleep all experience seems to be annihilated. What then is the difference between deep sleep and turīya? In the words of Gauḍapāda, 'Deep sleep (prajfla) does not know anything either of the Self or of the non-Self, either of truth, or of untruth. But turīya is ever existent and ever all-seeing.[5] Again he says: 'Dream is the wrong apprehension of reality. Sleep is the state in which one does not know what reality is When the false experience in these two states disappears turiya is realized.[6] In the following verse he makes a clear distinction between a man who is asleep and a man who is in turīya: 'In deep sleep the mind is withdrawn. But it is disciplined, and not withdrawn, in turiya. One whose mind is disciplined becomes one with Brahman—who is fearless and the light of whose knowledge shines in every direction.[7]

The real Self, the ultimate reality, remains unknown in the three ordinary states of consciousness. 'When, however,' says Gauḍapāda, 'the individual soul, sleeping under the influence of māyā (ignorance), is awakened, it then realizes nonduality, beginningless and endless.?[8]

The Self (or Ātman), as we know, is immortal, in that it has neither birth nor death. It is nondual, though it appears to be many, just as the one sun, reflected in many lakes, appears manifold. Describing the nature of the Ātman, Gauḍapāda says, 'This Atman is beyond all expression by words, beyond all acts of the mind. It is peace, eternal effulgence, absence of activity; and it is attainable when the mind becomes pure and tranquil.[9]

Gauḍapāda, like all the other saintly philosophers of India, points out the way to illumination within one's own soul. With patience and perseverance, he tells us, we should seek to control the vagaries of the mind; then through the practice of discrimination we must tearn to renounce the pleasures of the senses; and finally, by the practice of concentration and meditation, when we are quite absorbed in our devotions, we arrive at a kind of bliss, a lower stage of samādhi. We must also, Gauḍapāda insists, give up our attachment to this bliss if we would realize the supreme bliss. My master, Swami Brahmananda, also, used to tell us that we must not stop with the bliss we may find in deep contemplation but go deeper and deeper. In the words of Gauḍapāda:

> 'The mind should not be allowed to enjoy the bliss that arises out of the condition of absorption. It should be freed from attachment to such happiness through the exercise of discrimination. When the mind does not lose itself in inactivity and oblivion, or is not distracted by desires—that is to say, when the mind achieves quietness and does not give rise to appearances—it verily becomes Brahman. This, the highest bliss, is based upon the realization of Self; it is peace, identical with liberation, indescribable, and unborn. It is further described as the omniscient Brahman, because it is one with the unborn Self, which is the object sought by knowledge[10]

Gauḍapāda contends that the waking and the dreaming states are equally real and equally unreal. They are real only in a relative sense, and they are unreal as compared with the transcendental, turiya, which is identification with the ultimate reality, the unchangeable Self. The definition of Reality is that it is never contradicted at any time but persists forever. 'Anything which is nonexistent at the beginning, and also at the end, necessarily does not exist in the middle.[11] By this test, all experience of both dreaming and waking is unreal. And from the standpoint of the ultimate reality, experience of the waking state is but a prolonged dream. Shakespeare seems to have caught the dreamlike quality of this world of appearances in the famous lines:

...These our actors,
As I foretold you, were all spirits, and
Are melted into air, into thin air;
And, like the baseless fabric of this vision,
The cloud-capp'd towers, the gorgeous palaces,
The solemn temples, the great globe itself,
Yea, all which it inherit, shall dissolve,
And, like this insubstantial pageant faded,
Leave not a rack behind. We are such stuff
As dreams are made on, and our little life
Is rounded with a sleep.

Consistent with his philosophy of nondualism. Gauḍapāda did not believe in the absolute reality of creation. The one absolute, nondual Self, or God, neither created this universe nor did he become this universe. In reality there is no creation, for the one infinite Existence appears to be the manifold universe just as a rope may appear to be a snake. The universe is not a reality but something superimposed upon the Atman.

'There is no death,' says Gauḍapāda, 'no birth; there is no one in bondage, no one aspiring to knowledge; there is no seeker after liberation, no one liberated. This is the absolute truth,[12] In evident allusion to expressions such as these, S. Radhakrishnan observes: 'The general idea pervading Gauḍapāda's work, that bondage and liberation, the individual soul and the world, are all unreal, makes the caustic critic observe that the theory which has nothing better to say than that an unreal soul is trying to escape from an unreal bondage in unreal world to accomplish an unreal supreme good, may itself be an unreality[13]

Now if one fails to take into consideration the main contention of Gauḍapāda, the above criticism may apply. What is his main contention? That the highest good, that is, freedom, supreme bliss, is the very nature of the Ātman, an absolute reality which persists. The supreme good, therefore, is not, as Dr Radhakrishnan alleges, unreal, but something you already have. To seek to possess something that you already have is foolish fancy. To think that you do not have something, though you always have it, is delusion. The story is told of a man who had a towel on his shoulder but sought for it everywhere. He but needed to awake to the fact that the towel was where he had placed it. So it is with us. Thinking we are bound, we seek liberation, though the liberation we seek is already within us. We but need to awake from the sleep of ignorance to realize 'I am Brahman'. Either that we are bound or that we seek liberation is false.

Dr. Radhakrishnan further remarks: 'If we have to play the game of life, we cannot do so with the conviction that the play is a show and all the prizes in it mere blanks. No philosophy can consistently hold such a view and be at rest with itself. The greatest'condemnation of such a theory is that we are obliged to occupy ourselves with objects, the existence and value of which we are continually denying in theory[14]

To this one may reply with the question. Can we play the game of life if we take life itself as a reality? The game is then no longer a game but a burden. Only for a genuine yogi, who has seen life as mere play, is it possible to play with satisfaction the game of life. To him the prizes are not blanks but the bliss of a free soul. We can play the game of life well only when we recognize that it is not everlasting, that joys and sorrows are in their very nature impermanent. The genuine yogi enjoys the game, plays it better than does one who clings to the enjoyments of life and finds to his despair that they elude his grasp at every moment, howsoever he may 'bid the clouds to stay'. Howsoever one may try to fool oneself by asserting the reality of the world, there is no world when life ends in death. As one holds fast to life and its experiences, the prizes in the game become mere blanks. The fact is that Gauḍapāda does not in any way reveal a romantic desire to chase the shadows of life nor does he attempt lo hide his head in the sand. Rather does he boldly seize upon naked reality and fearlessly face the facts of life by rising above them, above life and death, above joys and sorrows, into the realization 'I am Brahman'.

ŚAṀKARA

Introduction

As prophet and as thinker, Śaṁkara stands among the greatest figures in the history of the world. He is, primarily, the unrivalled propounder of advaita Vedānta, the nondualistic aspect of the Vedic teachings. By means of his remarkable clearness, his supreme wisdom, and his profound spirituality he has so stamped himself upon Vedānta that it has remained the paragon of Indian philosophy, and has given solace to the sorrowful heart of a large segment of mankind.

Life of Śaṁkara

Beautiful and fantastic clouds of legend surround the austere, charming, boyish figure of Śaṁkara—saint, philosopher, and poet. But, historically speaking, we know very little about the circumstances of his life.

He was born in or around the year AD 686 of brahmin parents Kālādi, a small village of western Malabar, in southern India.[15] By the age of ten, he was already an intellectual prodigy. Not only had he read and memorized all the scriptures, but he had written commentaries on many of them, and had held discussions with famous scholars who came to him from every part of the country. Yet the boy was dissatisfied. At a time when most children are only beginning to study, he was already disgusted by the emptiness of book-knowledge. He saw, moreover, that his teachers did not practise die lofty principles they preached. Indeed, the whole society in which he lived was materialistic and pleasure-seeking. India was passing 'through a period of spiritual decadence'. Śaṁkara, burning with youthful zeal, resolved to make his own life an example which would lead men back to the paths of truth.

The death of his father set him puzzling over the riddle of life and death, and he determined to solve it. He would renounce everything in his search for the meaning of existence. It was then that he wrote the poem called 'Moha Mudgaram'—'The Shattering of Illusion'. Of this the following is a more or less literal translation:

Who is thy wife? Who is thy son?
The ways of this world are strange indeed.
Whose art thou? Whence art thou come?
Vast is thy ignorance my beleonged
Therefore ponder these things and worship the Lord

Behold the folly of Man:
In childhood busy with his toys,
In youth bew itched by love,
In age bowed down with cares—
And always unmindful of the Lord!
The hours fly, the seasons roll, life ebbs,
But the breeze of hope blows continually in his heart.

Birth brings death, death brings rebirth:
This evil needs no proof.
Where then, 0 Man, is thy happiness?
This life trembles in the balance.
Like water on a lotus-leaf—
And yet the sage can show us, in an instant,
How to bridge this sea of change.
When the body is wrinkled, when the hair turns
When the gums are toothless, and the old man's staff
Shakes like a reed beneath his weight,
The cup of his desire is still full.

Thy son may bring thee suffering,

Thy wealth is no assurance of heaven:
Therefore be not vain of thy wealth,
Or of thy family, or of thy youth—
All are fleeting, all must change.
Know this and be free.
Enter the joy of the Lord.
Seek neither peace nor strife
With kith or kin, with friend or foe.
O befoved, if thou woudst attain freedom,
Be equal unto all[16]

Śaṁkara now persuaded his mother to let him take the monastic''' vow, promising that he would return to visit her before she died. Then, having made arrangements for herneed, he set out in search of a teacher.

On the banks of the River Narmada he met Gauḍapāda[17] a famous philosopher and seer, who had attained knowledge of the Reality. Śaṁkara asked the old man for initiation, but Gauḍapāda refused. He had made a vow to remain absorbed in union with Brahman. However, he sent the boy to his foremost disciple, Govindapāda. Govinḍapāda initiated him and instructed him in meditation and in the whole process of yoga. Within a very short time, Śaṁkara achieved complete mystical realization, and himself went out to teach.

One morning, when he was on his way to bathe in the Ganges, he met a canḍāla, a member of the'lowest caste, the untouchables. The man had four dogs with him, and they were- blocking Śaṁkara's path. For a moment, inborn caste-prejudice asserted itself. Śaṁkara, the brahmin, ordered the candala out of his way. But the canḍāla answered: 'If there is only one God, how can there be many kinds of men? How can there be any distinctions of caste or creeds Śaṁkara was fillei' with shame and reverence. He prostrated himself before the canḍāla. This incident inspired one of Śaṁkara's finest poems, the 'Manīṣa Pancaka'. It consists of five stanzas, each one ending with the refrain:

> He who has learned to see the one Existence everywhere,
>
> He is my master—be he brāhmin or caṇḍāla.

Śaṁkara began his teaching among the scholars of the country, converting the teachers first, and then their pupils. One of the teachers was the famous philosopher Manḍan Miśra. Manḍan Miśra held that the life of the householder was far superior to that of the monk, and his opinion was respected and widely shared throughout India. Śaṁkara determined to argue with him, and journeyed to his home. When he arrived, he found thedoors locked. Miśra was holding a religious ceremony and did not wish to be disturbed. Śaṁkara, with the mischievous spirit of a boy in his teens, climbed a near-by tree and jumped down from it into the courtyard. Miśra noticed him among the crowd. He disapproved of monks—especially when they were so youthful—and asked sarcastically: 'Whence comes this shaven head?' 'You have eyes to see, sir,' Śaṁkara answered saucily: 'The shaven head comes up from the neck.' Miśra lost his temper, but Śaṁkara continued to tease him, and at length the two of them agreed to hold a debate on the relative merits of the life of the monk and the life of the householder. It was understood that Samkāra, if he lost, should become a householder, and that Miśra, if he lost, should become a monk. The debate lasted for several days. Bharati, the learned wife of Miśra, acted as umpire. Finally, Śaṁkara was able to convince Miśra of the superiority of the monastic life, and Miśra became his disciple. It was he who later annotated Śaṁkara's commentaries on the Brahma Sūtras.

Śaṁkara's life came to an end at Kedarnath in the Himalayas. He was only thirty-two years old. During this brief period, he had established many monasteries, and had founded ten monastic orders. This was the first time that Hindu monasticism had ever been organized in India, and

Śaṁkara's system still exists. He was a reformer rather than an innovator. He preached no new doctrine or creed. But he gave a new impulse to the spiritual life of his time. Separated by intervals of a thousand years, Buddha, Śaṁkara, and Rāmakrṣṇa dominate India's religious history.

Śaṁkara's literary output was enormous. He not only made i .commentaries on the Vedanta Sūtras, the principal Upaniṣads, and the Bhagavad-Gītā, but produced two major philosophical, works, .'the *Upadeśāsaharī*and the *Vivekacūḍāmṇi* (*The Crest-Jewel of Discrimination*). He was also the author of many poems, hymns, prayers, and minor works on Vedānta.

Brahman—the absolute exister knowledge, and blisses real. The universe is not real. Brahman and Atman are on.[18]

In these words, Śaṁkara sums up his philosopli.. What are the implications of this statement? What does he mean by 'real' and by 'not real'?

Śaṁkara accepts as 'real' only that which neither changes nor ceases to exist. In making this definition, he follows the teachings of the Upaniṣads and of Gauḍapāda, his predecessor. No object, no kind of knowledge, can be absolutely real if its existence is only temporary. Absolute reality implies permanent existence. If we consider our various experiences during the states of waking and dreaming, we find that dream-experiences are contradicted by waking-experiences and vice versa—and that both kinds of experience cease in dreamless sleep. In other wurds, every object of knowledge, external or internal (for a thought or idea is as much an object of knowledge as is the external world), is subject to modification and therefore, by Śaṁkara's definition, 'not real'.

What, then, is the reality behind all our experiences? There is only one thing that never leaves us—pure consciousness. This alone is the constant feature of all experience. And this consciousness is the real, absolute Self. In dreamless sleep, even, the real Self persists (as we realize on waking, there being no break in essential continuity), while the ego-sense, which we call 'ourself, or individuality, has become temporarily merged in ignorance (avidya) and has disappeared.

Vedānta philosophy occupies a central position between realism and idealism. Western realism and idealism are both based on a distinction between mind and matter; Indian philosophy puts mind and matter in the same category—both are objects of knowledge. Śaṁkara should not, however.'be regarded as a precursor of Berkeley: he does not say that the world is unreal simply because its existence depends upon our perception. The world, according to Śaṁkara, 'is and is not'. Its fundamental unreality can be understood only in 'relation to the ultimate mystical experience, this experience of an illumined soul. When the illumined soul passes into transcendental consciousness, he realizes the Self (the Atman) as pure bliss and pure intelligence, the one 'without a second. In this state of consciousness, all perception of multiplicity ceases, there is no longer any sense of 'mine' and 'thine', the world as we ordinarily know it has vanished. Then the Self shines forth as the One, the Truth, the Brahman, the basis of the apparent world. The apparent world, A it is experienced in the waking state, may be likened, says Śaṁkara, to an imagined snake which proves, on closer inspection, to be nothing but a coil of rope. When the truth is known, we are no longer deluded by the appearance—the snake-appearance vanishes into the reality of the rope, the world vanishes into Brahman.

Other systems of Hindu philosophy—Samkhya, Yoga, and Nyāya—maintain that the phenomenal world possesses objective reality, even though it may not be apparent to the eyes of an illumined soul. Advaita Vedānta denies this objective reality. The point is a vital one. . Mind and matter, finite objects and their relations, Śaṁkara holds, are a misreading of Brahman—and nothing more.

The Nature of the Apparent World

When Śarhkara says that the world of thought and matter is not real, he does not mean that it is nonexistent. The apparent world is and is not. In the state of ignorance (our everyday consciousness) it is experienced, and and it exists as it appears. In the state of illumination it is not experienced, and it ceases to exist. Śaṁkara does not regard any experience as nonexistent as long as it is experienced, but he very naturally draws a distinction between the private illusions of the individual and the universal, or world, illusion. The former he calls prātibhāsika (illusory) and the latter vyavahārika (phenomenal). For example, a man's dreams are his private illusions; when he wakes, they cease. But the universal illusion—the illusion of world-phenomena—continues throughout a man's whole waking life unless he becomes aware of the truth through knowledge of Brahman. Śarhkara makes, also, a further distinction between these two kinds of illusion and those ideas which are altogether unreal and imaginary, which represent a total impossibility or a flat contradiction in terms—Such as the idea of the son of a barren woman.

Here, then, we are confronted by a paradox—the world is and is not. It is neither real nor nonreal. And yet this paradox simply recognizes, the existence of what Śaṁkara calls māyā. Māyā, this apparent world, has its basis in Brahman, the eternal. According to Śaṁkara, it consists of names and forms. It is not nonexistent, yet it differs from the Reality, the Brahman, upon whom it depends for its existence. It is not real, since it disappears in the light of knowledge of its eternal basis. The apparent world is māyā; the Self, the Ātman, alone is real.

Superimposition or Māyā

The most difficult of all philosophical problems is that of the relation between the finite and the Infinite; the problem of how this finite world came into being. If we believe that the finite has an absolute reality of its own, and that it has emerged from the Infinite add is an actual transformation of the Infinite, or if we regard the Infinite as a transcendental first cause of the phenomenal world (a position held by most Christian theologians), then we must admit that the Infinite is infinite no longer. A God who transforms himself into the visible universe is himself subject to transformation and change—he cannot be regarded as the absolute reality. A God who creates a world limits himself by the very act of creation, and thus ceases to be infinite. The question 'Why should God create at all?' remains unanswered.

This difficulty is overcome, however, if we consider the world as .māyā; and this explanation of our universe is, moreover, in perfect accord with the findings of modern science.

'A soap-bubble with irregularities and corrugations on its surface is perhaps the best representation of this new universe revealed to us by the theory of relativity. The universe is not the interior of the soap-bubble but its surface—and the substance out of which this bubble is blown, the soap film, is empty space welded into empty time.[19]

Thus it is only when we analyse the nature of the universe and discover it to be māyā—neither absolutely real nor absolutely nonexistent—that we learn how the phenomenal surface of the soap-bubble safeguards the eternal presence of the Absolute.

The Upaniṣads, it is true, appear to consider Brahman the first cause of the universe, both material and efficient. They declare that the universe emanates from, subsists in, and finally merges in the absolute Brahman. Sarhkara never directly contradicts the Upaniṣads, although sometimes he appears to interpret them to suit his own views. The unherse, he says, is a superimposition upon Brahman. Brahman remains eternally infinite and unchanged. He is not transformed into this universe. He simply appears as this universe to us, in our ignorance. We superimpose the apparent world upon Brahman, just as we sometimes superimpose a snake upon a coil of rope.

This theory of superimposition (vivartavāda) is inseparably linked with the theory of causality. Causal relation exists in the world of multiplicity, which is māyā. Within māyā, the mind cannot function without causal relation. But to speak of cause and effect with reference to the Absolute is simply absurd. To seek to know what caused the world is to transcend the world. To seek to find the cause of māyā is to go beyond māyā—and, when we do that, māyā vanishes, the effect ceases to exist. How, then, can there be a cause of a nonexistent effect In other words, the relation between Brahman and māyā is, by its very nature, unknowable and indefinable by any process of the human intellect.

Māyā: A Statement of Fact as Well as a Principle

Thus, according to Śaṁkara, the world of thought and matter has a phenomenal or relative existence, and is super-imposed upon Brahman, the unique, absolute reality. As long as we remain in ignorance (that is, as long as we have not achieved transcendental consciousness), we shall continue to experience this apparent world, which is the effect of superimposition. When transcendental consciousness is achieved, superimposition ceases.

What is the nature of this superimposition? In the introduction to his commentary on the Brahma Sūtras, Śaṁkara tells us that 'Superimposition is the apparent presentation to consciousness, by the memory, of something previosuly observed elsewhere.[20] We see a snake. We remember it. Next day we see a coil of rope. We superimpose the remembered snake upon it, and thereby misunderstand its nautre.

Śamkāra foresees an objection to his theory and goes on to anticipate and answer it. We may challenie theory ofsuperimposition by pointing out that Brahman is not an object of perception. How can we superimpose a snake upon a rope which we do not perceive? How can we superimpose a world-appearance upon a reality which is not apparent to our senses? 'For every man superimposes objects only upon such other objects as are placed before him (that is, as come into contact with his sense organs.[21] To this, Śaṁkara answers:

'Brahman is not, we reply, non-objective in the absolute sense. For Brahman is the object of the ego-idea. We know quite well, by intuition, that the inner Self must exist, since the ego-idea is a presentation of the Self. Nor is it an absolute rule that objects can be superimposed only upon such other objects as are placed before us; for ignorant people superimpose a dark blue colour upon-the sky, which is not an object of sense perception.[22]

This statement needs some further explanation. Although Brahman is never apparent to our everyday sense perception, there is a manner in which we are aware of the Reality, the inner Self. Brahman, it has been said, is absolute existence, knowledge, and bliss. Only in transcendental consciousness can we know this fully. Yet Brahman is partly apparent, to our normal consciousness also. Brahman is Existence, and we all know that we exist. In this sense, every one of, us has an intuitive knowledge of the inner Self (the Ātman or Theinner Self, the Reality is never an object of sense perception, however—because, in our ignorance, we superimpose of a private individuality—of being Mr Smith or Mrs Jones—upon our awareness of Existence.

We are unable to understand that Existence is not our private property, that it is universal and absolute. The inner Self is therefore present in our normal consciousness as 'the object of the ego-idea'—a literal translation ofŚaṁkara's phrase. The superimposition of the ego-idea upon Existence is our first and most important act as human beings. The moment we have made this, central act of super-imposition—the -moment we have said 'I am I, I am private, I am separate, I am an individual'—we have made further super-imposition inevitable. The claim to individuality for ourselves implies individuality everywhere. It mtomatically superimposes a multiple world of creatures and objects upon the one, undivided reality, the Existence which is Brahman. Ego-idea and world-appearance depend upon each other. Lose the ego-idea in transcendental consciousness, and the world- appearance must necessarily vanish.

When and how did this act of superimposition occur? Was it at our latest individual birth, or in some previous life? Was there a historical moment—corresponding to that in which Adam is said to have fallen—in which the phenomenal world came into being as the result of the ego-idea? The futility of such questions should be self-evident. We merely go round in a circle. What is this world-appearance? Māyā. What causes it? Our ignorance. What is this ignorance? Māyā, also. If there always was, and is, and always will be one unchanging "reality, how can we possibly assume that māyā began at some definite historical moment in time? We cannot. Therefore we are forced to conclude, as Śaṁkara does, that māyā, like Brahman, is without-any beginning. Ignorance as the cause and the apparent world as the effect have existed always and will always exist. They are like seed and tree. The 'coupling of the real and the unreal', produced by our ignorance, is a process universally evident in our daily lives. Śaṁkara says: 'It is obvious and needs no proof that the object, which is the nonego, and the subject, which is the ego-idea (superimposed upon the Self), are opposed to each other, like light and darkness, and cannot be identified. Still less can their respective attributes be identified...Nevertheless, it is natural to man (because of his wrong ideas) not to be able to distinguish between these distinct entities and between their respective attributes. He superimposes upon each the nature and attributes of the other, uniting the real with the unreal and-making use, of such expressions as "I am that." "That is mine"[23]

Śaṁkara is speaking here of two stages in the process of super-imposition. First, the ego-idea is superimposed upon the inner Self, the existence-reality. Then the ego-idea, reaching outward, as it were, identifies itself with the body and the body's mental and physical attributes and actions. We say, as a matter of course, 'I am fat', 'I am tired', 'I am walking', 'I am sitting down'—without ever stopping to consider what this '1' really is. We go further. We claim purely external objects and names for our own. We say 'I am a Republican', or 'This house is mine'. As superimpositions multiply, extraordinary statements become possible and normal—such as 'We sunk three submarines yesterday' or carry a good deal of insurance'. We identify our ego, more or less, with every object in the universe. And all the while, the inner Self looks on, utterly detached from these moods and antics, yet making them all possible by lending to the mind that light of consciousness without which māyā could not exist.

That māyā is beginning less can be shown if we return for a moment to the image of the rope and the snake. The superimposition of the snake upon the rope is possible only if we can remember what a snake looks like: a child who had never seen a snake could never superimpose it. How then is it possible for the newborn child to superimpose the world-appearance (the snake) upon Brahman (the rope)' We can answer this question only if we postulate a universal snake-memory that is common to all mankind and that has existed from a time without beginning. This snake-memory is māyā.

Māyā, says Śaṁkara, is not only universal but beginningless and endless. A distinction must be made, however, between māyā as a universal principle and ignorance (a', avidyā), which is individual. Individual ignorance is beginningless, but it can end at any moment; it is lost when a man achieves spiritual illumination. Thus the world may vanish from the consciousness of an individual and yet continue to exist for the rest of mankind. In saying this, Śaṁkara's philosophy differs essentially from the subjective idealism of the West.

Brahman and Iśwara

In a sense. Brahman is the ultimate cause of the universe, since, by the action of māyā, the world-appearance is superimposed upon him. Brahman is the cause, māyā the effect. Yet Brahman cannot be said to have transformed himself into the world or to have created it. since absolute Reality is, by definition, incapable of temporal action or change. Another word, Iśwara, must therefore be employed to describe the creative principle. Iśwara is Brahman united with māyā—the combination which creates, preserves, and dissolves the universe in an endless and beginningless process. Iśwara is God personified, God with attributes.

According to the Sāmkhya system of philosophy, the universe is an evolution of Prakṛti—undifferentiated matter, composed of three forces called the guṇas.' Creation is a disturbance in the balance of these forces. The guṇas enter into an enormous variety of combinations—somewhat like the atoms in Western physics—and these combinations are individual elements, objects, and creatures. This concept of Prakṛti corresponds, more or less, to Śaṁkara's concept of māyā—but with this important difference: Prakṛti is said to be other than and independent of Puruṣa (the absolute Reality) while māyā is said to have no absolute reality but to be dependent on Brahma. Therefore, according to Śaṁkara, it is Iśwara, rather than Prakṛti, who can be described as the ultimate cause of the universe.

Are there then two Gods—one the impersonal Brahman, the other the personal Iśwara? No—for Brahman appears as Iśwara only when viewed in the relative ignorance of māyā. Iśwara has the same degree of reality that māyā has. God the person is not 'Brahman in his ultimate nature. In the words of Swami Vivekananda, 'The personal God is the highest possible reading of the Absolute by the human mind.[24]

The idea is thus ingeniously illustrated by Sri Rāmakṛṣṇa:

'Brahman may be compared to an infinite ocean, without beginning or end. Just as, through intense cold, some portions of the ocean freeze into ice and the formless water appears to have form, so, through the intense love of the devotee, Brahman appears to take on form and personality.[25] But the form melts away again as the sun of knowledge rises. Then the universe also disappears, and there is seen to be nothing but Brahman, the infinite.[26]

Although Iśwara is, in a. sense, a person, we must beware of regarding him as similar to, or identical with, the jiva, the individual human soul. Iśwara, like the jiva, is Brahman united with māyā, bin with this fundamental difference—Iśwara is the ruler and controller of māyā, the jiva is māyā's servant and plaything. We can therefore say, without paradox, that we are, at the same time. God and the servants of God. In our absolute nature, we are one with Brahman; in our relative nature, we are other than the Iśwara, and subject to him.

Devotion to the Iśwara, the Personal God,may lead a man very far along the path of spirituality; it may even make him into a saint. But by itself it does not give the ultimate knowledge. To be completely enlightened is to go beyond Iśwara, to know the impersonal Reality behind the personal divine Appearance. We can become Brahman, since Brahman is present in us always. But we can never become Iśwara, because Iśwara is above and distant from our human personality. It follows, therefore, that we can never become rulers of the universe. To rule it is Iśwara's function, and the desire to usurp this function is the ultimate madness of the ego. It is symbolized in Christian literature by the legend of the fall of Lucifer.

Vyāsa, the author of the Brahma Sūtras, makes the same point when he says that no one will acquire the power of creating, ruling, or dissolving the universe, since that power belongs to Iśwara alone. And Śaṁkara in his commentary discusses the problem as follows:

'If a man, *by* worshipping the qualified Brahman (Iśwara), achieves knowledge of the Supreme Ruler while still preserving his individual consciousness—is his power limited or unlimited? When this question arises, some will argue that his power is unlimited, and they will quote the scriptural texts (referring to those who achieve knowledge of Iśwara) "They attain their own kingdom", "To them all the gods offer worship", and "Their desires are fulfilled in all the worlds".'

'But Vyāsa answers this question when he adds: "Except for the power of creating the universe." The powers of Iśwara can be acquired by the liberated, but that power belongs to Iśwara alone. How do we know this? Because he is the subject of the scriptural texts concerning creation. These texts do not refer to the liberated souls, in any connection whatsoever. That is why he is called "the ever-perfect". The scriptures also say that the powers of the liberated are acquired by worshipping and searching after God; therefore the liberated have no place in the ruling of the universe. Again, because these liberated souls still preserve their individual consciousness, it is possible that their will may differ, and that, while one desires creation, another may desire destruction. The only way to avoid this conflict is to make all wills subordinate to some one will. Therefore we must conclude that the wills of the liberated are dependent on the will of the Supreme Ruler[27]

If there is only one consciousness, one Brahman, who is the seer and who is the seen? Who sees Brahman as Iśwara, and who is the jīva? Are they different or one?

As long as man is within the limitations of māyā, the One is seen as many. Ignorance can do no better than to worship Appearance; and Iśwara is the rules of all appearances—the highest idea which the human mind can grasp and the human heart can love. The human mind can never grasp the absolute, Reality, it can only infer its presence and worship its projected image, in the process of this worship, the mind becomes purified, the ego-idea thins away like mist, superimposition, ceases, Iśwara, and world-appearance both vanish in the blaze of transcendental consciousness, wherein there is no seer, no seen—nothing but Brahman, the single, all-embracing,' timeless fact.

The Problem of Evil

Every religion or system of philosophy has to deal with the problem of evil—and unfortunately it is a problem which is usually explained away rather than explained. 'Why', it is asked, 'does God permit evil, when he himself is all goodness?'

One of two answers is usually given to this question by Western religious thought. Sometimes we are told that evil is educational and penal. God punishes us for our sins by visiting us with war, famine, earthquake, disaster, and disease. He employs temptation (either directly or through the agency of the Devil) to test and strengthen the virtue of the good. This is the answer given by the Old Testament. It repels many people today and has become unfashionable—although, according to Vedānta, as we shall see in a moment, it contains a certain amount of truth.

The other answer—now more generally accepted—is that evil does not exist at all. If we view life *sub specie aeternitatis,* we shall know that evil has no reality; that it is simply a misreading of good.

Vedānta philosophy disagrees with both these answers—with the second even more radically than with the first. How, it asks, can evil be changed into good, merely by viewing it in a special manner? Pain and misfortune may be borne more easily than would otherwise be possible, if we fix our minds upon God, but they are very real experiences nevertheless, even though their duration is limited. Vedānta agrees that evil, in the absolute sense, is unreal. But it reminds us that in this sense good is unreal also. The absolute Reality is beyond good and evil, pleasure and pain, success and disaster. Both good and evil are aspects of māyā. As long as māyā exists, they exist. Within māyā they are real enough.

The question 'Why does God permit evil?' is, in fact, most misleadingly phrased. It is as absurd as if one were to ask 'Why does God permit good?' Nobody today would ask why rain 'permitted' a catastrophic flood; nobody would blame or praise fire because it burns One man's house and cooks another man's dinner. Nor can it be properly said that Brahman is 'good' in any personal sense of the word. Brahman is not good in the sense that Christ was good—for Christ's goodness was within māyā. The Reality itself is beyond all phenomena; even the noblest. It is beyond purity, beauty, happiness glory, or success. It can be described as good only if we mean that absolute consciousness is absolute knowledge, and that absolute knowledge is absolute joy.

But perhaps the question does not refer to Brahman at all. Perhaps, in this connection, 'God' means Iśwara, the Ruler of māyā. If this is granted, can Vedānta philosophy agree with the Old Testament that God is a law-giver, a stern and somewhat unpredictable father, whose ways are not ours, whose punishments and rewards often seem unmerited, who permits us to fall into temptation? The answer is yes and no. The Vedānta doctrine of karma is a doctrine of absolute, automatic justice. The circumstances of our lives, our pains and our pleasures, are all the result of our past actions in this present existence, and in countless previous existences, from a beginningless time. Viewed from a relative standpoint, māyā is quite pitiless. We get exactly what we earn, no more, no less. If we cry out against some apparent injustice, it is only because the act that brought it upon us is buried deep in the past, out of reach of our memory. To be born a beggar, a king, an athlete, or a helpless cripple is simply the composite consequence of the deeds of our other lives. We have no one to thank but ourselves. It is no use trying to bargain with Iśwara, or propitiate him, or hold him responsible for our troubles. It is no use inventing a Devil as an excuse for our weakness. Māyā is what we make of it—and Iśwara simply represents that stern and solemn fact.

Viewed from a relative standpoint, this world of appearance is a bleak place, and as such it often drives us to despair. The seers, with their larger knowledge, tell us otherwise. Once we become conscious, even dimly, of the Atman, the Reality within us, the world shows itself in a very different aspect. It is no longer a court of justice but a kind of gymnasium. Good and evil, pain and pleasure, still exist, but they seem more like the ropes and vaulting-horses and parallel bars which can be used to make our bodies strong. Māyā is no longer an endlessly revolving wheel of pain and pleasure but a ladder which can be climbed to consciousness of the Reality. From this standpoint, fortune and misfortune are both mercies—that is to say, opportunities. Every experience offers us the chance of making a constructive reaction to it—a reaction which helps to break some chain of our bondage to māyā and bring us nearer to spiritual freedom. Śaṁkara therefore distinguishes between two kinds of māyā—avidyā (evil or ignorance) and vidvā (good or knowledge in a relative sense). Avidyā is that which causes us to move farther away from the Self and obscures our knowledge of the Truth. Vidyā is that which enables us to come nearer to the Self by removing the veil of ignorance. Both Vidyā and avidyā are transcended when we pass beyond māyā into consciousness of the absolute reality.

It has been said already that māyā is the superimposition of the ego-idea upon the Ātman, the real Self. The ego-idea represents a false claim to individuality, to being different from, or separate from, our neighbours. It follows, therefore, that any act which, contradicts this claim will bring us one step back towards right knowledge, towards consciousness of the inner reality. If we recognize our brotherhood with our fellow men; if we try to deal honestly, truthfully, charitably with them; if we work for equal rights and equal justice, politically and economically, and for abolition of barriers of race and class—then we are in fact giving the lie to the ego-idea and moving towards awareness of the universal, nonindividual Existence. All such actions belong to what is known as ethical goodness—just as all selfish actions belong to ethical evil. In one sense, and in one sense only, goodness may be said to be more 'real', or more valid, than evil: since evil actions and thoughts involve us more deeply in māyā, while good thoughts and actions lead us beyond māyā, to transcendental consciousness.

The words sin and virtue are somewhat alien to the spirit of Vedānt philosophy, because they necessarily foster a sense of possessiveness with regard to thought and action. If we say 'I am good' or 'I am bad', we are only talking the language of māyā. '1 am Brahman' is the only true statement regarding ourselves that any of us can make.

St Francois de Sales wrote that 'even our repentance must be peaceful'—meaning that exaggerated remorse, just as much as excessive self-congratulation, simply binds us more firmly to the ego-idea, the lie of māyā. We must never forget that ethical conduct is a means, not an end in itself. Knowledge of the impersonal reality is the only valid knowledge. Apart from that, our deepest wisdom is black ignorance and our strictest righteousness is all in vain

The Supreme Goal

It may be objected that Vedānta philosophy, like every other system of religious thought, is based upon a central hypothesis. Certainly, the supreme goal of life is to know Brahman exists. But can we be sure of this? Isn't it possible that there is no underlying reality in the universe? Isn't it possible that life is just a meaningless flux, a dying and a becoming in eternal alternation?

What is so attractive about Vedanta is its undogmatic, experimental approach to truth. Śaṁkara does not tell us that we must accept the existence of Brahma as a dogma before we can enter upon the spiritual life. No-he invites us to find out for ourselves.

Nothing-no teacher, no scripture can do the work for us. Teachers and scriptures are merely encouragements to personal effort. But, as such, they can be very effective. Imagine that the, existence or nonexistence of God is the subject of a lawsuit and that you are the judge. Try to listen impartially to both sides. Consider the witnesses for Brahman—the seers and saints who claim to have known the eternal reality. Consider the circumstances of their lives, their personalities, their words. Ask yourself. Are all these witnesses liars or hypocrites or insane persons, or are they telling the truth? Compare the great scriptures of the world and ask. Do they contradict each other, or do they agree? Then give your verdict.

But mere assent, as Śaṁkara insists, is not enough. It is only a preliminary step toward active participation in the search for Brahman. Direct personal experience is the only satisfactory proof of his existence, and each of us must have it.

Modern science goes a long way towards confirming the Vedānta world-picture. It admits that consciousness, in varying degrees, may be present everywhere. Differences between objects and creatures are.

Only surface differences, varying arrangements of atomic pattern. Benients can be changed into other elements. Identity is only provisional. Science does not yet accept the concept of absolute reality, but it certainly does not exclude it. Sarhkara knew nothing of science, but his approach is fundamentally scientific. It is based upon the practice of discrimination—a discrimination to be apply d to ourselves and to every circumstance and object of our experience, at each 'instant of our lives. Again and again—thousands and thousands of times a day—we must ask ourselves. Is this real or unreal, is this fact or fancy, is this nature or only appearance? Thus we probe deeper *Had* deeper towards the truth. 'We all know that we exist. We are all aware of our own consciousness. But we hat is the nature of this consciousness, this existence? Discrimination will soon prove to us that the ego-idea is not the fundamental reality. There is something beyond it. We can call this something 'Brahman'—but 'Brahman' is only another word. It does not reveal the nature of the thing we are looking-for. *Can* Brahman be known as an existing substance or thing? Not in the ordinary meaning of the verb to know. To know something is to have objective knowledge of it, and such knowledge is relative, depending upon space, time, and causation. we cannot know absolute consciousness in this manner, because absolute consciousness is knowledge itself. Brahman is the source of all other knowledge; he comprises the knower, the knowledge, and that which is known. He is independent of space, time, and cause.

In this sense, the practice of discrimination differs from the method of scientific research. The scientist concentrates upon some object of knowledge, and pursues it beyond the range of physical sense perception, with the aid of mechanical apparatus, chemical analysis, mathematics, and so forth. His research extends like a journey, deeper and deeper into time and space. The religious philosopher; on the other hand, is trying to annihilate time and space, the dimensions of the ego-idea, and thus uncover the Reality which is nearer and more instant than the ego, the body, or the mind. He is trying to be aware of what he already and alw ays is, and this awareness is not an aspect of consciousness, but consciousness itself. The illumined seer does not merely know Brahman; he is Brahman, he is Existence, he is Knowledge. Absolute freedom is not something to be attained, absolute knowledge is not something to be won, Brahman is not something to be found anew. It is only māyā which has to be. pierced, ignorance which has to be overcome. The process of discrimination is a negative process. The positive fact, our real nature, eternally exists. We are Brahman—and only ignorance divides us from knowledge of the fact.

Transcendental consciousness, or union with Brahman, can never be investigated by the methods of scientific research, since such research 'depends ultimately upon sense perception, and Brahman is beyond the grasp of the senses. But this does not mean that we are doomed to doubt, or to blind trust in the experience of the seers, until we have reached the supreme goal for ourselves. Even a little effort in meditation and the spiritual life will reward us with the cuiction that this is really the way to truth and peace, that we are not simply deceiving or hypnotizing ourselves, that Reality is accessible. We shall '! have our ups and downs, of course, and our moments of uncertainty, but we shall always return to this conviction. No spiritual gain, however small, is ever lost or wasted.

By temperament, Śaṁkara inclined toward jñāna yoga, the way of pure discrimination, although he was capable of great devotion also.' Renunciation, discrimination, self-control—these are his watchwords. Some may find his austerity too forbidding, but it is precisely this austerity which supplies a valuable corrective to the dangers of an easy sentimentality, an excess of carefree optimism, a confusion of real devotion with mere emotional self-indulgence. Śaṁkara was under no illusions about this world of māyā; he condemns its apparent pleasures and delights with brutal frankness. For this very reason he was able to describe so powerfully the complete transformation of the universe which takes place before the eyes of the illumined seer. When Brahman is experienced, when all creatures and objects are seen in their real relation to the Absolute, then this world is indeed a paradise; it is nothing but Brahman, nothing but utter consciousness, knowledge, and peace.

To quote Śaṁkara describing the experience of an illumined soul: 'The ego has disappeared. I have realized my identity with Brahman, and so all my desires have melted away. I have risen above my ignorance and my knowledge of this seeming universe. What is this joy that I feel? Who shall measure it? I know nothing but joy, limitless, unbounded!

'The ocean of Brahman is full of nectar- the joy of the Atman. The treasure I have found there cannot be described in words. The mind cannot conceive of it. My mind fell like a hailstone into that vast expanse of Brahman's ocean. Touching one drop of it, I melted away and became one with Brahman. And now, though I return to human consciousness. I abide in the joy of the Atman.

'Where is this universe? Who took it away? Has it merged in something else? A while ago, I beheld it—now it exists no longer. This is wonderful indeed!

'Here is the ocean of Brahman, full of endless joy,. How can I accept or reject anything? Is there anything apart or distinct from Brahman?

'Now, finally and clearly, I know that I am the Atman, whose nature is eternal joy. I see nothing, I hear nothing, I know nothing that is separate from me.[28]

SELECTED PASSAGES FROM ŚAṂKARA'S VIVEKACUDAMANI

Crest-Jewel of Discrimination

The spiritual seeker who is possessed of tranquillity, self-control, mental poise and forbearance, devotes himself to the practice of contemplation, and meditates upon the Atman within himself as the Atman within all beings. Thus he completely destroys the sense of separateness which arises from the darkness of ignorance, and dwells in joy, identifying himself with Brahman, free from distracting thoughts and selfish occupations.

Those who echo borrowed teachings are not free from the world. But those who have attained samadhi by merging the external universe, the sense organs, the mind and the ego in the pure consciousness of the Atman—they alone are free from the world, with its bonds and snares.[29]

Be devoted to Brahman and you will be able to control your senses. Control your senses and you will gain mastery over your mind. Master your mind, and the sense of ego will be dissolved. In this manner, the yogi achieves an unbroken realization of the joy of Brahman. Therefore let the seeker strive to give his heart to Brahman.[30]

The self-luminous Atman, the witness of all, is ever-present within your own heart. This Atman stands apart from all that is unreal. Know it to be yourself, and meditate upon it unceasingly.[31]

When the mind achieves perfect union with Brahman, the wise man realizes Brahman entirely within his own heart. Brahman is beyond speech or thought. It is the pure, eternal consciousness. It is absolute bliss. It is incomparable and immeasurable. It is ever-free, beyond all action, boundless as the sky, indivisible and absolute.[32]

To taste, within his own heart and in the external world, the endless bliss of the Atman—such is the reward obtained by the yogi who has reached perfection and liberation in this lifes.[33]

The fruit of dispassion is illumination; the fruit of illumination is the stilling of desire; the fruit of stilled desire is experience of the bliss of the Atman, whence follows peace.[34]

Teachers and scriptures can stimulate spiritual awareness. But the wise disciple crosses the ocean-of his ignorance by direct illumination, through the grace of God[35]

Our perception of the universe is a continuous perception of Brahman, though the ignorant man is not aware of this. Indeed, this universe is nothing but Brahman. See Brahman everywhere, under all circumstances, with the eye of the spirit and a tranquil heart. How can the physical eyes see anything but physical objects? How can the mind of the enlightened man think of anything other than the Reality [36]

BHĀSKARA

Still another aspect of Vedānta, known as Bhedābhedavāda, or doctrine of identity in difference, finds its exponent in Bhāskara. Oudulumi originated the system, but his writings are not now available, and we know of him only through mention of him in the Brahma Sūtras of Vyāsa. Bhāskara wrote commentaries upon the Sūtras and in so doing explained his own and Oudulumi's philosophy. In the main he attempted an attack upon Śaṁkara's doctrine of māyā. He therefore lived after Śaṁkara—according to Indian authorities, in the early part of the ninth century.

The Philosophy of Identity in Difference

Brahman is one without a second, the unchangeable reality, endowed with blessed attributes, including the power to create, sustain, and dissolve the universe. He is the formless, personal God who in his causal state is transcendental—beyond time, space, and causation; in his aspect as effect, he has evolved or become transformed into the empirical universe. Since Brahman, the Infinite, has made himself finite, as finite ha is real, though he, the Infinite, is not necessarily conditioned by the finitude. Brahman as cause contains the whole universe potentially within himself, and the universe is the cause actualized, though in part only, since the cause has not exhausted itself in the effect.

Again, as effect, Brahman is both jīva, or the individual soul, and the world. He is endowed with power of two kinds: bhogya, the kind which evolves as the objective universe, and bhoktr, the kind which evolves as living souls. This power of Brahman is not māyā, but is real in the absolute sense.

Empirical existence therefore consists of (1) the subject, the experiencer, the jīva, and (2) the object of experience, the world of the senses. Though the empirical world of subject and object is not separate from Brahman, for it is Brahman that is evolved as the universe, yet again Brahman is not merely the universe of name and form—he is transcendental as well.[37]

Individual souls are many, and they are parts of Brahman. They are related to him as are the rays of the sun to the sun. They are neither absolutely different from God, nor are they absolutely identical with him. In the state of bondage—that is, ignorance—individual souls are different from God; and in the state of liberation—that is, knowledge—they become one with him. To the self, purified by spiritual discipline, is revealed the knowledge of Brahman, and as the self finally becomes one with Brahman, all consciousness of separation is dissolved. But this union is possible only after death, never at any time during life. In this respect the philosophy of Bhāskara differs from all the other systems we have studied.[38]

Union with Brahman is the supreme goal. As the means of achieving this, Bhāskara, like all other teachers of religion, offers the ideal of non attachment, the ideal of being in the world and yet not of it, and the worship of Brahman and meditation upon him

YĀMUNA

Viśiṣṭādvaita Vedānta, the Vedānta in its aspect of qualified non-dualism, traces its origin to the period of the Upaniṣads; at least it had gained followers at the time of the composition of the Mahābhārata, being identical with the doctrine of Pañcarātra mentioned in that poem. In the tenth century A.D. however, it received greater impetus and a brighter light from the teachings of the saint Yāmuna; and in the eleventh century the great teacher Rāmānuja, who had been influenced by Yāmuna, gave it a sound philosophical basis, and made it a popular religion, particularly in southern India. Yāmuna and Rāmānuja belong to the long line of Vaiṣṇava saints recognized in southern India and generally known as Ālvārs. Ālvār is a Tamil word which means lie who rules the world by his love of and devotion to God'. Many legends are told of these ancient Ālvārs, and all of them clearly express love of God and devotion and self-surrender to him.

One of the Alvārs was Nāṭhamuni, grandfather of Yāmuna. He was known to history as a great saint living in the early part of the tenth century. Born of a well-known brāhmin family, on the death of his son he gave up the life of the world and embraced a life of renunciation. He wrote two books which are regarded as authoritative by the Śrī Vaiṣṇava, the school of qualified nondualism.

Yāmuna, his grandson, was born in AD 953. At the age of twelve he became king of half the kingdom of Pāṇḍu. There is extant an interesting account, though obviously legendary, of how he ascended the throne.

The king of Pāṇḍu, it seems, had a court pundit who was very clever in debate; and it was the custom of the country that whoever challenged the scholarship of the pundit and defeated him in argument was appointed court pundit in turn; and whoever challenged the pundit and was defeated by him must pay him an annual sum as tax. Bhāśya, teacher of the boy Yāmuna, had been defeated by the pundit and had thus become subject to the penalty. Now it so happened that once the tax-collector appeared when Bhāśya was absent from home, and Yamuna, feeling the humiliation of his master, challenged the pundit to debate. Though the king and his pundit were amazed at the child's temerity, they were obliged to accept the challenge.

The boy was brought to court and accorded due honour and respect. The queen felt sure that he would be crowned victor, for she could see that he was no ordinary child. When she confided her thoughts to the king, he laughed and jokingly offered to lay a wager against him. The queen said, 'If the boy is defeated, I promise to be the slave of Your Majesty's slaves.' To this the king replied, 'If the boy wins, I will offer him half my kingdom.'

So the boy and the pundit entered into debate. To the surprise of all, the boy was victorious, and the pundit was obliged to acknowledge himself beaten at the hands of a child. The king, paying his bet, offered Yāmuna half his kingdom. The boy accepted the gift and ruled for many years at peace with all men.

The news of Yāmuna's elevation to the throne came to the ears of Nāthamuni, his grandfather, who was then living as a monk. Fearing lest his grandson should give himself over to worldliness, Muni charged Nambi, his favourite disciple, to watch over him and see that he did not lose himself in love of the world but that instead he sought the truth.

When Yāmuna was thirty-five years of age, and still reigning over his kingdom, Nambi appeared before him and said, 'Your grandfather has left a vast treasure with me. If it is your desire to find this treasure, you must follow me, and follow me alone.' So Yamuna left his kingdom and followed Nambi. As he associated closely with his grandfather's disciple, he came to admire his greatness, his love for God, his purity of conduct, and above all the peace and joy that shone in his countenance. And there arose, in the heart of King. Yāmuna a mighty longing to find God and attain peace. He lost all taste for the enjoyments of the world, even the desire to return to his kingdom. Both king and devotee retired to the temple of Śrī Raṅganātha. Thus Yāmuna became a monk and teacher.

In his later years Yāmuna wrote four famous books. He wished to write, in addition, a commentary on the Brahma Sūtras, but passed away before the fulfilment of this desire. As he lay dying, he expressed a wish that Rāmānura, whom he loved much, shuuld write the commentary. Hearing of this, Rāmānuja, who had already won fame for himself, hastened to him, but arrived too late. He promised, however, to carry out Yāmuna's wish, and succeeded in doing so.

Briefly—for we shall consider the doctrine of qualified nondualism in some detail in the chapter on Rāmānuja—the philosophy of Yāmuna consists of the following ideas.

God to the Supreme Being. He is the whole, of which individual souls are the parts. We are related to him as are the waves of the ocean to the ocean. The universe is a transformation of God. God is its soul; he visible world is his body.

The ideals of all-consuming love for God, and self-surrender to him, Yāmuna has expressed beautifully in a famous prayer:

'God is beyond the realm of speech and mind. He is the ground of speech and mind, and he is the ocean of mercy. How can we pray to him or praise him, who is worshipped and praised even by the great gods? In the ocean are drowned the high mountain and the small atom. No difference between them is felt by the ocean.

'My beloved, O thou Sweet One, "I" and "me" and "mine" all belong to thee. And if I am conscious of this truth that whatever I have—all—belongs to thee forever, then what can I offer thee?"

'1 am Thine': this expresses the attitude of the devotees of.Visistad-vaita. The Vaiṣṇava devotees of Bengal preach another beautiful truth.' 'Thou art mine.'

Elsewhere Yāmuna writes: 'Thou art father, thou art mother, thou,, art son, thou art daughter, thou art dear friend, thou art guru, thou art the supreme goal and refuge of the whole universe.' According to Yāmuna, the highest ideal is to take refuge in the Lord and surrender oneself completely to him. This ideal of surrendering oneself to God was developed by Rāmānuja, as we shall now see, into a complete philosophy.

RĀMĀNUJA

Since human beings possess widely differing temperaments, they conduct their lives upon different levels. For this reason, no one system of religion can equally well satisfy everyone, and there exist diverse forms of religious truth. And yet, however divergent they may be, they have an underlying unity, and all of them lead men by one path or another to a single goal. The varied scriptures of the world may be likened to a kind mother who cherishes her many children by granting their demands according to their needs.

After Śaṁkara, Rāmānuja ranks first among the greatest interpreters of Vedānta. Śaṁkara's philosophy, though it did afford spiritual comfort to many, yet did not meet the requirements of all aspirants. There are men in every age who hunger for a God whom they can love, whom they can worship. Now the Absolute of Śaṁkara becomes to such men entirely too much of an abstraction to be the object of love and worship. It is true that Śaṁkara does reserve a place in his system for a God of love, and there is room in it for devotion to him; but to many his Iśwara not wholly satisfying, for they regard him as but a lower aspect of Brahman, the Absolute. The Śaṁkara philosophy touches indeed such dizzy heights of abstraction, and at the same time offers such a surpassing degree of spiritual illumination, that it becomes extremely difficult, if not impossible, for most men either to comprehend it or to accept it. They are therefore inclined to regard this Absolute of Śaṁkara as, in the words of Dr Radhakrishnan, 'a bloodless Absolute dark with the excess of light.[39]

So the kind mother, the scriptures, spoke once more, this time through the lips of Rāmānuja and led the people to the bosom of truth.[40] Rāmānuja argues that God and the souls of men are not the same, though they are not separate from each other, and that the highest ideal and the ultimate goal are to love and worship God and surrender ourselves utterly and completely to him. The material world and human beings, though different, have a real existence of their own as the body of Brahman, who is their soul and controlling power. Apart from Brahman they are literally nonentities. So Rāmānujas philosophy is known as Viśiṣṭādvaita—that is, advaita, nondualism, with viśeṣa, or qualifications—because it admits the plurality both of matter and of souls.

Life of Rāmānuja

Rāmānuja was born at Śrī-perum-budur in southern India in the year AD 1017. His mother was the granddaughter of Yāmuna, the saint and philosopher who we have already met. In his youth Rāmānuja journeyed to Conjeevaram in order to study Vedānta with a teacher known as Yādava Prakāś.

Yādava Prakāś, a celebrated interpreter of Vedānta, wrote a commentary upon the Brahma Sūtras which has unfortunately been lost. We do know, however, that his interpretation closely followed that of Bhāskara, who, as we have already discovered, believed in the unity of the soul with Brahman in relation to transcendental knowledge, and acknowledged difference from him in relation to ignorance. In the view of Yādava, this difference is as real as is the unity. Like Bhāskara, Yādava interpreted the philosophy of Bhedābheda, or unity in difference.

For a time, the youthful Rāmānuja pursued his studies under the direction of Yādava, but their paths soon parted.'The fact was that the young man soon developed his own interpretation of the philosophy of Vedānta, and this seemed more reasonable to the other students gathered about the master than did that of the master himself. Yādava became furiously angry. He accordingly conceived a dislike and a consuming envy of his brilliant pupil.

Matters came to a head when Yādava was requested by the ruler of the country to heal his little daughter supposed to be possessed by demons. When the master failed, Rāmānuja was called upon. The story goes that at the young man's bidding the spirit left the girl, and she became quite well. Yādava now hated Rāmānuja, who was obliged to leave the master's school. But this was not enough, Yādava became so possessed by hate and jealousy that he even attempted to assassmate his young pupil, who was saved by warning given to him by a hunter and his wife. Many years later, however, Yādava recognized Rāmānuja's greatness, repented, and became his loyal follower.

Rāmānuja now returned to his mother's home, and at her request took upon himself the state of a householder by marrying a girl of her choice.

About this time, Yāmuna, head of the temple of Śrīraṅgam, being old and sick and hearing of Rāmānuja's learning and purity of character, desired to install him as his successor. When the aged saint was about to breathe his last, his disciples sent for Rāmānuja to come to his bedside, but he did not arrive till just as Yāmuna's body was being conveyed to the riever bank for cremation. As Rāmānuja viewed the corpse, he remarked that the three fingers of the right hand, remained closed. The disciples in explanation said that the closed fingers indicated the existence of an unfulfilled desire, which—as already mentioned—was a wish to compose a commentary upon the Brahma Sūtras. When Rāmānuja promised to take upon himself the fulfilment of this task, legend has it that the three fingers forthwith assumed their natural position.

After Rāmānuja's return to Conjeevaram, his spirit grew restless, for he could see no way to fulfil his promise. Accordingly, he sought advice of the head priest of the temple of Śrīraṅgam, who uttered a Sanskrit verse which seemed to be the word of God, and his will: 'I am the Supreme. The Truth is based upon distinction. Self-surrender is the surest way to the door of salvation. Whether man Struggles or not, salvation will come in the end. Accept the disciple ship of Periā Nambi.' So Rāmānuja set out to meet Nambi at the same time that Nambi was approaching Conjeevaram to meet him. They came together in a temple on the road, and Nambi initiated Rāmānuja into the mysteries of Vedānta.

Rāmānuja was not happy in his marriage, for in his heart he longed for the time when he might devote himself uninterruptedly to a life of worship and meditation. His wife, instead of aiding him to attain the spiritual ideal he desired, constantly irritated him by her thoughtless conduct. At last Rāmānuja, feeling the call of God from within, renounced all wordly ties, took monastic vows, and set out for Śriraṅgam, where the great saint Yāmuna had desired that he should live.

While he was a monk at Śriraṅgam, Rāmānuja became extremely popular, and man aspirants gathered round him. But still he remained unsatisfied. Now there was living at that time another saint, whose name was Gosṭhi-pūrna. Rāmānuja went to him and reverently begged to be initiated. Six times he went to him, and six times was refused.At last, however, seeing Rāmānuja's earnest 'devotion, Gosṭhi-pūrna initiated him with a holy mantra, a name of God, but warned him that he must never give that mantra to anyone, for if he did he would be damned, while whoever heard the sacred words would attain salvation. Upon hearing this, Rāmānuja went at once into he temple, gathered a crowd around him, and uttered the holy mantra 'Om namo Nārāyaṇāya', in the hearing of all. Gosṭhi-pūrna pretended to be very angry and rebuked him for his disobedience, but Rāmānuja replied, 'If by my damnation so many can be saved, damnation is my supreme desire.' Pleased, the saint answered, 'Because of your great love for humanity, the philosophy of Viśiṣṭādvaita shall henceforth be known as the Rāmānuja Philosophy.'

Rāmānuja now made Śrīraṅgam his headquarters, but travelled occasionally to various parts of the country, preaching and gathering many disciples. It was during this period that he wrote his commentary upon the Brahma Sūtras, as he had promised before the corpse of Yāmuna that he would do. This work is known as Sri Bhāsya, and is held in great respect by the followers of Śrī Vaiṣṇavism. He also wrote commentaries upon the Gitā and some original philosophical treatises propounding his doctrine. He passed away in the year AD 1137 after a fruitful life of one hundred and twenty years. He is worshipped today by thousands of his followers, and is regarded by all India as one of the greatest saints and philosophers in its history.

Viśiṣṭadvaita of Rāmānuja

At the beginning of our discussion of Rāmānuja's philosophy, we need to make quite clear the distinction between the definition of knowledge given by Śaṁkara and that given by Rāmānuja, for upon this distinction is based the entire difference between these two great philosophers. If properly understood, it will at once make clear in how many different lights the same truth may be viewed.

According to Śaṁkara, knowledge is self-luminous, light itself, It illumined objects of knowledge, and is therefore apart from and beyond the relation of subject and object. Relative knowledge is not true knowledge; it is not pure consciousness, though grounded upon it. Knowledge, by itself, is absolute. It is the Ātman, Light itself. Relative knowledge is infinite knowledge made finite.

Rāmānuja, on the other hand, does not take into consideration knowledge that is self-luminous and absolute. Knowledge, he declares is always relative, and in it there. is always a distinction between subject and object. In short, Rāmānuja does not admit nirvikalpa samādhi, the unitary consciousness, the experience of the Self as one with Brahman. He was at heart a bhakta, a devotee, who preserved his distinction from Brahman in order to enjoy the bliss of divine love. In consequence, his philosophy is one of devotion, although, being based on careful reasoning, it is not merely emotional in its nature.

One other point of difference between the two great philosophers should be noted. What Śaṁkara calls māyā, which is neither real nor unreal, and which, when joined to Brahman, the Absolute, attributeless and impersonal, becomes the personal Iśwara, or God, Rāmānuja calls Sakti, or power, which in its nature is real and eternally, coexistent with Brahman. Thus Rāmānuja does not accept the impersonal, attributeless Brahman of Śaṁkara, but rather aneternal personal Brahman, the repository of all blessed qualities.

Theory of knowledge

Perception, inference, and scripture are valid as sources of knowled ge and also, each on its own level, as an affirmation of reality. Unlike Śaṁkara, Rāmānuja does not admit a distinction between illusory perception and true perception, for he declares that even in illusory perception, so-called, there is some perception of reality. Thus all experience has its validity.

Rāmānuja's theory of dharma-bhuta-jñāna, or consciousness as an attribute and not the thing itself, explains his conception of the threefold function of knowledge: it gives reality; it has the power to reveal the truth: and it can reveal the truth of Brahman.

So long as man, owing to his imperfections imposed by karma, is crippled in knowledge. Brahman may not be revealed to him. But after he has been purified, he may have immediate intuition of God. This immediate intuition, as we have elsewhere remarked, is not the highest transcendental consciousness described in the Upaniṣads and by Śaṁkara as turīya, and as nirvikalpa samādhi by the yogis, but rather it is a transcendental experience of God in which there still remains the ego as distinct from him. The experience is described as savikalpa samādhi by\ the yogis, and it comes through absorption in meditation and devotion. This revelation of God in meditation possesses a self-certifying character, and, further, the fact that God is so revealed in the heart of man is borne witness to by the seers and saints of the Upaniṣads, as well as by the saints and seers of all ages and in all lands.

Brahman, or God

In the Upaniṣads we read, 'The knower of Brahman attains the highest'[41]. This text expresses the unity of the threefold nature of wisdom, namely: tattwa. or intellectual and philosophic understanding of Brahman: hita, or way to Brahman; and puruṣartha, direct perception of Brahman as the supreme goal.

Let us first try philosophically to comprehend the nature of Brahman. This is tattwa. Brahman is determinate and can therefore be defined by a statement of his essential attributes. In the words of the Upaniṣad, 'Brahman is satyam, or real, jñānam, or conscious, and anantam, or infinite.'[42] Śaṁkara does not consider these as attributes of Brahman. But Rāmānuja accepts them as essential.

Brahman is the basis of all existence, and since he is also the supreme good, he is also the supreme goal. The universe is composed of cit, the sentient, and acit, the nonsentient. Cit and acit have their source in Brahman, and he is the indwelling Self within all and the ruler of all.

Brahman is both the first cause and the final cause of the universe of the sentient and the nonsentient. 'Brahman ...wills to be many', we read in the Upaniṣads, and he divides himself into the manifold universe, of the living and of the nonliving. This fact does not mean, however, that the act of creation had an absolute beginning in time. The universe, as explained by all systems of Indian thought, alternates between the phases of involution and evolution. In the phase of involution it remains latent in Brahman, and creation or evolution is the actualization of the latent. The one becomes the many, not in the pantheistic sense of emanation, but in the sense that Brahman, by exercise of his will, evolves the twenty-four categories and the jīvas, or individual souls. Brahman is the material as well as the efficient cause of the universe. 'From him the universe has emerged, in him it exists, and unto him it returns.[43] As the web comes out of the spider and is withdrawn, as plants grow from the soil and hair from the body of man, so springs the universe from the eternal Brahman[44] God, as the source and support of the universe, has transformed himself into the cosmic manifold; and he is the indwelling Self in his creation, the ruler and director of the cosmic process. The evil that the universe contains is the result of the karma of individuals, for whom God is the dispenser of the law. He, himself, remains unaffected by evil, and is forever absolutely good.

God, though he has transformed himself into the universe of sentient and nonsentient forms, remains distinct from them. Matter is the object of experience, individual souls are the experiencing subjects, and God is the lord and ruler of all. He is defined in the Upaniṣads (as we have seen) as satyam, real: jñānam, conscious; and anantam, infinite. Rāmānuja, in commenting on this text, points out that because of these distinctive attributes God is above and beyond matter (which is changing phenomena) and distinct from individual souls caught in its meshes. Thus, though the universe is a transformation of Brahman, he remains by his nature beyond change, and though immanent, he is transcendent.

So does Rāmānuja define God as the repository of infinite, noble, and blessed qualities, and as one 'not only differentiating himself into the cosmos but remaining absolutely distinct from it'. Yet, again, 'he is its stuff and soul'.

Brahman, then, is related to the cosmos as the soul is related to the body. As a man has a soul and a body, and as the soul, though distinct from the body, yet controls and guides it, lives in it, and uses it as an instrument, similarly Brahman is the soul of the universe, the source and sustenance of all beings within it, and the ruler over all. In this body-and-soul connection between Brahman and the cosmos are included the three relations defined by Rāmānuja: 'ādhāra and ādheya—support and the supported; niyāmaya and niyamya—the controller and the controlled; sesin and śeṣa—the Lord and his servant'. Professor P. N. Srinivasachari, a deep student of Rāmānuja, speaks of this triune relationship thus:

'The relation of ādhāra and ādheya [support and the thing supported] is from the point of view of metaphysics which defines Brahman as real (satya), conscious (jñāna), and infinite (ananta). This relation emphasizes the inner unity of Reality. The relation of niyāmaka and niyamya [controller and the controlled] brings out the transcendental goodness of God and his redemptive impulse. The relation of śeshin and śesha [the Lord and his servant] satisfies the highest demands of ethics and aesthetics by defining God as the supreme Lord for whose satisfaction the world of chit [the sentient] and achit [the insentient] lives, moves and has its being. The relation of body and soul combines all the three together and serves as an analogical representation of a spiritual truth.[45]

God as the controller of the universe is absolutely good and the redeemer of all beings. Evil and suffering, be it repeated, are caused by the individual's karmas. Karmas—good or evil deeds—create happiness or misery; but by karmas alone man cannot redeem himself. Only the grace of God can save him; God is therefore the saviour. In his infinite love, his absolute goodness, he is forever merciful, for he even becomes flesh in human form in order to redeem the prodigal and to rejoice in the ecstasy of communion with his devotee. The Gitā, as we have seen, expounds the idea of avatār, or divine incarnation; Rāmānuja tells us that the central motive of God in descending to earth in human form is his love for humanity and his desire to save it.

The finite self is not a separate self-existent entity, but an organ, an element of Brahman. It is a part of Brahman, essentially different from him but inseparably bound to him. The finite self is anu, or atomic like the point of a goad, though it admits of no spatial division from the fact that it is spirit. The finite self, then, is an essential attribute (prākāra) of God; and as substance and attribute, though inseparably associated, are yet absolutely distinct from each other, so God as substance is absolutely distinct from the individual soul. As inseparably associated with God, the individual self is eternal; and at distinct from him, it has a personality of its own and a free will. Bus God, being also the inner ruler of the cosmos, which forms his body, 'makes the soul act'. Not that man's acts are good or evil as guided or forced by God—for God permits the individual to choose between good and evil. Eventually, however, by his grace God restores all souls to himself. Man's choice of good or evil, in short, is an exercise of his free will. That makes him responsible for his actions, while God remains unaffected by them.

Free will, furthermore, is given in order that man may eventually detach himself from the meshes of ignorance and grow into the 'personality of God'. Though Rāmānuja tries to refute the doctrine of māyā as expounded by Śarhkara, he is obliged to admit in the final analysis the existence of māyā, or ignorance, in m,in; for the self, he believes, has forgotten its divine origin and its divine destiny, and tends to identify itself with matter, until it becomes subject to the evils of sarhsara, or empirical existence. The true Self, which is an eternal mode of God, has degenerated into ego by becoming a mode of matter. We free ourselves from this ego when we surrender ourselves to God. Our free will, a gift of God, finds fulfilment of its purpose when we live in conformity with the will of God, who is our divine source and the Self of ourselves.

The poet Tennyson in two lines sums up the implications of free will and self-surrender:

Our wills are ours we know not how,
Our wills are ours to make them Thine.

The Supreme Goal

As we have already stated, God is the tattwa, the truth; he is the hita, the ways and means, and he is the puruṣartha, the supreme goal.[46]

Not only must we give intellectual assent to the truth that we live, move, and have our being in God, but we must have awareness or this truth. Like all true saints and philosophers, Rāmānuja held that God can be known and realized, that a vision of his being is possible for man, and that man must Strive to attain it. And he realized, like all saints, that the vision of God is vouchsafed to man by God himself out of his infinite love and grace.

Self-effort and divine grace are not opposed to each other; neither is divine grace conditional. In the words of Śrī Rāmakrṣṇa, the breeze of divine grace is blowing, but we must set sail to catch it. In the same way Rāmānuja explains how we must love God, serve him, and meditate on him: and then, as spiritual hunger grows within us, we experience love and divine grace flowing from him and flooding our whole being. The culmination of spiritual experience, he says, is then realizing God's unbounded love and finding complete refuge in him. To find complete refuge in him is the ideal of self-surrender, or prapatti, which is not extinction of self, but rather a union of our will with the will of God.

Rāmānuja did not believe in a complete identity of man with God. For him kaiṅkarya. or living in the service of God, was the supreme ideal. This ideal of service, however, must not be confused with a modern Christian ideal, that of helping God to realize his own fullness. In this Christian ideal there exists a strong element of egotistical pride. The truth is that God does not need our help; we realize our own fullness by loving and serving him.

Rāmānuja did not, however, believe in jīvanmukti, or liberation in this life, but rather in videha mukti, or liberation after death—death, for him, being a passing 'through the path of light' to our permanent linme in God. In death the self realizes union with God as his body, his part. his attribute. Never is there a dissolution of jīvahood, or individual personality. Professor P. N. Srinivasachari has beautifully summarized this ideal of freedom in the following words:

'Release is not freedom in embodiment but freedom from embodiment; it refers to the return of the prākāra or mukta [released soul] to his home in the absolute. [Rāmānuja's absolute, however, is not the Absolute proper—but the Personal God.] Mukti [freedom] is beyond the range of materialism and mentalism and involves the intuition of the infinite as well as its attainment. The finite has its roots in the infinite and in mukti there is she coalescence of content without the abolition of existence. When the freed self sees God face to face, its logical outlook becomes a spiritual insight, and freed from the nescience of empirical life, it expands into omniscience. It has a sense of the infinite and sees everything with the eye of the all-self. When the self is Brahmanized, it is stripped of its self-hood and sense of separateness, shakes off the shackles of karma based on kāma [desire] and effaces itself in spiritual service and solidarity. The finite remains, but the fetters of finitude and individualism are removed.[47]

The Ways and Means of Attainment

In explaining hita, the practical aspect of his philosophy, Rāmānuja insists that God is the Lord of Love, and he prescribes bhakti yoga. 'Bhakti yoga', explains Swami Vivekananda, 'is a real, genuine search after the Lord, a search beginning, continuing, and ending in Love. One single moment of the madness of extreme love of God brings us eternal freedom.[48]

Śaṁkara laid great stress upon jñāna yoga, the path of knowledge, but Rāmānuja laid stress upon bhakti yoga, the path of love. Both these saintly philosophers admit the need of love and devotion as well as the need of knowledge; only Śaṁkara preaches love as a means to knowledge and Rāmānuja preaches love as both means and end. Rāmānuja, on the other hand, admits knowledge as a means to love, whereas Śaṁkara insists that knowledge is both means and end. I do not believe that there exists, after all, any real difference between their explanations of the means. Swami Vivekananda declares, it is a distinction without much difference. When Rāmānuja speaks of knowledge as a means, he has in mind not transcendental knowledge but intellectual analysis; and when Śaṁkara speaks of love as a means, he has reference to an inferior form of worship. 'Each seems', says Swami Vivekananda, 'to lay a great stress upon his own particular method ofworship, forgetting that with perfect love true knowledge is bound to come, even unsought, and that from perfect knowledge true love is inseparable.[49]

As he explains what meditation is, Rāmānuja also explains what true love is, and how with love and devotion we necessarily must meditate upon God. In his commentary upon the first aphorism of the Vedānta Sūtras, he gives an illuminating explanation of this interlocking of love and meditation:

'Meditation is a constant remembering (of the thing meditated upon), which flows like oil poured from one vessel to another. When this kind of remembering has been attained (in relation to God) all bonds break. Thus the scriptures speak of constant recollectedness as a means to liberation. This remembering again is the same as seeing, because it has the same significance, as is evident from the passage, "When He who is far away and near is seen, the bonds of the heart are broken, all doubts vanish, and all effects of karma disappear." He who is near can be seen, but he who is far away can only be remembered. Nevertheless the scriptures say that we have to see Him who is near as well as far away, thereby indicating to us that the above kind of remembering is as good as seeing. This remembrance when exalted assumes the same form as seeing...Worship is constant remembering, as may be seen from the principal texts of the scriptures. Knowing, which is the same as repeated worship, has been described as constant remembering...Thus the memory, which has attained to the level of direct perception, is spoken of in the Sruti (scripture) as a means of liberation. "This Ātman is not to be reached through various sciences, nor by intellect, nor by much study of the Vedas. Whomsoever this Ātman desires, by him is the Ātman attained; unto him this Ātman reveals himself." Here, after saying that mere hearing, thinking, and meditating are not the means of attaining this Atman, the passage continues—Whomsoever this Atman desires, by him the Atman is attained. The extremely beloved is desired; he by whom this Atman is extremely beloved becomes the most beloved of the Atman. So that this beloved may attain the Atman, the Lord himself helps. For it has been said by the Lord: "Those who are constantly attached to Me and worship Me with love—I give that direction to their will by which the come to Me." Therefore it is said, to whomsoever this remembering, which is the same as direct perception, is very dear, because it is dear to the object of such memory-perception, he is desired by the Supreme Atman, by him the Supreme Atman is attained. This constant remembrance is denoted by the word bhakti (love).[50]

With respect to the method and means of attaining bhakti, Rāmānuja remarks: 'Its attainment comes through discrimination, control of the passions, habitual practice of religious disciplines, sacrificial work, purity, strength, and suppression of excessive) joy.'

By discrimination is meant the distinguishing, among other things, of good food from bad. Body and mind being interrelated, purity of food is important, especially for beginners, because it enables them to think pure thoughts.

Control of the passions is the strengthening of the will and its guidance toward meditation on the Lord. 'By practice and non-atttachment is it to be attained.'

Sacrificial work refers to the five great sacrifices mentioned in the Vedas.

Purity is both external and internal. In the list of qualities conducive to purity. Rāmānuja enumerates the following: satya, truthfullness; ārjava, sincerity; dayā, doing good to others; ahimsā, noninjury; abhidyā, noncovetousness, not thinking vain thoughts, not brooding over injuries received from others. Strength is vigour of mind.

Lastly is suppression of excessive joy. Excessive joy fritters away the energies of the mind, and yet we must be cheerful. Swami Vivekananda rightly says:

'The person who aspires to be a bhakta must be cheerful. In the Western world the idea of a religious man is that he never smiles, that a dark cloud must always hang over his face, which, again, must be long-drawn with the jaws about collapsed. People with emaciated bodies, and long faces are fit subjects for the physician, they are not yogis. It is the cheerful mind that is persevering. It is the strong mind that hews its way through a thousand difficulties. And this, the hardest task of all, the cutting of our way out of the net of maya. is the work reserved only for giant wills.[51]

Rāmānuja makes some slight distinction between bhakti, or devotion, and prapatti, or self-surrender. When love for God arises in the heart, the highest attainment comes in the surrendering of our wills to God's will and in our living, literally, in the service of God. But, as we have seen, according to Rāmānuja there never comes complete union of man and God, of the lover and the beloved. And yet the greatest lovers and devotees tell of the ultimate consummation of love in mystic union—'I and my Father are one'—the union which knows neither separation nor distinction.

To the student of Western philosophy, Rāmānuja's ideas concerning God and the soul bear an astonishing resemblance to ideas on the same subjects with which Scholastic philosophy concerned itself during the Christian Middle Ages. The personality and the attributes of God the Heavenly Father, the relation of man to God. the question of free,will and divine grace, the submission of the will of man to a higher will than his, the union of human and divine, the relative positions of reason and love in the divine scheme, the vision of divine love and grace, and the release of the soul from bondage after death—It was principally on these topics that the Schoolmen speculated through many hundreds of years, from St Augustine until the final synthesis of faith and reason in St Thomas Aquinas. And Rāmānuja, living in the tenth century, might well have been the spiritual father of the Christian Dante. It is true that medieval Christianity placed far greater emphasis upon the sense of sin than is to be found anywhere in Hindu philosophy, but in the teachings of Rāmānuja all the other mysteries of

Christian theology seem to find their counterpart. We may add in this connection that the greatest Christian mystics atained the height of realization by following bhakti yoga, or the path of love and devotion, the same method of attainment that was taught by Rāmānuja.

NIMBĀRKA

There are four chief schools of Vaiṣṇavism (Vedanta in its devotiona, aspect)'. Śrī, of which Rāmānuja is the principal exponent; Sanakal founded by Nimbārka in the eleventh century; Brahma, founded by Mādhwa in the twelfth century; and Rudra, founded by Vallabha in the sixteenth century. To these should be added the Bengal Vaiṣṇavist school, whose founder was Sri Caitanya, the prophet of Nadiā. We are here concerned with Nimbārka only.

Very little is known of Nimbārka's life, but he is held in reverence as one of the greatest saints of India, and the monastery he is said to have founded is still a celebrated place of pilgrimage.

Nimbārka's philosophy remains unique in that it never attacked other schools of philosophy. Nearly all of those who wrote commentaries on the Brahma Sūtras in the wake of Śaṁkara attempted to refute his doctrine of nondualism, but without much success. In my discussion of certain of these: philosophers I have avoided their endless disagreements with Śaṁkara and with one another in favour of points of agreement and harmony. Infinite is God and infinite are the ways to apprehend and comprehend him—and such was the opinion of Nimbārka also as he approached the fundamental problems of God, the universe, and the human soul.

According to Nimbārka's philosophy of Bhedābheda, or dualism in nondualism, Brahman has two aspects, the absolute and the relative, or, in other words, the impersonal and the personal. In his personal aspect, Brahman possesses attributes, and from him as person has issued the universe of name and form. But Brahman has not exhausted himself in the creation of the universe, for he is also transcendental and impersonal, without attributes, and as such he is greater than the universe.

The universe is, however, one with, as well as different from, Brahman, even as the wave is one with but different from the ocean, or a ray of the sun is one with but different from the sun. Such also is the relationship between individual souls and Brahman; they are at once one with him and different from him. It is not merely a distinction between part and the whole that we have in mind, for they are both a part of Brahman, and one with him.

Thus there exists almost an identity between the philosophy of Nimbārka and that of Bhāskara, but with the important difference that according to Bhāskara the individual soul is a part of Brahman only so long as it remains in ignorance—that in knowledge and emancipation it becomes one with him; whereas Nimbārka declares that the individual soul is a part of Brahman, and is also one with him, both in the state of ignorance and in that of knowledge and emancipation.

In the state of ignorance—according to Nimbārka—the individual soul experiences the empirical world of phenomena, while in the State of liberation it attains the superconscious, transcendental vision of the noumenal. the absolute Brahman, at the same time that it realizes itself as living both in union with Brahman and separate from him.

Nimbārka lays stress upon both knowlege and devotion as means of attaining freedom. Knowledge reveals the.' true nature of Brahman, and devotion culminates in all-absorbing love for him and in complete surrender of the finite will to the infinite will, although in both the love and the surrender the individual self remains.

For the followers of Nimbārka, Kṛṣṇa and his divine consort Rādhā embody both supreme will and supreme love.

MĀDHWA

Mādhwa, another celebrated commentator upon the Brahma Sūtras, founded the Vaiṣṇava sect known as Brāhma or Sad Vaiṣṇavism.

He was born in the year A.D. 1199, of brāhmin parents, in the village of Biligram, which is near the modern town of Udipi in the western part of what is now the Madras Presidency. He was sent to the village school but proved himself to be more an athlete than a scholar. Physically strong and swift, he defeated his playmates in running, in jumping, in swimming, and in other athletic feats. But he left school at an early age and continued his studies of the sacred scriptures at home alone. In later years, his learning was shown in his knowledge of these scriptures, especially the Purāṇas, and of the science of logic.

During the period of his study at home, he was seized with a burning desire for renunciation, and at the age of twenty-five he took monastic vows and devoted himself to the Vedānta philosophy under the guidance of a teacher who expounded its nondualistic aspect. Soon, however, Mādhwa began to differ from his guru in his interpretation of Vedanta. He wrote an independent commentary upon the Gītā, revealing scholarly ability and logical penetration. As a result of his studies, he soon developed a school of philosophy of his own.

In the course of, extensive travels in the peninsula of India, he encountered the exponents of many systems of thought, discussed ideas with them, and attempted with success to gain a hearing for his doctrines. He passed away at the age of seventy-nine.

Mādhwa wrote commentaries upon the Upaniṣads, in addition to those on the Brahma Sūtras and the Gītā already mentioned, and also many treatises in which he expounded his own views and attacked others, particularly Śaṁkara's theory of māyā. In the following paragraphs are summed up main aspect, of his philosophy. The proposition on which Mādhwa bases his realism is that both the knower and the object of knowledge must be real, for otherwise no knowledge would be possible. Knowledge necessarily implies them. All knowledge is relative. Absolute knowledge, or the transcendental consciousness, in which all distinction between knowledge, knower, and known vanishes—as absolute knowledge is defined in Yoga and by Śaṁkara—cannot be admitted. 'No knowledge can be known', says Mādhwa, 'without the knower and the known.'

Pramāṇas. the means and instruments of knowledge, are perception, scriptural texts, and inference. Whatever is known through these is directly related to the object of knowledge, which has a reality of its own.

On this theory of knowledge, Mādhwa erects his theory of the objective reality of the world. The world is real because it is perceived as such. The objects presented to our perception may be either subject or not subject to change, and the fact that an object is fleeting and chagneable does not mean that it is not real.

Our experience is the experience of difference. We see things and things, people and people, and we perceive them to be different from one another. Different from all living beings and nonliving things is God, who exists in order that his law may be fulfilled in the universe, and in order that finite souls, less limited than nonliving things in power and intelligence, may find release from the sufferings and bondage of the world in loving him and surrendering themselves to him.

Mādhwa's whole philosophy is thus based upon the idea of difference or distinction. And distinctions are known to be five in number: (1) God is distinct from individual souls;

(2) God is distinct from nonliving matter: (3) one individual soul is distinct from every other; (4) individual souls are distinct from matter; and (5) in matter, when it is divided. the parts are distinct from one another.

The universe is divided into two categories: Swatantra, independent being, and aswatantra, dependent beings. God is the only independent being. He is the one omnipotent, omniscient, and omnipresent being. How God, who is distinct from individual souls and nonliving things, can be omnipresent is explained by saying that he is not limited by time and space and that the dependent beings 'do not form a resisting medium to his presence'.

(1) Matter is distinct from God and human souls and in itself is only a dependent being. (2) God is the ruler of the universe, but the universe is real and eternally existent.

Each soul is distinct from every other, and all souls are distinct from God though they have dependent existence in him. By nature souls are intelligent. Each soul when born into this world and invested with body and senses is in a state of bondage, but by continued struggle through many lives release from this bondage may be obtained.

Moreover, although souls are distinct from one another, they fall into classes. Of these there are three, differing in their essential nature as well as in their destiny. One class, who are moral and devoted to God alone, will attain salvation and enjoy the eternal felicity of heaven—an abode called Vaikuṇṭha. The second class will never attain salvation but will remain subject to rebirth, experiencing in life after life both happiness and misery. The third class, who revile Viṣṇu and his devotees, will never attain salvation but will be subject to damnation.

This belief of Mādhwa, that only a few attain salvation while the rest cannot, and some even suffer damnation, is contrary to the teachings of all other Indian religious schools.

Mādhwa may possibly have been influenced by certain Christian missionaries who during his time may have penetrated into India.

Only such souls as are devoted to Viṣṇu will attain salvation—that is, go to Vaikuṇṭha and enjoy the beloved company of God. But even in Vaikuṇṭha there are gradations of souls and therefore differences between them.

Mādhwa may possibly have been influenced by certain Christian missionaries who during his time may have penetrated into India.

Only such souls as are devoted to Viṣṇu will attain salvation—that is, go to Vaikuṇṭha and enjoy the beloved company of God. But even in Vaikuṇṭha there are gradations of souls and therefore differences between them.

Foot Notes:

1. See chap. 16, p.

2. Badarikāśrama, in the Himalayas, is a well-known place of pilgrimage, where devotees from throughout India gather in great numbers every summer. At Other times of the year the roads to it are covered with heavy snow. The place has in it a famous temple, dedicated to the worship of Nārāyaṇa. I had the privilege of visiting this holy shrine in 1916.

3. Forword to *Māṇḍūkyopanishad with Gauḍapāda's Kārikā and Sankara's Commentary* (Swami Nikhilananda trans., Sri Ramakrishna Ashrama: Mysore, 1949), p. v.

4. *Ibid.,*. pp. vi-vii.

5. Kārikā. I 7. 12. This and the following passages from the Kārikā have been translated by the author.

6. Kārikā

7. *Ibid.,* III 35.

8. *Ibid.,* III 17, 16

9. *Ibid.,* III 37.

10. *Ibid.,* III 45, 46, 47.

11. Kārikā, IV. 31.

12. *Ibid.,* II 32.

13. *Indian Philosophy,* vol. II, p. 463.

14. *Indian Philosophy,* vol. II, p. 463.

15. The date is that given by Pandit Rajenda Nath Ghosh, a noted authority on—Śaṁkara. S. Radhakrishnan writes (*Indian Philosophy*, vol. 11, p.447): "According to Telang. Śaṁkara flourished about the middle or the end of the sixth century A.D (His argument is that Pūrṇavarman referred to in Śaṁkara's commentary on the Brahma Sūtras was a Buddhist king of Magadha about that time.) Sir R.G Bhindarkar proposes AD 680 as the date of Śaṁkara's's birth, and is even inclined to go a few years earlier. Max Müller and Professor Macdonell hola that he was born in AD 788 and died in AD 820. That he flourished in the first quarter of die ninth century is also the opinion of Professor Keith.supported by the investigations made by Prof. Max Mullerand Prof. Macdonell as well as by Prof. Keith and Dr Bhāndarkar. Prol Telang, on the *basis of* a reference to Pūma Varman, the Buddhist king of Magadha, in the *Sūtra Bhaṣya* of Sanrnra. pleads that he

must have lived in the sixth century A.D. (*Prabuddha Bharata*, November. 1957)

To an Indian scholar, A. V. Sankaranarayana Rao, I owe the following recent statement:

The date of Saṅkara has not been definitely arrived at and is still a matter of controversy. It is the consensus of opinion that he lived after Bhagavān Buddha. The dates assigned to him vary from sixth century BC to eighth century AD. The traditional date is Kaliyuga 2593 or 509 bc. It has been generally accepted by many modern historians that he lived between 788 and 820 AD. This has been more or

16. Translated by Swami Prabhavananda and Christophe Isherwood.

17. There is difference of opinion regarding the meeting of Śaṁkara with Gauḍapāda. See chap. xv.

18. *Brahmajñānavalīmālā*, v. 21.

19. Sir James Jeans.

20. Commentary on I i. 1.

21. *Ibid.*

22. *Ibid.*

23. Commentary on I i. 1.

24. *Complete works of Vivekannda*, vol. III, p. 37.

25. *Kathāmṛta*, vol. v, p. 40.

26. *Ibid.*, vol. IV, p. 255.

27. Commentary on the Brahma Sūtras, IV. iv. 17.

28. *Vivekacūḍāmaṇi*, vv. 481-5.

29. *Vivekacūdāmaṇi*, vv. 481-5.

30. *Vivekacuḍāamaṇi*, vv. 355, 356.

31. v. 368. 32. v. 380. 33. v.108.

34. v.-118. 35. v.-119.

36. Vivekacūḍāmaṇi v. 321.

37. Na prapañcamātram Brahma.

38. Compare this philosophy of union with God after death with the Pauline—interpretation of the teachings of Christ.

39. The above remark reminds one, by way of contrast, of the bold,impersonal thinkers of the Vedic age who asked, 'Who has seen the first-born, when he taht had no bones bore him that has bones?' (Rg-Veda, i. 4. 164, quoted by S. Radhakrsihana, *Indina Philosophy*, vol. I. p. 93.)

40. Ramanuja did not originate the philosophy associated

with his name, but he is its chief exponent.

41. Taittiriya, II. i.3.

42. Taittiriya, II. i. 3.

43. *Ibid.,* III. i.

44. Muṇḍamka, I. i.7.

45. *Cultural Heritage of India,* vol. I, p. 567.

46. Cf.: 'I am the way, the truth, and the life' (John xiv. 6).

47. *Rāmānuja's Idea of the Finite Self pp. 98-9.*

48. *Complete Worksof Vivekananda,* vol. III, p. 31.

49. *Ibid.,* vol. III, p. 34.

50. Vivekananda's translation; *Complete Work of Vivekananda,* vol. III, pp. 34-5.

51. *Complete Works of Vivekananda,*vol. III, p. 69.